ISBN 978-1-332-32878-9
PIBN 10314772

1 MONTH OF
FREE
READING

at

www.ForgottenBooks.com

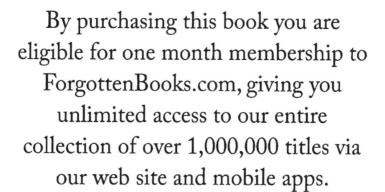

By purchasing this book you are eligible for one month membership to ForgottenBooks.com, giving you unlimited access to our entire collection of over 1,000,000 titles via our web site and mobile apps.

To claim your free month visit: www.forgottenbooks.com/free314772

English
Français
Deutsche
Italiano
Español
Português

www.forgottenbooks.com

Mythology Photography **Fiction**
Fishing Christianity **Art** Cooking
Essays Buddhism Freemasonry
Medicine **Biology** Music **Ancient
Egypt** Evolution Carpentry Physics
Dance Geology **Mathematics** Fitness
Shakespeare **Folklore** Yoga Marketing
Confidence Immortality Biographies
Poetry **Psychology** Witchcraft
Electronics Chemistry History **Law**
Accounting **Philosophy** Anthropology
Alchemy Drama Quantum Mechanics
Atheism Sexual Health **Ancient History**
Entrepreneurship Languages Sport
Paleontology Needlework Islam
Metaphysics Investment Archaeology
Parenting Statistics Criminology
Motivational

TRANSACTIONS

of the

AMERICAN SOCIETY

OF

MUNICIPAL IMPROVEMENTS

For 1917-18

Twenty-Fourth Year

BLOOMINGTON, ILL.:

CHARLES CARROLL BROWN

SECRETARY

CONTENTS

PAPERS

(ii)

INDEX

INDEX

THE PRESSING OF SEWAGE SLUDGE

By Kenneth Allen, Engineer of Sewage Disposal, Board of Estimate and Apportionment, New York City.

NOTE. Wherever used in this paper the word "gallon" refers to the standard U. S. gallon of 231 cu. in., and the word "ton" to the short ton of 2,000 pounds, unless otherwise specified.

Introductory.

For some time after the middle of the last century it was believed that irrigation furnished a satisfactory solution of the sewage disposal question, but with the rapid growth of towns and cities the areas required for this process became so large as to be burdensome; and where settling tanks were in use the accumulations of sludge became an increasing nuisance.[1] These conditions led in the seventies to the more intensive treatment by chemical precipitation[2] which met the first objection, but there remained even larger volumes of liquid sludge from the new process to be disposed of. From seaboard towns it could be carried to sea and dumped, but with inland towns it was more of a burden than ever.

This led to the device of dewatering the sludge by filter presses which produced a moist cake having but a fifth of the volume of the wet sludge and which was in a condition to be handled by a spade. It was, too, comparatively free from objectionable odor.

The first sludge pressing plants were established in England between 1880 and 1884 at Aylesbury, Merton and Wimbledon, and in Germany about 1887,[3] where, however, they have only been used in connection with the lignite or "Degener" process at Spandau, Potsdam and Tegel.[4]

Sewage irrigation experienced but a limited development in the United States, chiefly in Massachusetts and the far west, but between 1887 and 1900, chemical precipitation was adopted at Coney Island (1887), Round Lake, White Plains, the 26th Ward, Brooklyn, Sheepshead Bay, New Rochelle and Far Rockaway, N. Y.; Long Branch and East Orange, N. J.; the Mystic Valley and Worcester (1890), Mass.; Canton and Alliance, O., and

---

[1] At Birmingham several acres were covered to a depth of 4 ft. with sludge and "the stench became so great, and the complaints so frequent, that an injunction was finally served against the city." Rep. Mass. St. Bd. Hlth. 1876, p. 330.

[2] By 1886 fifty English cities and towns, and by 1894 two hundred and thirty-four, had adopted chemical precipitation. See Rep. Mass. St. Bd. Hlth. on Drainage of Mystic, Blackstone and Charles Rivers and "Principles of Sewage Treatment." Dunbar.

[3] "Principles of Sewage Treatment," Dunbar, p. 97.

[4] It is also understood to have been tried out at Halle and Oberschoeneweide. See "Sewage Sludge," Elsner, Spillner, Allen, p. 65.

Providence, R. I. (1900).[5] Of these the sludge has been pressed at Long Branch, East Orange, Worcester, Alliance and Providence, but has been abandoned at all these towns but Worcester and Providence.

Sewage Sludge.

The density, composition, appearance and odor of sludge depend on the sewage from which it is derived, whether from the separate or combined system, domestic or with a large proportion of trade wastes, fresh or stale, etc., and also on its manipulation, whether by mere settling, chemical precipitation, digestion in septic or Imhoff tanks or aeration in the activated sludge process.

The volume produced daily per 1,000 population is, according to Dr. Imhoff, 1.57 cu. yds. in the sedimentation tank, 0.79 cu. yd. after drawing off the supernatant liquor, 0.262 cu. yd. after digestion from combined sewers and 0.131 cu. yd. from separate sewers.[6]

SLUDGE DATA

Derived from	Moisture %	Cu. Yd. per m.g.	Lb. per cu. yd.	Dry Matter Tons per m.g.
Imhoff tanks............	80–85	2–4	1740–1840	0.161[7]
Plain sedimentation......	88–96	4–10	1700–1780	0.580[7]
Chemical precipitation....	86–94	20–30	1710–1790	1.435[7]
Activated sludge process..	98–99	20–80	1690–1700	0.67[8]

With strong sewages or those carrying much grit, especially where treated by plain sedimentation or in Imhoff tanks, these figures may be exceeded. The weight of sludge from chemical precipitation is, of course, increased by the chemicals added.

The weight of sludge after dewatering may be readily determined by the well-known formula:

$$X = \frac{100S}{100-P}$$

in which

X=lb. of sludge after dewatering.
S=lb. of solids in wet sludge.
P=per cent. moisture in product.

---

[5] The process was recommended here in an elaborate report made to the city after an inspection of European plants by Samuel M. Gray in 1884. It was also, with the pressing of the sludge, considered for the Charles and Mystic Rivers in a report made to the Mass. State Board of Health by Charles H. Swan in 1888, but the project finally adopted developed later into the present North Metropolitan Sewerage District involving dilution in Boston harbor.

[6] Eng. News, March 14, 1913.

[7] Worcester experiments.

[8] Cleveland experiments.

For example, a cubic yard of sludge, 90% moisture, weighing 1,740 lbs. would weigh, after dewatering to 60% moisture,

$$\frac{100 \times (10\% \text{ of } 1740)}{100-60} = 435 \text{ lb.}$$

Different sludges vary in their adaptability to pressing. Plain settled sludge or a sludge greasy in its nature is difficult to press. If fine in composition it flows too freely thru and then clogs the filter cloths, leaving the cake in a pasty condition that will not cohere.

Septic sludge varies greatly in consistency depending on the thoroness of digestion. Ordinary septic tank sludge is fine in composition and offers much the same difficulty as plain settled sludge in passing thru the filter. Elsner, however, claims that septic sludge, as well as lignite sludge, is more amenable to pressing without the addition of chemicals than plain settled sludge.[9]

Considering the granular condition of well-digested Imhoff sludge, and its freedom from matter of a viscid or mucous nature, it would seem probable that this might be readily dewatered by pressing, provided a fine filter-medium be used. Experiments in pressing Imhoff sludge, which will be referred to later, have been carried on at Cleveland. But as such sludge can be easily air-dried at slight cost and without offense, there seems little likelihood of it being pressed to any extent.

Precipitated sludge is most favorable for pressing because the lime used in precipitation gives it a certain "body", enabling the cake to cohere without becoming pasty and smearing up the filter cloths.

Sludge may be dried by air-drying and by artificial heat, or it may be dewatered by centrifugal machines or by filter presses. It may, also, be produced with a consistency suitable for handling, altho containing 80% moisture, by the Dickson process, first employed on a large scale at Dublin. This consists, essentially, in the addition of 0.5% of yeast to the raw sludge, allowing it to ferment for from 20 to 24 hrs. at a temperature of from 90 degrees to 94 degrees F. and then, as the sludge floats at the top, drawing off the underlying liquor.[10]

Under certain conditions any one of these processes may be impracticable or undesirable. The present discussion will be confined to filter-pressing which, except air-drying, has been the one most commonly employed.

Preliminary Operations.

Before pressing the sludge from sedimentation or precipitation tanks it is usually drawn or pumped to a sludge-setting or con-

[9] "Sewage Sludge," Elsner, Spillner, Allen, p. 67.
[10] Experiments by treating the sludge from 0.5 m.g.d. of sewage by this process have been recently made near the outlet at South Fifth Street, Brooklyn.

centration tank, dosed with milk of lime, settled for from 12 to 24 hours and the supernatant liquor drawn off. This reduces the contained moisture to 85 or 90% and the volume perhaps 50%. Altho the cost of treatment and disposal of sludge cake and the volume of the latter are all increased by this addition of lime, this is more than counter-balanced by the reduction in the time and cost of pressing.

Sulphuric acid, where used in connection with a greasy sewage, is also valuable in concentrating the sludge. The most notable works of this kind are those at Bradford, England, which comprise 128 presses delivering 3,700 lbs. of cake each per run, the largest sludge pressing plant in the world.[11] The sewage, which contains 440 p. p. m. of grease, is first screened, then precipitated with 2.8 tons of sulphuric acid per million U. S. gallons of sewage. This produces 40 tons of sludge per m. g., containing but 80% moisture, which is again screened, heated and delivered to the presses.

Sulphuric acid is also used for sludge concentration at Oldham, by Dr. Grossman. Here 0.3% by weight of acid is added to sludge of 87 to 90% moisture and after resting the clear liquor is drawn from beneath, leaving the concentrated material with from 70 to 74% moisture.[12]

In this country experiments in the use of sulphur dioxide have been made on Boston sewage by Mr. E. S. Dorr and Prof. R. Spurr Weston, particularly with reference to the recovery of grease and fertilizer.

The method of treatment is patented and is known as the "Miles" process.

It was found that one ton of sulphur dioxide per m. g. of sewage produced, after settling 8 hours, 6.7 tons of sludge, 85.8% moisture. By further settling for 26 hours there can be obtained 4 tons of concentrated sludge 80% moisture in a condition suitable for pressing.

The advantage claimed in the use of sulphur dioxide is the thoro separation of the grease from the sewage and the low moisture in the sludge.

In general it is found best, if not always necessary, to add lime to almost any sludge before delivering to the press. Even this may not be sufficient where the sludge is high in grease, as was found at Frankfort. Here, to render the process effective, resort was had to the addition of sulphate of alumina and heating the presses, but this procedure was abandoned on account of the cost. A preferable way is to crack the grease with sulphuric acid, as is done at Bradford, England, settle, draw off the clearer liquor and press the sludge, now reduced to 80% moisture, in hot presses. The cake is thus relieved of the greater part of the

[11] Joseph Garfield, Sewage Works Engineer.
[12] Jour. Chem. Ind., June 15, 1915.

grease, which passes off with the drainage liquor, is recovered and sold.[13]

A similar process was tried at Cassel, Germany, a few years ago, producing dried fertilizer and grease as at Bradford. But here, tho the wet sludge averaged 18% grease, the process was abandoned after 3 years' trial on account of the fuel required to heat the wet sludge and dry the cake.

The amount of lime which should be added to sludge before pressing depends, as has been said, on the character of the sludge, on the amount previously used for precipitation, etc. In English practice it usually varies from 0.5 to 1.0% by weight of the wet precipitated sludge or from 3 to 7% of the pressed cake.

Some interesting experiments were made on the effect of lime by John T. Thompson, Chemist and Acting Manager of the Knostrop Sewage Works at Leeds, England.[14]

The sludge was screened thru 1-in. perforations in a plate, concentrated by settling, and then pressed. With fresh, plain, settled sludge, pressing occupied 3 hours, while with the addition of 1% quicklime this was reduced to 50 minutes. Partly digested septic sludge with 1% lime took 3½ hours to press and even then was soft in the middle, while old septic sludge with 1% lime could not be properly pressed and with 3% lime took 3 hours to produce a good cake. It was found difficult to remove cake made from septic sludge from the cloths, which were rotted more rapidly by the latter.

Mr. Thompson concludes that good cake, 60% moisture, may be readily produced from fresh sludge by the addition of 1% lime and suggests the following simple test for the foreman to apply:

"If the press effluent is just alkaline to phenol phthalein a good cake can usually be obtained in 45 minutes, but if the effluent gives no color reaction it may take 1½ to 2 hours to get the same result."

Amounts used in several English plants are mentioned by Elsner as follows:

	Lb. per cu. yd.	Lb. per 1,000 gal.
Chorley	8.4	41.6
Bury	10.1	50.0
Willisden (greasy)	37	183
Colchester	47	232
Ealing	84	416

Septic sludges, however, have required as much as 9.6% of the weight of the pressed cake at Nelson, 10% at Rochdale, and 15% at Burnley. At York, the cost of lime for pressing septic

[13] "The Separation of Grease from Sewage Sludge," K. A., *Engineering and Contracting*, vol. xl, p. 601.
[14] *Surveyor & Mun. & Co. Eng.*, July 23, 1915.

sludge was so great as to be prohibitive and at Oldham much difficulty was experienced in the operation.[15]

According to Metcalf and Eddy[16] as much as 100 lbs. per 1,000 gallons has been found necessary with septic sludge.

This excess of lime required above that for mere precipitation, should not be added before the latter treatment, as it has an unfavorable effect on the effluent, promoting secondary putrefaction, deposits of sludge on the stream bed and the clogging of filters, while it retards nitrification.

The amount of lime used at Worcester and Providence, which are examples of well-operated American plants, is given in the following statement.

	Worcester		Providence	
	1915	*1916*	*1915*	*1916*
Sewage treated, m.g.	4367	5869	6594.6	7790.666
Tons solids per m.g. sewage.	1.24	1.23	1.07	0.82
Lime used, tons............	2290	2460	1443	1588
lb. per m.g., total.......	1048	838[17]	438	408
Sludge produced, m.g.	23.347	31.168	18.026	14.484
cu. yd. per m.g..........	26.4	26.4	13.55	9.20
Per cent. moisture........	92.31	93.74	90.13	89.09
Sludge pressed, m.g........	15.233	13.742	13.803	12.192
Lime used for pressing,				
lb. per m.g. sewage	312	308	198	150
lb. per 1000 gal. sludge ...	58.4	57.9	72.5	80.6
% wt. of sludge	.070	0.70	0.88	0.93
Cake produced, tons	16,973	13,192	24,709	23,511
tons per m.g. sewage.....	5.9	5.1	3.74	3.02
tons per m.g. sludge pressed	1110	960	1790	1930
% moisture.............	71.2	72.8	70	72

Altho lignite sludge can be pressed without the addition of lime, the cake, according to Spillner[18], contains 8 or 10% too much moisture, so that it disintegrates easily if exposed to the rain. For this reason it should be stored under cover.

It is produced (as noted at Spandau) by adding finely ground lignite mixed with water and then, as it passes thru a baffled trough, a solution of sulphate of alumina. Ten tons of sludge, 90% moisture, are produced at Spandau from 2.4 million gallons of sewage containing 1,000 p. p. m. of solids daily. The sludge is in a condition for pressing as it comes from the tanks, and as the latter are enclosed (of steel) the process is nearly odorless.

[15] See Rep. V. Royal Com. Sew. Disp., p. 168. "Sanitary Engineering," Moore & Silcock, vol. II, p. 692. "Sewage Disposal," Kinnicutt, Winslow and Pratt, p. 177. "Sewage Disposal," Kershaw, p. 141.

[16] "Am. Sewerage Practice," vol. III, p. 490.

[17] Low, due to lack of supply.

[18] "Sewage Sludge," p. 137.

Activated sludge, which has been pressed without lime at Milwaukee, will be referred to in more detail later.

Before the sludge is pumped to the presses it should be coarse-screened to remove any rags, sticks or other coarse material that may have accidentally found admission and which might clog pipes or channels or bring unequal pressures to bear on the plates of the press, causing them to crack.

Screening may be accomplished by a downward discharge of the sludge thru a basket or cage screen above the sludge concentration tank, by forcing it or allowing it to flow thru a bar screen or rack on its passage from the tank to the presses, or by the operation of a coarse band screen at either of the above points or in the sludge tank itself.

Conveying Sludge by Channels and Pipes.

From the concentration tank the sludge usually flows to a pump well, whence it is pumped to the presses. If it flows by gravity, the required slope of the chute or pipe depends upon the condition of the sludge. According to Elsner, "for any easy, automatic flow (in a chute) with settled sludge containing at least 90% of water, a slope of 1:10 to 1:15 is necessary, depending on whether there is much sand and coarse material, or whether there is a fine fluid sludge. Very liquid sludge with about 95% of water and but little sand may under some circumstances be given a slope of 1:100, but 1:80 is better. For sludge obtained with interrupted operation a fall of 1:40 to 1:50 is necessary. The plants of the Emscher Association have slopes of 1:20 to 1:40, while the pipe conduits at Elberfeld have 1:30. At Fitchburg a slope is provided of 1:90, while the new concrete channels for Imhoff sludge at Columbus are given a slope of 1:56.

In Germany sludge has been transported a distance of 3,000 ft. in this way.

To avoid undue resistance, force mains for sludge should preferably be not less than 8 in. in diameter, altho at Mannheim it is conveyed 1¼ miles by 'a 150 m. m. (5.85 in.) iron pipe. On curves the radius of the centre should be about five times the diameter. According to Mr. Blamey Stevens[19], in order to keep the inner surface of the pipe scoured, the velocity of the sludge in meters per second should not be less than $P \div 287 \ D$[20], in which

P= friction head of sludge÷friction head of water,
and D=diameter of pipe in meters.

Changes of cross section should be avoided to prevent clogging, but if unavoidable, means for back-flushing should be provided.

An acid sludge tends to keep the inner surface of the pipe

[19] "Sludge," Student's Paper No. 448, Inst. C. E.
[20] This corresponds to the critical velocity for cast iron pipe, above which the flow is turbulent. Prof. O. Reynolds, Phil. Trans., 1883.

clean, but one containing chlorine in excess will produce rusting, and unslacked lime or an excess of lime tends to cause deposits. Either rust or deposits interfere with the flow and may result in clogging the pipe.

If allowed to stand for a considerable time in pipes, especially if permitted to drain, sludge may adhere in the form of cake on the inner surface and be difficult to remove. Nevertheless, with proper precautions, long lines of sludge mains are satisfactorily maintained in operation.

At Birmingham the digested sludge from septic tanks at Saltly is first screened and then, about once a week, pumped to the drying beds at West Orton, a distance of four miles. There are two mains, one 9 in. and one 12 in. in diameter.

At Bradford, too, some 330 tons of sludge per day is forced after screening thru five miles of 8-in. steel pipe from the tanks at Frizinghall to the press house at Esholt. In this case the operation is continuous.

At Glasgow there are three plants—the Dalmuir, the Shieldhall and the Dalmarnock. At the latter plant a part of the sludge is pressed and the balance, amounting to 89,090 tons in the fiscal year 1915-16, is pumped thru a 9-in. main to the Shieldhall Works, a distance of nearly five miles, where it is taken by steamer and dumped at sea.

Pumping Sludge to the Presses.

Screened sludge may be pumped by almost any type of pump if designed for this service, including pulsometers, ejectors, chain pumps, bucket elevators, the air lift, membrane pumps, pneumatic receivers, centrifugal pumps, and plunger pumps.

Pulsometers, chain pumps and ordinary *ejectors* are inefficient and suitable only for occasional or emergency use, or where the volume is so small that economy of power may be disregarded.

The *Shone Ejector* is well adapted to such use, being automatic in operation and with few moving parts, but operates only when the sludge is received under pressure. It is employed at Worcester and Providence to pump the sludge from the precipitation tanks to a storage tank. The capacity of each ejector at these plants is 500 gallons. In the opinion of Mr. Harrison P. Eddy, based on experiments at Worcester, 17% is about as high an efficiency as can be expected with Shone ejectors operative with sewage. [Proc. Inst. C. E., 1916.]

The *Air Lift* has been used for pumping Imhoff sludge abroad and in Fitchburg, Mass. There seems to be no good reason why it would not be applicable to other sludges, altho the released air might increase the amount of odor, which at best is often offensive where sludge is handled.

The *Membrane Pump*, found more particularly in Germany,

consists of a cylinder, A, connected at each end by pipes with a second cylinder, B, containing a plunger. A diaphragm or membrane of rubber in each end of the first cylinder, A, transmits the fluid pressure exerted by the plunger of B thru ports in the cylinder head to the contained sludge, which is alternately drawn into and expelled from the central space between the membranes thru ball valves placed, respectively, below and above the center of the cylinder B.

At Hanover one of these pumps, having a capacity of 150 gallons per minute with a lift of 43 feet, required 5 or 6 h. p. for operation. The rubber membrane lasts from 8 to 10 months. Otherwise there is little to wear out or get out of order.

The *Air Receiver* is in common use, especially abroad. It consists essentially of a receptacle, similar to a boiler, furnished with large inlet and outlet sludge connections and an air pipe leading from an air compressor or vacuum pump.[21] The receiver is filled by gravity or by exhausting the air inside and the sludge is then expelled by admitting air under pressure by automatically controlled valves. In practice these receivers are usually in pairs, so that while one is discharging the other is filling. An advantage is that air left under pressure in one receiver after expelling the sludge may be utilized by conveying it to the other receiver without allowing it to exhaust to the atmospheric pressure.[22] Their efficiency has been stated to be not over 16%, but there are obvious advantages in freedom from moving parts, automatic control and adaptability to wide ranges of pressure, so that it is one of the best devices for pumping sludge.

The size may vary within wide limits. At Elberfeld, Fig. 1, the capacity is 160 cu. ft., at Frankfort 210 cu. ft., at Providence 600 cu. ft., while at Bradford, where exceptionally large volumes are handled, the capacity of each receiver is 1,350 cu. ft.

A special type of receiver known as a *Monte-jus* is used in England and Germany for this purpose. It is nearly spherical in form, both for greater strength and to prevent deposits, and holds from one to three charges for a press. Pressures as high as 100 lb. per square inch have been used with these. The valves are often operated by hand.

The *Centrifugal Pump* is also used for sludge but should be specially designed with large clearances. It has a higher efficiency than the air receiver—usually from 20% to 40%—but, as in the case of the air lift, it is not adapted to pumping thick sludge under high pressures.

Reciprocating or Plunger Pumps are usually to be preferred to centrifugal pumps and in small installations are sometimes the best to adopt on account of their simplicity and ability to operate

---

[21] At Frankfort the receiver while being filled is under a vacuum of 300 mm.

[22] "Sewage Purification and Disposal," Kershaw, p. 138.

Fig. 1.   Air Receiver in Sludge Plant at Elberfeld, Germany.

under sudden and large variations of pressure.   At Birmingham two direct-acting pumps of this type having a capacity of 250 gallons per minute each are used to pump thru the long force mains already described.   But under ordinary conditions and for large plants the air receiver or Shone ejector is believed to be preferable.

Sludge Pressing.

There are several forms of filter press.   That most commonly used consists of a series of parallel plates from 30 to 54 in. square and with depressed surfaces, so that when the rims are in contact they enclose a series of cells from ¾ in. to 2 in. thick.   The plates are usually of cast iron from 2 in. to 3 in. thick at the rim and where in contact are machined so as to form a true and tight joint.   The depressed surfaces are either grooved vertically, in concentric circles and radially, or else in two directions at right angles to each other forming numerous little pyramids, in order to facilitate drainage.   Each plate has a 6-in. hole in the center thru which the sludge flows by gravity from a tank or is pumped to the series of cells.   The pipe to the press is usually 8 in. in size.   Fig. 2.

Between each pair of plates there are placed two pieces of cloth with holes 4 in. to 6 in. in diameter in the center, opposite the holes in the plates.   The two cloths on the opposite sides of each plate are then sewed or clamped together at the hole to prevent the sludge from entering and escaping between.

Fig. 2.   Plate for Filter Press as used at Providence, R. I.

A modification of this is the "frame plate" used in Germany, in which a series of plates of uniform thickness, i. e., with plain faces except for the drainage grooves, alternate with frames. The grooves in the plates lead to drainage ducts below and a sieve is placed over each face. The cloth is then folded over each plate and clamped by the adjacent frame. The sludge enters by a continuous duct near the upper edge of the plates and frames. Fig. 4.

The plates, usually 50 to 100 in number, are held together tight by tie rods passing thru their upper corners or lugs projecting therefrom. A head casting at one end and a follower at the other hold the plates between, while the sludge is subjected to a pressure of from 50 to 120 lbs. per sq. in. This pressure may be derived directly from the air receiver or it may be applied after the press is filled by means of a screw operated by hand or motor.

As the pressure continues, the drainage liquor, which is putrescible and offensive, flows thru ½-in. holes in the bottom of the plates to a drain pipe by which it is carried back to the sedimentation tank to be again treated with the sewage. Pressure is maintained until the drainage is insignificant, which may be anywhere from 15 minutes to 1½ hours, altho at Oberschoeneweide, in order to secure a firm cake from lignite sludge, and elsewhere with greasy sludge, it has been necessary to maintain the pressure for 12 hours or more.

One of the most important sludge pressing plants is that at Leeds, where about 900 tons of cake (containing 317 tons dry solids) are produced in a week of 53 working hours.

The sewage amounts to 21 million U. S. gallons per day, of which 4.6 million are industrial waste. After passing a screen and a grit chamber, it is dosed with 10 to 100 p.p.m. of lime and the sludge is pumped by Tangye pumps to three sludge tanks of 360 tons capacity, milk of lime being introduced in the pump section, 3 1-3 tons per tank. The limed sludge, 90% moisture, is then settled for 12 to 18 hours and the supernatant water drawn off. This usually amounts to from 8 to 12% of the volume. Two pairs of rams 6 ft. in diameter by 12 ft. deep force the concentrated material under a pressure of 100 lb. per sq. in. to the presses, each feeding four of the eight installed, but this is increased to a final squeeze of about 1,700 lb. per sq. in. by hydraulic thrust blocks.

Each press has 64 cells 52 in. by 52 in. by $1\frac{1}{2}$ in. in size, and therefore produces about five tons per run. The cake drops to bogies below holding 50 cu. ft. each and drawn by a locomotive. Eight laborers attend to the presses and four to the bogies.[23]

At Glasgow the Dalmarnock plant consists of 18 (?) presses of 41 cells each. The air pressure is 100 lb. 150 tons of cake, 66% moisture, have been produced in five runs per day, equivalent to $2\frac{3}{4}$ tons or $3\frac{1}{4}$ cu. yd. per million gallons of sewage.[24] The moisture is reduced from 90 to 66% by the process.

The plant at Worcester, Mass., Fig. 3, consists of 4 Bushnell presses of 125 39-in. circular plates each. Sludge is pumped into the presses by two triplex pumps having 6-in. bronze ball valves. Between the pumps and the presses there is a 1,130-gal. equalizing tank supplied with compressed air as a cushion at the top and from the bottom of which a 10-in. main with 6-in. branches feeds the presses. The follower or rear end plate of the press carries a 10-in. hydraulic ram with a 48-in. travel which brings the plates into close contact so as to prevent leakage, and the sludge is then pumped in under a pressure of 80 lb. per sq. in. The cake produced is 36 in. in diameter and $\frac{3}{4}$ in. thick. On falling from the cloths it is carried by a conveyor to a car holding 3 cu. yd., run to a trestle and dumped. Four sludge cars and two motor cars are provided. Each press will produce, with 8 fillings, 16 cu. yd. of cake per day.

In 1916 a daily average of 37,600 gallons of sludge, 93.74 per cent. moisture, produced 36.1 tons of cake, 72.8 per cent. moisture, containing 1.23 tons of solids per million gallons of sewage. The cost of pressing was $7.05 per million gallons of sewage, or $5.71 per ton of solids.

---

[23] *Surveyor & Mun. & Co. Eng.*, July 23, 1915.

[24] Owing to alterations in operation this was cut down to 90 tons in 1915-1916.

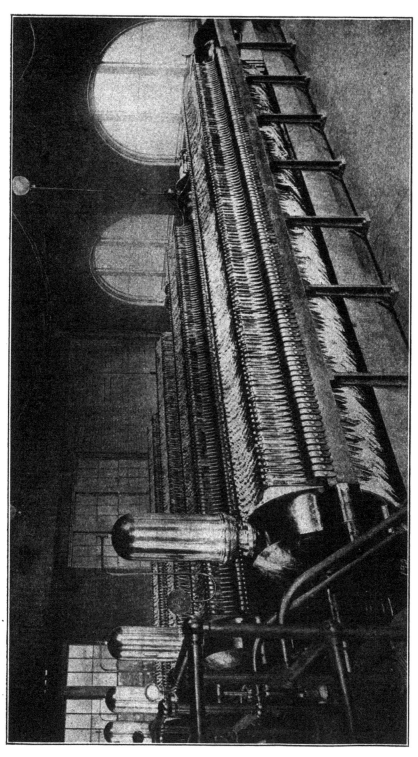

Fig. 3. Four Filter Presses at Worcester, Mass.

At Providence there are 18 presses of from 43 to 54 plates each. These are filled with sludge under a pressure of 60 lb. per sq in. The cake, 36 in. square and 1¼ in. thick, amounts to 64 tons per day.

At Spandau the sludge from a population of 80,000 is forced from cylindrical steel receivers under a pressure of 33 lb. per sq. in. to the 8 presses. The plates and frames are 3.6 ft. square and made of wood. Each plate has 2 inlet slots near the top and vertical drainage grooves leading to drainage ducts in the bottom. Fig. 4.

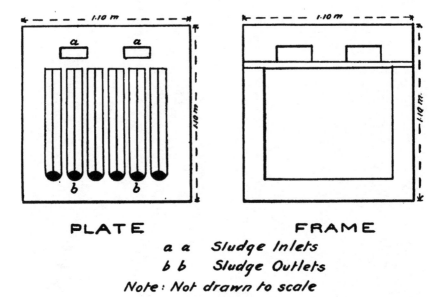

PLATE   FRAME

a a   Sludge Inlets
b b   Sludge Outlets
Note: Not drawn to scale

SPANDAU

Fig. 4. Diagrams of Wooden Plate and Frame used at Spandau, Germany.

After filling, the presses are subjected to an increased pressure by a hand pump and the sludge is left under a pressure of from 60 to 75 lb. per sq. in. for 20 hours. The cake is then 1¼ in. to 1½ in. thick and contains 60% moisture. On opening up each press the sludge drops into 4 tip cars for removal. It is then either sold at 4.6 ct. per cu. yd. (1913) or air-dried and used for fuel. It has no appreciable odor.

At York, England, where the grease makes the sludge particularly difficult to press, milk of lime is flushed into the press in advance of the sludge, which has already received its dose.

Another plan when dealing with such sludge is to heat the presses by injecting steam and, as at Bradford, heating also the sludge itself in advance. The grease then passes off in large part with the drainage liquor.[25]

The author was told at the works that the cake here contains but 27 or 28% moisture. The power required for pressing is given by Kershaw as from 7 to 13½ b. h. p. per ton (8 to 15 b. h. p. per long ton) of cake pressed per hour, depending on the size of the plant and the moisture and other characteristics of the sludge.

The cloths are a little more than twice the size of the plates over which they are folded. They are made of jute, duck or other fabric; at Worcester of 11 oz. duck 40 in. wide. Their life varies greatly, depending on the sludge, the pressure to which they are subjected, whether they are cleaned periodically, etc., but is usually rather brief from rotting. Elsner states that the life of (probably jute) cloths may be as much as 4 weeks if first treated with a tar composition. At Spandau they were said to last from one to two months; at Worcester, according to Metcalf and Eddy, 6 to 9 weeks is regarded as reasonable when operating at the rate of 12 cleanings per day of 10 hours. Stated another way, 2.44 sq. yd. of duck are required per ton of dry solids.

A septic sludge or one containing particles of lime—especially if left unslaked—or particles of rust from the plates shortens the life of the cloths. Probably for the last reason wood has been used for plates in Germany instead of iron.

At Leeds it was decided, after trying different cloths, to adopt 54-in. 3-ply twist twilled jute sacking, 30 oz. per yd. Experiments were then made to increase the durability of the cloths, first by shrinking and then by treating with different oils. The best results were secured by oiling an 8-inch strip around the edge of each cloth, around the center hole and where the bosses on the plates meet with "Golden-Bloomless" mineral oil costing 23.7 ct. per gal. or "Black Oil," a crude petroleum costing 10 ct. per U. S. gal. The effect of oiling seems to be to render the material more elastic and so prevent its rupture under strain. One gallon sufficed for 5 cloths, increasing their average life from 156 to 200 pressings. The saving effected is shown by the following statement:[26]

	Price per yd.	Cost of pressing per ton (2,000 lb.) of cake.
Year ending March 31, 1913	21.5 cts.	39.8 cts.
Year Ending March 31, 1915	28.6 cts.	36.5 cts.

It is estimated that about $1,450 is thus saved annually.

---

[25] The grease is recovered from the press liquor, in the last fiscal year owing to the high price of fats, to the value of $387,000. Joseph Garfield, Sewage Works Engineer.

[26] *Surveyor & Mun. & Co. Eng.,* July 23, 1915.

After drainage is complete the pressure is released, the plates are separated and the sludge falls or is scraped off the cloths onto a conveyor or into a tip car, by which it is removed for disposal. This operation takes from 10 to 30 minutes or more. The entire operation of filling, pressing and emptying ordinarily takes from 45 minutes to 2 hours.

Sludge Cake.

In practice precipitated sludge is reduced to cake having about 20% its original weight and containing from 50 to 70% moisture. The moisture is not uniform in the cake, being greatest near the point where admitted to the press. The weight of this cake is about 8 2-3 tons per million gallons of sewage (Rideal). The cakes run from an inch or less in thickness to 1½ or 2 in. if greasy and well dosed with lime. On breaking it up the weight per cu. yd. is reduced to about 1,350 lb. when the voids are found to be about 40%. By air-drying under cover this weight may be further reduced by about 50%.

Analyses of sludge cake as produced at Chorley and Dorking, England, are given in the Fifth Report of the Royal Commission on Sewage Disposal. The sewage in each case is domestic. At Chorley, with combined sewage, 9 grains per Imp. gal. of alumino ferric is used for precipitation, and at Dorking, which is partially sewered on the separate system, 5 grains per Imp. gal. of lime. The cake as delivered contains about 50% moisture, but the samples analyzed were dried at 110 degrees C.

	Chorley	Dorking
Grit	25.30	6.84
Oxides of iron and aluminum	9.37	3.46
Lime	10.32	23.16
Phosphoric acid	0.98	0.66
Nitrogen (total)	1.28	0.89

At Leeds in the year 1913-14 the average composition of the cake was as follows:

Water.. 60.1 per cent.
Volatile matter.. 16.7 per cent.
   Nitrogen, 5.9 per cent.
   Total grease, 6.3 per cent.
Mineral residue .... 23.2 per cent.
   Calcium phos., .94 per cent.   —————
                             100.0 per cent.

The solids from the sewage normally comprised 35.3% of the cake.

The average of 4 analyses of commercially dried (10% moisture) activated sludge, with especial reference to their fertilizing value, are given by William R. Copeland as follows:[27]

   Nitrogen as ammonia................................4.68%
   Available phosphoric acid.........................0.57%

[27] *Eng. Rec.,* Oct. 7, 1916.

Cost of Pressing Sludge.

The cost of pressing is given by the Royal Commission on Sewage Disposal for two typical groups of towns:

Group I—For towns of 30,000 persons or more employing chemical precipitation followed by sedimentation or sedimentation alone and where no special addition of lime is required on account of industrial waste. Sludges under such conditions will require lime equivalent to from 2 to 4% of the weight of the pressed cake.

Group II—For towns of less than 30,000 persons and for those where, because the sludge is greasy or derived from septic tanks, it is necessary to add lime equivalent to from 5 to 20% of the weight of the pressed cake.

The moisture in each case is assumed to be 90% in the wet sludge and 55% in the pressed cake.

COST OF PRESSING SLUDGE.
In cents per ton of 2,000 lb.

Wet Sludge—	Group I	Group II
Operation	9.6—12.0	14.5—24.4
Operation and fixed charges	13.2—15.6	18.1—28.0
Pressed Cake—		
Operation	43.5—54.4	65.2—109
Operation and fixed charges	59.7—70.6	81.4—125

Moore and Silcock give the cost of pressing in England at from 32.6 ct. to 54.4 ct. per ton of cake; Elsner at $4.50 per million gallons of sewage. According to Schiele the cost of producing one ton of cake from 5.8 cu. yd. of wet sludge, including fixed charges, varies from 41½ ct. to $1.28, and averages 85 ct.

In a list of 18 British cities Metcalf and Eddy find the cost of pressing to vary from 6 to 43 ct. per ton of wet sludge or from 27 to 93 ct. per ton of cake.

At the Dalmarnock Works at Glasgow 171,476 tons of crude sludge were pressed to 291,045 tons of cake in the year ending May 31, 1916, at a cost of $2.16 per million gal. of sewage, or 67 ct. per ton of cake.

At the Knostrop works at Leeds in the year ending March 31, 1915, 42,321 tons of cake, 60% moisture, were produced at a cost of $15,480, exclusive of interest and amortization, and $6,681 for disposal or, for pressing, per ton of cake, 36.7 ct.; per ton dry solids, $1.03.

For German conditions Reichle and Thiesing mention from 63½ to 85 ct. as fair limits (before the war).[28]

Estimates based on foreign practice cannot of course be applied directly to American conditions. The following is the distribution of cost based upon figures estimated for Wimbledon by Santo Crimp:

[28] "Sewage Sludge," p. 69.

Wages 36.0%
Lime 40.0%
Coal 9.6%
Cloths 12.8%
Oil, etc. 1.6%

Total 100.0%

American cost data are practically limited to experience at Worcester and Providence, data for which are as follows:

COST OF SLUDGE PRESSING.

Range	Worcester	Providence[29]		
	1899 to 1912	1903	1910	1916
Per mil. gal. sewage....	$3.85 to $6.76	$2.44	$4.06	$2.78
Per ton of dry solids...	3.39 to 4.64	2.27	2.54	3.38
Per ton of cake........	0.91 to 1.37	0.67	0.72½	0.94½

The above figures are in general based upon precipitated sludge. Owing to the greater amount of lime required it will cost perhaps a third more to press fresh or septic settled sludge.

Disposal of Cake.

The cake may sometimes be disposed of for a nominal sum, say 10 to 25 ct. per ton, to farmers, but if there is no demand for it, it may be used for filling at about an equal cost. When deposited in depths up to 12 feet in water-soaked land near Leeds[30] it was observed to shrink about 33% in two years and to generate more or less heat.

While there is more or less odor in the press house this does not carry far, and if kept under cover it is quite inoffensive. Fresh cake kept moist by rain, especially if the weather is warm, will give off a certain amount of odor, but, if first air-dried to 20 or 30% moisture, objectionable odors are usually prevented.

An advantage in lignite sludge, besides being inodorous, is that it can be utilized by burning under the boiler, and experiments by W. L. Stevenson at Philadelphia show that by the addition of a small amount of combustible material to ordinary air-dried sludge from plain sedimentation there will be obtained a material having a moderate value as fuel.

The foregoing remarks have been confined to the plate type of press, often spoken of as the "Johnson" filter press, this having

[29] Costs include disposal.

[30] In 1914, 13,868 short tons were used for manure and 26,634 tons for filling in land.

been almost universally used for the pressing of sewage sludge heretofore. There are, however, several other more recent types which deserve mention.

The Kelly Filter Press.

The Kelly Filter Press, Fig. 5, consists of a steel frame supporting a cylindrical "press shell" at one end and a carriage for inserting into and withdrawing from the other end a series of longitudinal filter leaves. Each leaf consists of a horizontal pipe above connected to a similar pipe below by a mesh of double crimped No. 0.105 gage wire. This wire mesh enters a slot in each pipe for the removal of the filtrate, to which it is strongly riveted or welded. A bag of extra heavy twill or duck is drawn over each leaf and the end sewed up by hand, forming the filtering medium. The leaves are uniformly spaced but of different heights, depending on their position with reference to the press shell.

Fig. 5. The Kelly Filter Press.

At each end of the filter carriage are plates for supporting the leaves, one of these providing the head of the press shell when the leaves are inserted. By means of a groove in the head plate corresponding to an annular projection on the end of the shell, which are forced together on a gasket and held by a special locking mechanism, all leakage during operation is prevented.

In operation the carriage and leaves are inserted in the shell and the head is locked. The shell is then filled with sludge by a pipe, while the air is released by an overflow valve at the top. This, it is claimed, takes but about four minutes. When filled the overflow valve is closed and about 40 lb. pressure applied to the sludge pipe. The cake forms on the surface of the bags as the filtrate passes thru and is carried off by the frame pipes and drains.

After the cake is built up the sludge supply is shut off and compressed air admitted from above, displacing the remaining wet sludge and aiding in drying the cake. This is then removed from the bags by shaking, by loosening with a wooden spade, or by compressed air introduced thru the drainage pipes.

The following data are taken from a circular of the manufacturer:

Size of shell	30″ x 72″	40″ x 108″	48″ x 120″
Capacity of shell—			
cu. ft	32	75	120
gal	240	560	900
Number of leaves	4–9	6–8	6–10
Filter area, sq. ft	60–130	180–250	260–450
[31]Weight of cake 1½″ thick	667	1333	3333
[31]Average weight of cake in tons per 24 hours	3⅓–6⅔	13⅓–26⅔	33⅓–66⅔

The economies claimed for this press are due to the small amount of labor required, lack of wear on filter cloths and the avoidance of breakage of plates.

The Sweetland Filter Press.

This consists, Fig. 6, of a number of parallel circular leaves consisting of a heavy wire screen hung from a casting above. Each leaf has an outlet nipple at the top connecting with a drainage duct in the above casting, is bound by a stiff U-shaped frame on the edge and covered with suitable canvas. The entire series of leaves is enclosed in two semi-cylindrical castings, the lower of which can be swung to one side on a hinge.

The sludge is forced in thru a channel in the bottom of the lower casting and flows up between the leaves and as the filtrate passes thru the canvas and out thru the drainage duct the solids form a cake on each side of every leaf. When the process of filtering becomes slow, compressed air is introduced, blowing the wet sludge in the bottom of the cylinder back into the storage tank and drying the cakes. The lower casting is then swung to one side and the dewatered sludge drops out, aided by reversing the air pressure thru the leaves. This back pressure serves as well to keep the filter surfaces clean. The operation of dumping is claimed by the manufacturer to occupy but from 8 to 20 minutes.

In a press of this kind used by R. W. Pratt at the Cleveland Sewage Testing Station the leaves were 2 ft. in diameter. The average moisture in the wet sludge was about 86% and that of the cake between 62 and 76%. Mr. Pratt mentions the importance of keeping the cakes from adhering to each other by providing sufficient clearance. Where the leaves were even as much as 3 in. between centers no cake was obtained with less than 70%

---

[31] Assuming weight of cake 66⅔ lb. per cu. ft.

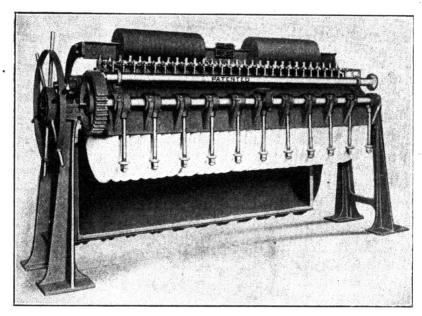

Fig. 6. The Sweetland Filter Press.

moisture, and it was concluded that there should be a clearance of not less than 3 nor more than 4½ inches. Pressures of from 30 to 35 lb. were sufficient except for short periods at the end of the run when as much as 50 lb. were sometimes used. As to the time required the best results were with a half hour for forming the cake, ¾ hour for drying or 1¼ hours for the entire run.

These tests were mostly with Imhoff sludge, but as there is no exposure of the sludge to the air, Mr. Pratt is of the opinion that "in large installations the Sweetland press could be operated without odors or nuisance" with ordinary sludge.

RESULTS OF PRESSING IMHOFF SLUDGE.

Condensed from Table 61, Report Sewage Testing Station, Cleveland, 1914.

Number of leaves..........	16	16	14	14
Spacing center to center....	1½"	3"	3"	4½"
No. of runs averaged.......	4	7	2	4
Time in hours				
Pressing...............	.94[32]	1.15	1.65[33]	.50
Drying................	.12½	.36	.58[33]	.75
Total..................	....	1.51	....	1.25
Spec. grav. of raw sludge....	1.05	1.06	1.11	1.07[34]
Per cent. moisture				
Raw sludge.............	89	86	82	86
Cake..................	68	72	75	64
Pressure—lb. per sq. in.....	53[34]	43	43	42
Lb. cake per run	242[34]	314	139	90

[32] Average from 2 runs.
[33] Result from 1 run.
[34] Average from 3 runs.

The Worthington Filter Press.

The Worthington or "Berrigan" press, Fig. 7, has been tried out in particular at Milwaukee in connection with activated sludge.

The sludge is placed in each of a number of unbleached muslin bags inclosed in a bag of special fine canvas. The bags are hung vertically between two plates, which, being drawn together by means of a toggle joint, squeeze the superfluous water from the sludge and thru the bags. As the pressure continues, the motion, which is automatically controlled, decreases, but the pressure may be increased very greatly.

Fig. 7. The Worthington or Berrigan Filter Press.

The plates are grooved and faced with wire to facilitate drainage. In size they are manufactured 36 in. by 48 in., 72 in. by 108 in., and 96 in. by 120 in.

The Milwaukee experiments were made with a 72-in. by 108-in. press, with 10 bags. The sludge, 98% or 99% water, is first concentrated to 96 or 97%. The best way to accomplish this, whether by decanting the supernatant water after settling from 1 to 3 hours or scraping or sucking up the deposited sludge, remains to be settled. It is a material factor in the economy of operation, as every per cent. reduction means a large saving in the volume of sludge to be handled and consequently in the cost of the plant.

The concentrated sludge is fed into the bags without any addition of lime and then subjected to a pressure gradually increasing to about 60 lb. per sq. in. After draining the pressure is released, the bags are lifted out and emptied by gravity. They keep fairly clean in this way, but, if sludge adheres to the surface, it is removed by a jet of steam.

The Milwaukee machine will produce from about 2 m. g. of sewage, a ton of cake 1 in. thick per run, which, by further drying to 10% moisture, will yield about 1,000 lb. in a condition, after grinding, to be used as fertilizer, for which it is said to be particularly well adapted. The time required is about 5 hours per operation, so that the above press will produce some 5 tons of cake per 24 hours of 75% moisture.

One laborer, according to Mr. T. C. Hatton, Chief Engineer of the Milwaukee Sewerage Commission, can attend to 5 presses, so that the cost of attendance is low, and as to the power required, the designer, Mr. Berrigan, claims that a 15-h. p. motor will suffice for 5 machines.

The following conclusions were based upon the Milwaukee experiments with activated sludge[35]:

"Sludge can be dewatered satisfactorily from 96% to 75% moisture by either a plate press or pressure press without the addition of lime or other base.

"The filter bags used in the presses must be cleansed frequently to maintain efficiency. This can be done by soaking in a bath of dilute caustic soda and hot water.

"Sludge after pressing can be stored in a building without creating offensive odors more than 50 ft. away, and can be easily handled."

After drying (to 10%) this sludge contains from 4.5 to 5% of ammonia, for which there is, ample market as a fertilizer.

The cost of a press such as has been described complete is stated to be about $4,000, exclusive of overhead charges, to which should be added $800 for an accumulator, or $500 for a pump of capacity to serve 20 presses.

An estimate of the cost of operation is given by Mr. Hatton in the Report of the Commission for 1916, as follows, based upon a plant capable of handling the sludge from 100 m. g. d. of sewage:

COST PER TON OF CAKE.

Labor (3 shifts of 8 hours)	$1.36
Bags (cleaning and upkeep)	.64
Power	.09
Contingencies	.16
Overhead charges, 10% of cost	1.21
Total	$3.46

or, since 1 m. g. d. of sewage produces ½ ton of cake, the cost of pressing is about $1.73 per m. g. of sewage.

[35] Rep. Mil Sew. Com. 1916. See also W. R. Copeland in *Eng. Rec.*, Oct. 7, 1916.

According to Mr. G. W. Fuller the cost is about $3.00 per ton of dry solids or $2.70 per ton with 10% moisture.[36]

ESTIMATED COST OF PRESSING ACTIVATED SLUDGE

In the Stockyards District, Chicago, by Langdon Pearse and W. D. Richardson.[37] Based on 96 tons of Dry Material per day.

Cost per dry ton.

Supplies:		
Duck at $1.75 per lin. yd., 120 in. wide..................$1.37		
Miscellaneous .... .24		
	$1.61	
Labor $1.13		
Power 3.24 h. p., equals 2.42 kw.-hr. at 0.7 cts. per hr. .41		
	1.54	
Operating expenses		$3.15
Fixed charges		2.57
Grand total		$5.72

While this press has been shown to be well adapted to the dewatering of activated sludge, Mr. Berrigan claims that it will also be found satisfactory with plain settled or septic sludges without the addition of lime, but the writer is not aware that this has been conclusively demonstrated as yet.

Conclusion.

Dewatering sewage sludge by filter pressing with the plate type of press has been brought to a point where its efficacy and cost can be closely predicted. With fresh settled or precipitated sludge and the addition of from 0.5 to 3% of lime and a pressure of 70 or 80 lb. per sq. in. a firm satisfactory cake can be produced.

Several of the newer forms of press promise an improvement on the older plate press, but experience with them in handling sludge has been so very limited that their comparative merits are not yet definitely known.

The great demand for sludge pressing in the past was the result in large measure of the practice of chemical precipitation. This kind of treatment is unquestionably on the decline for normal sewages, but in the meantime the activated sludge process has appeared and promises to be adopted with success in many situations, and the necessity of promptly dewatering the large volumes of watery sludge may lead to an increased demand for sludge pressing in the next few years. Moreover, the fact that new processes for recovering the valuable ingredients in sludge

[36] *Eng. Rec.,* Oct. 7, 1916.
[37] *Eng. & Cont.,* July 11, 1917, p. 28.

combined with the increasing demand for grease and ammonia all tend to a development of methods of dewatering, in which filter pressing, up to the present time, is the most prominent.

Quoting Mr. John T. Thompson of Leeds:

"Progress already made in this direction shows that in time it will be possible by artificial processes to get rid of all sludge without causing any nuisance, and make sufficient by the sale of by-products at least to pay the full cost of disposal."

The present paper is intended to present the main features of the practice as carried out in the past with the hope that those members of the Society who have a more intimate and practical knowledge of the subject will add their more valuable personal experience and views regarding the present status and the lines on which future development may be expected.

NOTE

Aside from personal notes, municipal reports and articles in the engineering periodicals, the author has made free use of data found in the following treatises:

Sanitary Engineering, Moore and Silcock;
Sewage, Rideal;
Principles of Sewage Treatment, Dunbar and Calvert;
Sewage Disposal, Kershaw;
Sewage Disposal, Kinnicutt, Winslow & Pratt;
Sewage Disposal, Fuller;
Sewage Disposal Works, Raikes;
Sewage Sludge, Elsner, Spillner, Allen;
American Sewerage Practice, Metcalf & Eddy.

PROCEEDINGS FOR 1917-1918

This is the first of three numbers in which the papers and committee reports for the fall of 1917 will be published during the Society year. The second issue will appear in January and the third in April. They will be paged consecutively and an index will be printed in the last number so that they can be bound if desired.

Members are urged to send to the Secretary as soon as convenient, written discussions of the papers and reports appearing in the issue, that they may be published in the January issue. Papers by members and others will be very acceptable to the Committee on Publication and should be sent as near December 15th as possible, that they may appear in January. Committee reports not yet sent are due at the same time. Send them to the Secretary, 2535 North Pennsylvania Street, Indianapolis, Ind.

SPECIAL FORMS OF CONTRACTS FOR UNUSUAL CONSTRUCTION AND TO MEET PRESENT CONDITIONS OF LABOR AND PRICES

By T. Keith Legaré, City Engineer, Columbia, S. C.

Much has been written lately in regard to letting contracts for construction work on the basis of cost-plus-percentage, or some other method, and the following notes along this line may be of interest.

The City of Columbia, South Carolina, is situated on a plateau sloping in all directions and bounded on the west by a large river, from which the water supply is taken at a point about opposite the center of the city. In order to dispose of the sanitary sewage from the northeast, north and northwest sections of the city, it was decided to construct a pipe sewer outfall, 6¾ miles in length. The route of this proposed sewer is along a valley formed by a creek north of the city, and thence along the east bank of the Columbia Canal, which is parallel to the river, to a point below the water works, where it will empty into the river. Several surveys were made in order to locate the best possible line, but in some places there was very little choice, on account of the steep hills, and it will be necessary to place nearly 4,000 ft. of the sewer on concrete trestles and a great deal of it thru solid rock. Before proposals were asked for on the construction of this sewer, it was realized by the writer that, on account of the difficult construction and the unusual conditions of local labor, bids submitted by contractors would probably be excessively high, therefore, with the intention of forming a contract that would be satisfactory and fair to both contractor and municipality, the following method was outlined in the proposals.

Cost-Plus-Fixed-Sum-Contract.

For furnishing, without cost to the City of Columbia, South Carolina, all tools, appliances or machinery necessary or proper for performing and completing the work, maintaining same in proper working condition, and workmen's compensation and public liability insurance; and furnishing all necessary labor and completing the entire undertaking for the sum of............................ Dollars, plus the actual cost of the labor. We guarantee the cost of labor and the contractor's fee not to exceed the total sum of ....Dollars. Should the total cost of this contract exceed this amount, the City of Columbia, South Carolina, will not be held liable for the excess amount, and should the total cost be less than this amount, the contractor is to receive one-fourth of the difference, in addition to the above fee. Date on which we propose to complete the above work.........................

It will be noted that the contractor, under this form of contract, is to furnish at his own expense all equipment and liability insurance, the cost of which together with whatever profit he considers that he is entitled to, makes up the "contractor's fee"; and that he also has the opportunity of making additional profit if the actual cost of the work is less than the "guaranteed cost." Also that, if by inefficient management, or on account of other causes, the work should cost more than a stated sum, the municipality will not pay this additional cost. Some contractors object to the "guaranteed cost" feature of this contract because their profit may be reduced or eliminated thereby, but if they are willing to accept a contract on the lump-sum basis why should there be objection to this method? The municipality could not afford to guarantee to a contractor a certain profit regardless of the final cost of the work and it seems only fair to insist that the contractor place a limit on same. It is not claimed by the writer that this form of contract is without objectionable features, but that it has less than some of the ordinary forms: notably the cost-plus-per-centage contract, which the writer has had the opportunity of studying to a large extent recently.

The proposals submitted for constructing the sewer described herewith did not prove a favorable test for the cost-plus-a-fixed-sum contract, as all contractors bidding on the work are now engaged on large government contracts, in connection with the army camps being constructed at Columbia and other cities nearby, and they do not seem anxious for any new work unless there is a large profit certain. As all bids were considered entirely too high, they were rejected and the work will be done by a city force under the writer's direction.

THE CLEARING HOUSE OF INFORMATION

Members are reminded that the services of the Clearing House of Information are at their command at any time. If data are not on file from which a question can be answered, a circular letter will be sent out to the cities represented in the Society membership, about 270 of them, and responses to such requests for data are always prompt and full, and in considerable numbers. This is a good way to make yourself feel that you are making up for the loss of the convention this year.

THE REQUISITES OF AN EQUITABLE STREET IMPROVEMENT LAW

By Samuel D. Newton, Municipal Engineer, Cleveland, Tenn., and Charlotte, N. C.

The following remarks are put together rather hastily, not with the idea of adding to the general fund of knowledge as regards the different methods used for initiating and administering street improvements, but in the hope that they may serve as a hook on which to hang a discussion looking towards greater uniformity in this important department of municipal work. The subject, perhaps, better fits the pen of a lawyer than that of an engineer, but as it perforce falls to the lot of the municipal engineer to administer the laws and the ordinances based thereon after they have been put upon the statute and minute books, and as, consequently, the municipal engineer is usually more thoroly conversant with the shortcomings and excellencies of the various and different statutes, the writer feels that no apology need be offered for venturing to present these remarks.

The varieties of improvement laws are like the Gadarene demons, their name is Legion, and very often their provisions are such as to tempt the infested swine—no reflections intended—into a mad plunge sea-ward. There are many more varieties than there are States in the American Union; in the State of Tennessee alone there are four of general application, referring to cities and towns of different specified populations, as well as an indefinite number intended to apply to single towns only, and all of them vary in minutiae as well as in some of their more general features.

Essentially, however, all street improvement laws fall under two general heads; those in which the entire costs are to be borne by the municipality thru general taxation, usually deferred thru a greater or less period of time by means of bond issues, and those in which part or all of the expenses are proposed to be borne by the various abutting property owners, which latter are generally known as Abutting Property Laws. The former are usually special in their character, applying to some one particular town and commonly limiting the expenditure to some definite fixed sum which the municipality is specifically authorized to raise by a definite bond issue, while the latter are usually general, applying in common to all towns within certain specified limits of population, according to the latest Federal census. It is of these latter that this paper more especially treats, altho many of the remarks may be germane to either class.

I. Methods of Initiating Proceedings.

Usually these fall under two general classes; those in which proceedings start with a petition from the abutting holders, and those in which the first action is in the shape of an ordinance of the corporation's governing body. Something may be said in favor of either method. Generally, a more comprehensive program may be obtained if the city's council, or other governing body, take the initiative, as such a body, at least in theory, has a more comprehensive view of the needs of the town in general, while the individual holder has in view merely the needs, or fancied needs, of his own particular street or of his own lot. The corporation is supposed to have an expert to advise it, in the shape of its City Engineer or Street Commissioner. Unfortunately, however, the advice of this expert is not usually called for until the boundaries and limits of the Improvement District are already fixed. On the other hand, the petition plan more nearly satisfies the "consent of the governed" dogma, and affords the individual citizen, if intelligently used, a better opportunity of expressing his views. In general, I believe that the first plan is the better, altho provision should be made for considering petitions signed by a substantial majority of abutting owners.

As to what constitutes a substantial majority, and the method of reckoning it, customs differ. Usually, a two-thirds or three-fourths majority is specified; two-thirds ought to be sufficient. Such a majority is usually reckoned either on a per capita, a front-footage or a lot-area basis. Any one of these methods may at times seem to do injustice to individual lot owners. For an extreme instance, take a district in which nine-tenths of the property is owned by one person, while two or three small lots are owned by others. The small minority of front-footage could very easily get up a legal petition on the per capita basis over the head of the demurring major property owner and force him into a large expenditure of money when perhaps there would be no real call for street improvements for many years to come, and where the minority holders are gainers out of all proportion to their several investments. On the other hand, one large property holder could, on the front-footage method, hold the whip-hand over his smaller neighbors, retarding the material growth of a district which would otherwise develop naturally into valuable property. The lot-area method, in a district in which the lots are of irregular shapes and sizes, is inequitable, the holder of a narrow lot of considerable back-area having an unfair advantage over the holder of a shallow lot with a large frontage.

Perhaps the most equitable arrangement would be to combine the first two plans by specifying that a petition must be signed by the holders of at least a two-thirds majority of the front-footage, and a straight majority of all property holders irrespective of the sizes of their holdings. In any case, the governing body should hold a veto over any petition (except, perhaps, in the case where the abutting owners foot the whole bill), and this, so far as my knowledge goes, is always the case, since lot owners can not legally compel a city to appropriate money to defray the city's share of the costs. In all cases, the city's officials should have jurisdiction over the actual operations of improvements, the work being done on city's property. Of course, the Abutting Property Law never applies to privately owned passageways, altho, even in such instances, on the theory that such passageways will eventually become city streets and open to the public, it might be well to require the work to be done under the direction of the City Engineer.

II. Classes of Improvements.

Practice varies largely, also, as to the classes of improvements which may be carried on by an Improvement District under the Abutting Property Law. Usually, it is specified that the improvement must be permanent in nature, but so-called "permanent" improvements vary all of the way from water-bound macadam, even without curbs, gutters, underground drainage, and the like, to granite block paving, and may perhaps be held to embrace simple excavation or embankment work to specified grade with no kind of wearing surface whatever. In some cases the improvements may not be made to the street proper at all; the writer has personally built sanitary sewer laterals with no accompanying surface improvements, under the provisions of an Abutting Property Law. He can see no reason why, in a village or town totally unprovided with a sanitary drainage system, such a system, or even a purification plant, could not equitably be built on the abutting plan; but as it is the universal practice to build such systems under funds provided by general taxation, it seems highly inequitable to ask some outlying small district to pay, either entirely or in very large part, for an improvement, out of their own funds, when the remainder of the town has been sewered out of public funds; especially as the proper sanitation of any single district may spell the preservation of health and freedom from contagious diseases of the whole community.

To return, however, to the subject under discussion, it would seem that the term "permanent improvements" should be held to include only such classes of improvements as can be expected to outlast the bond-issue with which they are paid for; and, after the wearing out of the surfacing material, there should be left something permanent, over which a new surface can be built. In other words, no paving should be considered "permanent" which is not built upon some kind of foundation—concrete, either of Portland or bituminous cement, or its equivalent—which can be presumed to be durable.

Abutting property improvements may be held to embrace street pavements or merely sidewalks, or both. In the case of sidewalks, however, it is an open question in the writer's mind, whether the entire cost should not be borne out of the pocket of the abutting owner. Of course, the city should have the right to compel the owner to build sidewalks, and to build them under standard specifications thru the direction of the City Engineer, or the further right to build them at the owner's expense, protecting itself by a lien on his property, should he refuse.

Many Abutting Property Laws provide that neither maintenance nor resurfacing, to say nothing of entire renewal, can be chargeable in any part to abutting owners, and this is, I believe, in accordance with existing court decisions. But in such cases, if a makeshift is built at the start, an undue burden is laid upon the city when its temporary nature becomes fully apparent. Even in cases where there is no objection to making additional betterments under the statutes, it is exceedingly hard to get the citizens, having paid for one improvement, to go down into their pockets to buy a new one, or to determine what part of the new one is actual betterment, and so chargeable, either in whole or in part, against the abutting owner, and what part is mere renewal or repairs, not chargeable to the abutting owner. Personally, aside from the court holdings on the subject, I can see no good reason why the upkeep of a pavement in front of a man's place is not just as much the province of the citizen as the original building of it.

Also, under the head of permanent improvements, the proper drainage, or storm-sewerage, of any district, as determined by the judgment of a competent engineer, should be compulsory. It is as much the height of folly to depend upon surface drainage where storm-sewerage is really required as it is to depend upon a "fly swatter" where house screening is necessary. The subject of the proper drainage of the sub-grade is entirely too frequently neglected, often cutting down the life of the pavement by many years. At the same time, all "house connections," whether for improved or unimproved property, and all other underground structures, so far as they can be foreseen, should be laid before the permanent paving is put down. This is almost axiomatic, but in order that no loop-hole be left for evasion, provision for these things should be written into the law in unmistakable terms.

III. Proportioning of Expenses.

There are usually three grand divisions made of the expenses of paving under the abutting property plan, as between

(1) The street railway, if any, or other public service system, including steam railways, occupying any portion of the street to be paved;

(2) The city in general, and

(3) The abutting owners.

(1) *The Street Railway.* It is usually provided that both original cost and maintenance or renewal of such portions of the pavement as fall within what may be termed the right of way of the street or steam railway are to be borne entirely by the traction or railroad company using the street. This is hardly equi-

table, as a strip so occupied is still a portion of the street, open to the usual vehicular or pedestrian traffic, sometimes in preference to the remainder of the street. However, there is no question but that the major use of such a strip lies with the traction company or railroad; trucks or pleasure vehicles can turn out, street cars cannot. Moreover, such a section of the street is liable at any time to be torn up for the purpose of making track repairs or the like by the tenant company. Therefore, the preponderance of the expense should be borne by the traction company and the balance pro-rated in the usual way between the city and the abutting owners. Merely as a basis of discussion, I would suggest that one-eighth would be about the right proportion of the expense to be borne in such cases by the public and abutting owners.

As to the width of the strip so held to be occupied by the utility, and the major part of the expense of paving which (and keeping it in repair) should be borne by the utility, practice differs, some laws calling for nothing outside of the outer rails, and others providing for one, two or more feet, as the case may be. The usual length of a cross-tie is 8 ft., and, in tie renewals, about 6 in. of the pavement beyond the ends of the ties must be torn up, making a right-of-way strip in all about 9 ft. wide; or, using a standard gage track laid with rails having a normal width of head, the paving of a strip about 2 ft. wide on the outer side of the outside rails would seem to be properly chargeable in greater part to the traction company or railroad. Looked at in another way, the space occupied by the ordinary street car, plus safe clearance on either side, would more than take up such a 9-ft. right-of-way. In the case of double or multiple tracks, all of the space included between tracks, as well as the 2-ft. space on the outside of the outer rails, should be considered as within the traction company's or railroad's right-of-way.

(2) *City's Share.* Fundamentally, there are certain portions of the expense of paving which, irrespective of the ratio of division predetermined upon as between the individual holders and the city in general, naturally fall to the city's share. These are

(i) Intersections. It seems inequitable to charge the property holder for anything which does not lie immediately in front of his premises, and he is, theoretically at least, no more interested in paving street intersections than is any other taxpayer. Therefore, the entire cost of paving and improving street and alley intersections, except insofar as it is borne by the traction company or other semi-public corporation, naturally falls to the city's portion. Some writers of Abutting Property Laws, however, have assumed the theory that the care of the intersection falls to the intersecting streets, and, in one law with which I am familiar, it is provided that the cost of paving intersections shall, after being divided on the usual ratio between the city and the abutting owners, so far as the abutting owners' share is concerned, be pro-rated over the frontage of abutting lots for half a block in all directions over both improved and unimproved streets. This very largely increases the work of making out the assessment rolls (each half-block necessarily stands as a unit by itself), is difficult to explain to the citizens, is, to the writer's mind at least, founded on an erroneous theory and unjust to abutting owners, and should therefore be condemned.

(ii) Storm Sewers. For the reasons already stated when discussing the matter of sanitary sewers, and for the additional reason that it is difficult and often impossible to design a storm sewer or system of storm sewers intended to take care of the drainage of any particular district without in many instances, both for outlets and for other portions of the structures going outside of the limits of such district, it would seem that the cost of all storm-sewerage and of all other publicly owned underground structures should be charged to the city at large; and, in fact, this is usually, but not universally, done.

(iii) Sub-Grade. Usually, but not universally, the cost of shaping and compacting the sub-grade is borne by the city at large. However, the writer is not so clear as to the justice of this charge as of the others mentioned. Of course, if the grading, either cut or fill, is excessive, it may easily become a damage rather than a betterment to any particular piece of property, and as such excessive grading is clearly for the benefit of the city at large and not for individual property holders, it should be chargeable to the city; and, probably, as it is difficult to draw a strict line between excessive and ordinary grading, or to tell whether, or in how great a degree, any particular grade may be a betterment to the individual lot, and, further, as the cost of ordinary grading bears rather a small proportion to the entire cost of any particular improvement, it is just as well to write the entire cost of all grading and compacting of the sub-grade as belonging to the city in general.

(3) *Property Holders' Share.* Fundamentally, the improving of the street in front of a man's property is held to constitute a betterment to his property, and the selling value of the land is usually increased in a greater degree than the cost of the improvement charged against the land and made a lien thereupon. This is the basic theory on which the Abutting Property Law is written.

Practice varies widely as to the established ratio between the city's and property holders' shares of the expenses, after making the deductions embraced in the previous discussions, and it is difficult to say what is equitable in all cases. I believe that the ratio more commonly adopted is one to two—one-third to the city, and two-thirds to the abutting owners—and this is probably about right on the average. However, on a street where the thru traffic is heavy and the local traffic light, the city's proportion should be increased, and on strictly residence streets, leading nowhere, and where there is absolutely no thru travel, it is doubtful whether the city should pay any portion of the cost, except, perhaps, for intersections, storm-sewerage, and sub-grade. Probably the best way to determine the proportion would be by means of an official traffic census; but here difficulties arise again. In the first place, it is practically impossible to differentiate betweeen thru traffic and local traffic; time is usually so limited that it is impracticable to take an intelligent traffic census, which should be of considerable duration; and, again, what constitutes a very heavy traffic for a street in one town would be almost negligible for a street in a larger city. It is suggested that the law might designate a traffic census to extend over a normal period of one week or more, so as to arrive at a fair average, and that a sliding scale be then adopted, varying the ratio for dividing the expense according to the weight of the traffic and the population of the town. It is fully recognized that this method is bunglesome, and would have to be worked out very carefully in order not to put an injustice on either side. It would also delay proceedings, which are in almost every instance taken up too late in the season at the best.

As to the methods of proportioning the property holders' expenses among themselves, practice again varies widely. One law with which the writer is familiar provides that the costs be proportioned according to the unimproved values of the separate properties. This necessitates the working out of the areas of the several lots, and the appointing of a special valuation board from among the several abutting owners. It is inequitable for various reasons. For instance, if an improvement district (such as I have known several times to occur in practice) extends from out of a region of high class property into a region of low class property, the high class property pays more than its share of the expense, while the low class property pays less than its share. Again, a single property of high valuation, on account, for instance, of depth, and consequent large area, but with a small frontage of the improved street, pays more than its share, and vice versa. A corner lot is generally assessed higher than an inside lot, and pays a larger pro rata. Then, when the cross street comes to be paved, trouble ensues. This method is apt to engender a large amount of squabbling and hard feelings as between neighbors over their respective valuations. However, if assessments are to be made on a property valuation, this valuation should take no account of improvements, as otherwise the man who has highly improved his lot is penalized, while the man who has allowed his lot to remain unoccupied is rewarded for his unprogressiveness.

Another method of pro-rating the assessments is by the area of the lots; but here, again, injustice creeps in, as a deep lot with a small frontage would pay an assessment out of all proportion to what is paid by a wide and shallow lot.

Probably the best method is to assess the costs according to foot-frontage. However, for obvious reasons, even this method is by no means perfect. Nevertheless, it is the easiest one to administer, comes nearer to true equity than any other which has been suggested, and is the one the writer would recommend.

It is usually provided that certain properties be not taxed with any assessment at all, and that no property be assessed over a certain proportion (perhaps 50%) of its valuation. In such cases, either the city at large has to pay the assessment, or excess assessment, which would normally fall to such a lot, or else it is divided among the other abutting owners. It would seem to be more equitable to charge such costs to the city. The most common provision is, I believe, that properties not subject to special taxation, or, in other words, strictly public properties, pay no assessments, and it has been held by the courts that properties used for religious, benevolent, or educational purposes, or for purposes of burial, while usually not subject to general taxation, are subject to special taxation and can therefore be held for their assessments under the Abutting Property Law.

In one law with which I am familiar no exception of this kind is made, except for a provision that no property can be assessed for over 50% of its last valuation for taxation purposes. The interpretation in this case would seem to be that such properties as we are discussing, not being valued for taxation purposes, and half of such valuation consequently being nil, are not liable for paving assessments, and the entire costs of the assessments which would naturally fall to them must be borne by the city at large.

Valuations for taxation purposes are usually very low—in some cases ridiculously low—and it would seem more equitable to have a special valuation placed upon any lot claiming exemption from part or all of its assessments on these grounds.

IV. Designation of Materials to be Used.

Here, again, practice varies greatly. Some laws leave the designation of materials to be used to be determined by petition of the abutting owners, and, to a superficial view, this would seem to be fair, but when it is considered what a wide scope this provision allows to the activities of the paving promoter, and how little the average citizen really knows as to the general properties of the various paving materials, the absurdity of the provision becomes apparent. Other laws require the city governing board to narrow down the call for bids to the use of some particular predesignated paving material, with the consequence, especially when a patented material or method is specified, that very often but one bona fide bid is received, with one or two other contractors bidding high in order to keep the designated paving contractor in face. At least one State requires that bids shall be received on a number of different specified types, that thereafter selection shall be made from among them, and new bids received on the one particular type selected. This would seem to be a costly and cumbersome method without any apparent benefits to offset the cost and delay. Probably the most reasonable method of procedure is to call for bids on a number of different specified types, and then, after intelligent comparison, taking into account not only the first costs, but also all other relative advantages of the several types, as set forth by expert advice, to select the material that seems on all grounds to be best fitted for the purpose in hand, and to let contract to the best and lowest responsible bidder on that type.

Some paving laws provide that the city can, at its option, be its own contractor, purchasing materials in the open market and doing the work by day labor. This is an excellent provision for cities which do work enough to afford the purchase of the necessary equipment.

V. Financing.

It is almost universally provided, I believe, that the city's portion of paving costs may or must be deferred by bond issues of fairly long term. Sometimes these bonds are made to run for fifty years or more, or until after the improvements they are intended to cover are worn out twice over. Of course, this is bad financing. No bond issue for street improvements should run over twenty years at the outside; and, even then, at 5% interest, not compounded, the original cost is doubled. A ten or fifteen-year period would be better. It is the usual custom, wisely, or unwisely, to require a three, five, or eight-year guarantee on street improvements. Pavements usually long outlast their guarantee periods, but their average life is probably not over fifteen years, and no bond period should, under any circumstances, be longer than the expected life of the improvement it covers. Bonds are usually of the sinking-fund type, but may be of other types. There is an illuminating discussion in "Engineering News-Record" for August 30, 1917, as to the relative desirabilities of different types of bonds, and the decision there arrived at is that the serial type of bond is the cheapest and best. The overwhelming objection to the sinking-fund bond is that cities are so proverbially careless in providing for and administering their sinking funds.

The abutting owner usually has a short period (perhaps five years) in which to make payments on his share of the costs, the deferred payments to bear interest. No objection is seen to this provision. Payments to the contractor are in the meanwhile covered by means of short-term bonds, and it frequently happens that the contractor has to accept these short-term bonds as part payment for his work. This latter is bad financing and is apt to be reflected in the price he bids for the work.

It is a moot question whether a bond-issue for street improvements should be put to a vote of the citizens or not. Usually the Abutting Property Law clothes the city's governing body with power to issue bonds for such purposes without such a referendum, but, as has been previously remarked on another point, the "will of the people" would be more nearly reflected by a popular vote. The objection is that the imagination of the average citizen is short flying, his inertia is great, and it is usually difficult enough to get improvements started at present without any further impediments being placed in the way.

It seems to me that the whole question of the form to be taken by the Abutting Property Law might well be made a matter of study by a special committee of this Society. Such a committee should make a collection of as many different forms of Abutting Property Laws as possible, tabulate their special provisions, and then draft a model form for recommendation to the several State legislatures. If the different States could be brought to adopt such a model form, uniformity, if not greater equity, would result, and this is a "consummation devoutly to be wished."

REPORT OF COMMITTEE ON WATER WORKS AND WATER SUPPLY

As a brief preliminary report the Committee on Water Works and Water Supply would call attention to the value of an investigation of drinking fountains made by H. A. Whittaker, director of the Division of Sanitation of the Minnesota State Board of Health at the University of Minnesota. Seventy-seven fountains, representing fifteen different types, were examined for their efficiency in preventing contamination by users, and as to the length of time such contamination continued if it occurred. All these fountains were found to be improperly constructed to prevent contamination of them by the user.

Experiments were continued to determine what forms of drinking fountains would be free from contamination and one form was designed and constructed which is shown by experiment to be thoroly safe so far as contamination by the user of the fountain for drinking purposes is concerned.

The paper has been published by the U. S. Public Health Service in Reprint No. 397 from the Public Health Reports (pp. 691-699), and can be obtained from the Superintendent of Documents, Government Printing Office, Washington, D. C., at 5 cents a copy.

F. W. CAPPELEN, Chairman.

REPORT OF THE COMMITTEE ON SIDE-
WALKS AND STREET DESIGN

S. Sammelman, Chairman, St. Louis, Mo.

Having carefully studied the "Report of Special Committee for Revising and Standardizing Committee Work," Page 491, Proceedings of the 1915 Convention, we find among other duties defined, that the Committee on Sidewalks and Street Design is to report on "everything having to do with the physical treatment of a street and not covered by Committees (1), (3), (4), (5) and (6)," and yet said Committee is admonished against the "discussions of well-known ideas or descriptions of commonplace work."

Further, it is hardly probable that all engineers agreed entirely with the excellent report of your committee last year; however, not sufficient interest was evoked to cause a discussion of same. Either the subject is one in which each engineer is so well satisfied with his own methods as not to seek further enlightenment, or he considers this subject of so little importance that he is unwilling to discuss difference of opinion on detail, or that practice differs so widely that a common meeting ground on which definite discussion can be had has not been reached as yet. We are pleased to assume the latter condition to prevail.

Your Committee on Sidewalks and Street Design, in presenting this report to you, begs your indulgence for what might seem to be an unnecessarily long and detailed presentation of practices in connection with so simple a subject. We feel that it is your object to standardize design thruout the nation in a manner similar to that undertaken on standard forms of specification, and as this is but the second year of the above Committee's existence, we believe it necessary to present the chaff as well as the grain, in the form of positive recommendations, to the end that discussion will be had, and then, when thoroly threshed, the golden grain will stand out as best practices to be followed. Further, there then will be a nearly permanent set of rules to be guided by, as the occasion for changes is much less than in any other of the interesting subjects your honorable Society has under consideration.

Plans and Preliminary Survey.

I. We recommend that detailed plans of the street to be improved be made in advance of the letting of the contract for construction and that said plans be made a part of the specifications, instead of the practice of disposing of the various problems thruout the entire period of construction, which results in less well planned work and delay. The plans should be equally as complete in detail as plans are for sewer, bridge, or building construction. As nearly as is possible, all contingencies should be anticipated in order that the field engineers on construction need not go into the office for additional notes, and that public utility corporations and property holders may adjust their railway tracks, poles, manholes, meter boxes, pipes, conduits, fire plugs, etc., to line and grade in advance of the street contractor beginning his work. In general, the plans should contain the survey notes for the location of the line of the street, bench mark elevations, all improvements that are to be met or adjusted within the lines of the street to be improved, profile of center line on old ground surface, together with profile of the new street grade, which shows the excavation and embankment at any point at a glance, the profiles of the curb grades, details of the corners showing location of radius hubs with respect to street and alley corners, crown sections, summary of curb required, summary of sewer inlets to be built, rebuilt, or adjusted to line and grade, profile of streets in the vicinity from which earth may be borrowed or on which it may be dumped, profiles of water pipes to be lowered, the preliminary estimate of work to be done in the form of bid items and quantities, and all instructions that can be more plainly shown than described in the specifications.

In preparation of said plans it is necessary to make a preliminary survey of the street to be improved. To provide a working basis, the following detailed recommendations are made.

In making the survey, locate corners of alleys and all intersecting streets, including those that have been improved, by reference to permanent buildings, crosses on sidewalks, or setting monuments. Elevations on monuments to be recorded. By the use of the word "Found" (initials of engineer and date) indicate monuments and marks of the original survey that remain intact. Locate all poles, lamp posts, fire plugs, sprinkling plugs, valve boxes, stop boxes, inlets, manholes, trees, curbs set on intersecting improved streets, street railway tracks, sidewalks running parallel to street, and anything else that in your judgment will probably need adjustment during construction of the street.

Particular care should be given to the location of inlets that are in the circle of a curb-rounding, for the purpose of specifying exact lengths of rounding stones.

In addition thereto the elevations on all improvements on the property abutting the street that might influence the grade to be established should be taken, to-wit, elevation of ground or walks on street line at entrance to yards, bottom and top steps to houses. If building is used for business purposes and is flush with street line, door sills, window sills, etc., should be taken. The street should be cross-sectioned from street line to street line at intervals not greater than 50 ft. between stations.

Levels are to be taken on all the above mentioned objects, not including poles. Bench marks used in taking levels, if found not to be correct, should be noted in field book. Should any of the intersecting streets be improved, take elevations of curb, crown and gutter line, also note width of roadway said curb has been set for.

In determining the direction of a street, north, south, east or west, do not use compass designations, use house numbers for your guide. If the house numbers run north and south, designate the street as running north and south, likewise east and west, and record notes accordingly.

Grades.

II. We recommend that a center line grade of the street be used to indicate the grade to which the improvements on the street be made to conform to, and that it be called the "established" grade. Further, that the curb be set so that the average of the two elevations of the tops of the curbs, at points of intersection of a straight line drawn perpendicular to the center line of the roadway with the curb line, be equal to the established grade. When at all possible the curb grades on the opposite sides of the roadway should be level. Should it be found necessary to "hang" the curb (meaning to place the curb on one side of the street at a higher or lower elevation than that opposite), the maximum hang should be not greater than at the rate of 1-10 ft. for each 6 ft. of roadway width, and in such instances, that the roadway pavement be adjusted to somewhat eliminate hang in same, by placing a shallow gutter line on the side of the low curb and a deep gutter line on the side of the high curb. The minimum depth gutter line to be 4 in. and the maximum not greater than 10 in. The normal depth of gutter line below top of curb, when curbs are level, to be 7 in. This depth permits of the use of economically sized curb and also the resurfacing of the roadway without disturbing the base course. The longitudinal rate of grade of the gutter line to be not less than one-half of 1% or greater than 5% along straight curb, and along roundings not less than 1½%, or greater than the rate of the grade of the steeper of the two intersecting streets. (N. B., "Curb grade" as here used corresponds to the average use of the term "side line grades").

Crowns.

III. We recommend that the "crown" of the roadway be construed to be the difference in elevation of the top of the wearing surface at the center line of the roadway and the average elevation of gutter lines, the three named points being in a straight line at right angles to the center line of the roadway. This you will see does not necessarily constitute the high point on the pavement. In fact, it is only so when the gutter lines are of the same elevation.

The crown of the roadway varies and is governed by the width of the roadway, steep or flat grades, and material to be used as a pavement. From the point of wear it is desirable that the water be drained into the gutters as rapidly as possible, however the height of crown is limited by traffic uses. It is obvious that too high a crown will be the cause of automobiles skidding toward the gutters, which is a source of danger to be avoided. Some engineers have worked out formulas to determine the crown, and others have arbitrary tables of crowns arrived at in their community from what they consider good practice from past experience. Due to the fact that the crown affects the life of the pavement and its maintenance, this question should be gone into thoroly by this Society.

The following arbitrarily fixed table of crowns is offered as a basis for discussion. The use of a different crown for each change in the rate of grade is discouraged because of the difficulty met with on construction:

Width of Roadway	Wood Block Concrete	Brick Granite	Asphalt Bitulithic	Bituminous Macadam
24 ft	3 in.	4 in.	5 in.	6 in.
30 ft	4 in.	5 in.	6 in.	7 in.
36 ft	5 in.	6 in.	7 in.	8 in.
42 ft	6 in.	7 in.	8 in.	9 in.
50 ft	7 in.	8 in.	9 in.	10 in.
60 ft	8 in.	9 in.	10 in.	11 in.

Roadway Paving Surface.

IV. We recommend the use of a parabolic curve for the transverse section of the wearing surface of the roadway. Of the methods advocated, it is the best practice because of the simplicity with which it can be conformed to, both in the setting of the grades by the Engineer on construction, and by the contractor; also, the ease with which a grade stake can be replaced by the inspector or overseer on the job in the absence of the engineer. When the curb has been set, the final shaping of the subgrade is begun. It is common practice to stretch a string from curb to curb and to use an ordinary 2-ft. rule to measure the distance below or above said string and mark the grade of the intended finished surface of the pavement on stakes driven at regular intervals. Upon investigation you will find that the distance or "drop" from the string line to the intended surface of the finished pavement (if the string be stretched so as to coincide with the surface of the finished pavement at the center line of roadway and be of equal height—the crown height—above the gutter line of each curb) is obtained by squaring the fraction made up of the distance from center line of roadway to point at which the drop is desired, over one-half the width of the roadway, and multiplying the result by the "crown" of the roadway. This method also has the advantage of not making it necessary to determine or arbitrarily set the high point in your pavement when the curb hangs or the gutter lines are not of equal elevation. The high point automatically shifts from the center of the roadway toward the high side, and back again as the hang varies at different points.

Radii of Curb Roundings.

V. We recommend that at alley intersections with street roadway, a "rounding" or "circle" of 2 ft. radius be set, thence on the alley line from the point of tangency of said "rounding" to the outside edge of the proposed sidewalk, straight curb be placed. At the corners of street intersections large radius roundings are preferable. We recommend the use of the smaller width of sidewalk space on the intersecting streets as the length of radius to be used. In so far, however, as it is usually desirable to pave an intersecting street to the line of the street under construction, it is found to be more practical in the setting of roundings to use the width of the sidewalk space on the street under construction as the length of the radius. This is good practice providing the point of tangency does not extend more than three feet over the frontage of the abutting property.

Slope and Spacing of Sidewalk Paving.

VI. We recommend, in business districts, to pave the entire width of sidewalk space. Where full sidewalk space is paved, set grade of walk next to curb at the same height as curb and raise from curb to street line at the rate of ¼ in. per foot.

In the partially built or built up residence sections the walks should be placed midway between the curb line of the roadway and the street line, provided that a minimum distance of 4 ft. be had between face of curb and outer edge of walk. The sidewalk paving should slope toward the roadway at the rate of ¼ in. per foot; the unpaved portion, 1 in. per foot.

In laying out new subdivisions where fences, hedges, terraces, etc., are yet to be placed, we recommend that the sidewalks be placed so that the inner edge of the walks and the street line coincide. This serves as a definite location of the street line as well as providing more lawn and tree planting space between the outer edge of the walk and the curb.

Location of Poles, Fireplugs, Inlets, Etc.

VII. We recommend that the roadway side of all poles, fireplugs, meter boxes, house connection boxes, etc., be placed not nearer to the face of the curb than a line parallel to, and 1 ft. back of said face of curb.

We recommend that no iron grate paving surface sewer inlets be used, and further, that no inlets be placed in the curb roundings. Should the street grades pocket at a street corner, an inlet should be placed at each end of the rounding, and should the street grades on the intersecting streets be continuous in the same direction, an inlet should be placed at the end of the rounding that will intercept the water and prevent a large volume to flow in the rounding gutter. As to the spacing of inlets along the roadway, the water should be carried by the sewer rather than on the surface. There should be at least one inlet to every 500 linear feet of curb; the steeper the street grade, the more inlets should be placed.

In Conclusion.

Your Committee on Sidewalk and Street Design asks the full cooperation of the members in discussion and correspondence on this subject, that the best practices may be determined and then be set forth as a standard which will be as helpful a guide to the engineer as the standard specifications are.

Respectfully,

S. SAMMELMAN,
Chairman,
H. A. VARNEY,
J. E. BALLINGER.

COMMITTEE REPORTS

Chairmen of committees who did not have sufficient notice to prepare their reports in time for this issue of the Society's publication are requested to complete them and forward them to the Secretary, 2535 North Pennsylvania Street, Indianapolis, Ind., in time for the next issue. He should have them in hand by December 15th.

Sub-Committees of the General Committee on Standard Specifications, should send their reports to the Chairman of that Committee, George W. Tillson, Boro Hall, Brooklyn, N. Y. Copy may also be sent to the Secretary.

Discussions of the Committee reports in this issue, as well as of the papers is invited.

If you did not receive a copy of the booklet of Instructions to Committees, ask the Secretary for one.

MUNICIPAL FINANCE IN CONNECTION WITH PAVEMENT CONSTRUCTION AND RENEWALS

By George C. Warren, Boston, Mass.

This is one of the most important subjects with which municipal officials have to deal, especially in these times of public demand for more and better pavements and roads, following the advent of the automobile for pleasure and business purposes. It is also, in the writer's judgment and observation, one of the most neglected subjects, to the extent that the tendency is to continue operations under systems and laws inaugurated a quarter or half century ago, which, tho adequate and best at the time, are now quite uneconomic. The tendency in each locality is to patch up the old systems and to avoid a general change of system, with the result that in many places financing is unnecessarily costly and in others the system is such as to make it practically impossible to finance for improvements to the extent the public interests demand improvements should be made.

The several systems of finance for street improvement in the order of undesirability as the writer sees them are:

I. The municipality pays the entire cost,
>   A. On a bond basis,
>   B. On a cash basis.

II. The municipality assesses the whole or portion of the cost on the abutting property improved by the pavement,
>   A. Cash.
>   B. On a deferred payment or installment plan.

Let us consider each of these systems and their practical results.

I. *Municipality Pays Entire Cost.*

If the entire original cost of pavement and renewals is paid by the municipality out of its general funds, it necessarily means either or all: .

a. Streets so paved and maintained as to inadequately meet the public demand.

b. A high tax rate at which officials and taxpayers always shudder.

c. A high bonded indebtedness with which the taxpayers must reckon sooner or later.

In some municipalities the system for a quarter or half century or more has been to assess the abutting property owners either with the entire cost or a portion of the cost of the first pavement, the municipality paying the entire cost of repairs and renewals. The iniquities of this system are:

a. The tendency of abutters to urge and use every possible influence toward the adoption of the cheapest, which, generally speaking, means the poorest, type of construction which will "get by" the officials and the assessment period.

b. It only very temporarily overcomes the difficulties of excessive general taxes and bond issues.

In Boston the cost of the first improvement is assessed on the abutting property and all subsequent repairs and renewals are paid for from the general budget. The results are:

First, the almost universal tendency of property owners to accept and urge the adoption of the cheapest form of roadway and sidewalk construction which can be laid. In connection with the opening of a street in which I am interested, the other abutters favored gravel roadway and sidewalk, and when I protested that this class of construction is entirely inadequate to meet modern traffic conditions they said:

"But the city must keep the road in repair, and if later a better class of improvement is necessary, we will not be assessed for the cost."

Second, there are so many miles of roadway thus inadequately improved it is impossible for the city out of its limited tax budget and limit of bonded indebtedness to lay modern pavements to anything like the extent they should be laid to meet present traffic and economic conditions, and at the same time meet the enormous expense necessary to keep the old roadways in safe, passable condition.

As a result Boston now has approximately 400 miles of antiquated macadam roads, extremely expensive to maintain in even passable condition under present traffic conditions and affording no further economic use than as a foundation for a modern wearing surface adaptable for such a foundation. Such reconstruction of the macadam roads in the city of Boston would entail a bond issue of between ten and fifteen million dollars. If such bond issue were on either serial or sinking-fund ten-year basis (a longer term than which would be uneconomic) it would necessitate a tax levy of, say, one and one-half to two million dollars per annum to meet principal and interest. This additional burden to a municipality, the outstanding bonds and tax rate of which are about as high as economic, efficient finance would permit, is hardly practicable.

New York City has much the same law as Boston with respect to initial assessments and subsequent maintenance of the pavements, with the result, like Boston, that almost universally the initial pavement adopted was gravel or stone macadam and other cheap types of construction.

New York, however, has more generally succeeded in the reconstruction of pavements with those of more modern type, but has done this thru the issuance of millions and millions of bonds for long terms of years—very much longer than the reasonable life of pavements under the prevailing traffic conditions, until now it has been publicly stated that New York has many miles of streets which have been reconstructed two and sometimes three times from the proceeds of such long-time bond issues, before the first bond issues have been paid.

So very few municipalities pay the entire cost of pavements from the general fund on a cash basis, except from the proceeds of bond issues, that a discussion of that as a general plan for improvement of streets is not worth while.

The fact, as the writer believes, that payment for street improvement or renewals entirely from general funds of the municipality is a very uneconomic system of finance, is perhaps best proven by the fact that, naming a city which has followed that . plan for a considerable number of years, you have almost if not absolutely to a certainty named a city which is either poorly paved or is carrying the load of a heavy bonded indebtedness created for the laying of pavements. Generally both such undesirable features are the result of such a system.

II. *By Special Assessment.*

There are many different systems of payment for street pavements in whole or in part by "Special Assessment" against the abutting property.

In St. Louis, Mo., the entire cost of all street pavements and renewals is assessed on the abutter, and the contractor is given "tax bills" bearing six (6%) per cent. per annum interest against each individual property. Altho the interest is at a high rate for a municipality enjoying high credit, and altho the tax bill is a lien which takes precedence over mortgages and all other liabilities except other city taxes, thus providing the very best security, the tax bills are not salable except at a heavy discount, because investors generally do not want to carry paper, the collection of which requires so much red tape, and is issued in such odd amounts (many of them quite small) payable in annual instalments.

If St. Louis and other municipalities enjoying good credit would guarantee its Special Assessment paper and the cities themselves dispose of the securities, pay the contractor cash and collect the assessments, they would not only save the taxpayers a very considerable portion of the interest rates, but would also be able to sell the securities at par or a premium and thus save in lower contractors' prices the discounts and carrying and collection charges which the conservative contractor must include in his contract prices when he is paid in paper for which he must find a market.

The foregoing briefly outlines three extreme examples of what seem to me to be very unwise systems of financing street improvements. Between them are all shades of variation in vogue, some of them such that the contractor has to discount the paper given him in payment for his work as much as 15%, all of which, it is needless to say, comes out of the pockets of the taxpayers in either higher cost of work or poorer construction, or both, and certainly provides a most unwise system of finance.

For thirty years the writer has, in connection with the street paving business in which he has been engaged, given a great deal of thought to the best method of financing street pavements as practiced in the hundreds of municipalities in which the companies have done street paving business during that period. Recognizing the fact that one of the most difficult governmental problems is that of an equitable apportionment of taxes and that, under any system which can be devised, there will be more or less inequality, he has come to the conclusion that the most economic, efficient and equitable system which has been devised for financing the original construction and permanent maintenance of first class streets is briefly described as follows:

1. Assess the greater part (say two-thirds to three-fourths) of the original cost and cost of renewals and resurfacing against the abutting property. This on the theory which cannot be questioned as an almost universal fact that:

a. The abutting property is directly improved in value and comfort very much in excess of the cost of such assessment.

b. The general public has the use of the streets and should pay a portion of the cost of construction.

2. The city, from its general funds, to pay the entire cost of minor repairs up to the time that the street requires entire renewal or resurfacing.

3. Never issue bonds or other municipal paper to cover either the general tax or the special assessment portion of the cost of street pavements for a term greater than the reasonable life of the pavement and a good factor of safety. In the writer's judgment ten years is a proper general period for such municipal paper. If it is argued that pavements should last more than ten years, my answer is: "Granted, but it is better to be safe than sorry." It is a capital principle to expect that a pavement will be in existence for several years after it is finally paid for, rather than to take the chance of having two or more successive pavements unpaid for on the same street.

Even tho a longer term than ten years is provided for the general tax portion, never under any circumstances permit the property owners' share to run for more than ten years with interest.

4. Make the assessments absolutely payable in annual instalments with interest, with the privilege on the part of each tax-

payer to pay in cash if he so elects within one month after the levying of the assessment.

5. Preferably issue serial bonds for the portion of the cost to be paid for out of the general funds of the city. It is abundantly proven that serial bonds are far safer and more economical than sinking-fund bonds. Of course no bond issue should be made without adequate plan for annually raising funds to meet the bonds on maturity.

6. Be sure to make the rate of interest high enough so that the bonds will surely sell at par or better. If the bonds sell at a premium, the premium can be used to retire a portion of the bonds at the earliest legal opportunity and no loss entailed.

7. Make the rate of interest to the abutter on special assessments within ½% as low as the city pays on the bond, thus making the assessment as easy as possible to the assessed abutters. This ½% is ample to pay the cost of collection and possible loss on irregular assessments if the city collects its special assessment thru the regular financial channels, machinery and laws for collecting taxes.

8. The city pledge its credit for the payment of its Special Assessment bonds, which it can do without loss because it is secured by the assessments, which are a first lien against property far more valuable than the amount of the assessment.

9. Make the Special Assessment bonds, as well as general bonds, in round amounts payable at certain dates with coupons covering both interest and instalment payments of principal. Those dates as to the assessment bonds to be about one month after the due dates of the corresponding assessments. This gives the city one month to "exercise the power of the law" against any taxpayer who defaults on prompt payment of any assessment.

The writer formerly resided from 1888 to 1903 in the city of Utica, N. Y., which now has a population of about 90,000, and had something to do, by way of suggestion, with the plan of finance for street pavements which was adopted in that city. He feels a pride in the resulting safe, sane, equitable, easy system now in vogue for twenty-five years in Utica. Note the practical result under the system, which, briefly stated, is as follows:

1. The city pays one-third the cost of all original pavements and all renewals thereof, and provides for this out of the annual tax budget, the paving fund thus created being an annual tax of less than an average of $1 per capita of population, which is not enough to hurt any. No bonds are issued for the city's one-third.

2. The remaining two-thirds of the cost of original pavements and all renewals is assessed on the abutting frontage, each individual person assessed being given the option of paying the whole or any part of his or her assessment in cash, or deferring payment for six annual instalments with 6% interest. To recover

the deferred assessments the city issues six paving bonds, each for one-sixth of the whole amount of such deferred assessments, and payable in one, two, three, four, five or six years with 5% interest, the due dates of the bonds and assessments being coincident. The city loses nothing on account of the credit it gives the taxpayers, and the premium the city gets for the bonds and the 1% extra interest charged the taxpayers more than pays all clerical or other expense of the city in the transaction.

3. The city at large pays for minor repairs required between the time of laying the original pavement and the necessity of reconstruction or resurfacing.

The result of this system, after twenty-five years' practical trial, is that there are few cities in the United States and Canada which, as a whole, are as well paved today as is Utica, practically every street in the city now having a modern pavement, and the work having been done so easily and steadily that no one has felt the financial burden.

The practical working out of the system can be illustrated by the typical result on Oneida street. In 1892 the street was newly paved at a cost of about $200 per lot of 50-ft. frontage, the assessment being payable in cash or at the option of each taxpayer in six annual instalments of about $33 with interest, say $35 per year, for six years, including interest. The last instalment of the assessment was paid in 1898. Then came thirteen years' respite and in 1911 the street was resurfaced at a cost of about $90 for each lot of 50-ft. frontage, or if any desired to pay in six annual instalments at a cost, including interest, of less than $16 per annum. Note that all this—a thoroly well-paved city—has been accomplished by a general tax of less than $1 per capita per annum.

Of course it may properly be said that in larger cities, where traffic is more congested, the relative cost would be somewhat greater and the necessity of pavement renewals more frequent, but it may also be said, in answer, that the renting and selling values in the larger cities are enough greater so that the relative burden of such a system could be no greater than in smaller cities.

The city of Portland, Ore., having a population of 210,000, is another example of a well-paved city. It has more than 150 miles of bitulithic pavement, about 100 miles of asphalt pavement, large areas of granite block, vitrified brick and creosoted block pavements, making a total of about 350 miles of well-paved streets, practically all of which have been built within the past fifteen years. The entire cost of this vast area of pavements, together with curbing and sidewalks, was assessed against the property owners abutting upon the streets on the front-foot basis, the city simply extending credit to the property owners and holding liens on the property as security.

Upon completion of each contract the city issues certificates or tax bills against each of the abutting owners for their pro rata part of the cost, which tax bills are payable within thirty days of their issue. The tax bills are delivered to the contractor in payment for the work. Each property owner may pay his tax bill to the City Treasurer within the thirty days, or he may execute an application to have the payments extended so that one-tenth, with interest at 6%, will be payable each year for ten years, in which case he is required to assent to the amount of the assessment, agree to pay as it becomes due, and further agree that the assesment shall be a lien upon his property until paid, and waives all right to contest the assessment.

These liens take precedence over mortgages and all other obligations except direct city taxes. The city then issues 5% bonds, which are direct obligations of the city, secured by the liens on property, to the amount of the face value of the assessments which have been assented to. These bonds usually sell at a substantial premium, and the proceeds thereof, together with the cash payments received from those not desiring extended payments, are used to pay the cerificates or tax bills given to the contractor. City bonds so issued and secured are not considered to come within the debt limit of the city. It should be noted that the premium received from the sale of bonds and the additional interest of 1% per annum paid by the property owners provide more than sufficient funds to pay the cost of all clerical work, advertising and printing of the bonds.

Tax bills which are not paid when due, and where no application has been made for extended payments, are turned over to the legal department for collection in the same manner as other delinquent taxes. The city of Portland, Ore., paving bonds have always had a ready market among eastern investors and doubtless many of them are locked up in the coffers of some of our Boston citizens who are opposed to the city of Boston borrowing money for use on the streets.

Under the Portland plan a person owning a lot on a 30-ft. street having a frontage of 50 ft. can secure a first class pavement costing $2.50 per sq. yd. for the moderate sum of $208.33 and can pay for same at the rate of $20.83 per annum and interest for ten years. The value of the property is usually immediately enhanced by more than the total cost of the pavement, and the property owner knows that he is receiving a personal benefit from the expenditure, and further that he is not contributing to the cost of pavement in front of property owned by others for which he receives comparatively little direct benefit.

What owner of a home would not cheerfully contribute the small cost of thus improving his property? Could not the owner of a property which is rented secure in additional rent more than the moderate cost of the improvement? The paving of Portland, Oregon, has been accomplished at the sole expense of the property owners in spite of the fact that no street can be paved except with the consent of the abutters owning a majority of the frontage on the street. Furthermore, the law gives the property owners the right to select the kind of pavement they desire for their street. To reiterate, about 350 miles of modern pavements have been laid in Portland during the past fifteen years at the entire expense of abutting property owners, the owners of a majority of the frontage on each street making the decision: First, what streets shall be paved; second, what kind of pavement shall be used in front of their property.

The writer's contention is that the Utica and Portland systems of financing for pavements are, with modification, easily and equitably adaptable to other cities and to nearly all other factors of the broad matter of "City Planning"—parks, boulevards, pavements, sewers, shade trees, etc.—and that most municipalities of the United States and Canada can well look to Utica, N. Y., and Portland, Ore., for some good, sound, sane lessons in municipal finance for street pavements.

PARK ENGINEERING

Parks and Park Engineering is the title of a book by William T. Lyle, professor of Municipal Engineering at Lafayette College, Easton, Pa., which applies to the field of park and boulevard construction some of the principles of municipal engineering, making the modifications desirable to adapt these principles to the special conditions of park and boulevard traffic and the requirements of beauty as well as utility.

The artistic side of park development is not considered except in the minor details, but after a few words on the possibilities in the line of park development and organization, the author proceeds to show in clear and brief manner the methods of making the selection of lands, the topographical and hydrographical surveys, designing and constructing under-drains and sewers, grading, bulkheads, walls, pipe lines, paths and drives, and lighting systems. Contracts and specifications are worked out in some detail, covering only such lines of construction as are commonly required for parks. These are not exceedingly full nor are they always fully up-to-date, the use of concrete in such construction, for example, not being fully exploited.

In brief, the book is intended to aid the young engineer in applying the engineering knowledge which he has acquired in school to the particular field of park construction, and thus covers a line which has not heretofore been developed separately. It is published by John Wiley & Sons, New York.

REPORT OF SECRETARY FOR YEAR ENDING SEPTEMBER 30, 1917

Charles Carroll Brown, Indianapolis, Ind.

. The account of the changes in membership during the year is made up as follows:

	Sept. 30, 1916	Additions During Year		Losses During Year		Membership Sept. 30, 1917
		Admitted	Transferred	Withdrawn	Transferred	
Active...............	411	110	....	51	5	465
Affiliated...........	14	....	5	3	....	16
Associate...........	127	24	....	26	....	125
Total..........	552	134	5	80	5	606

The following credits for municipal membership dues received from the A. S. P. S. have not yet been taken up:

Boston, Mass.—4 delegates.

Columbus, O.—4 delegates.

Norfolk, Va.—3 delegates.

Pasco, Wash.—3 delegates.

S. Omaha (now Omaha), Neb.—3 delegates.

The accompanying table shows the receipts for the year from membership dues, active and municipal, associate, and affiliated; from the volume of proceedings, including copies sold, advertisements in proceedings and program, reprints of papers, and copies of specifications sold; and the receipts from the Exhibit Committee, being the balance left after paying the expenses of the exhibit. The table also shows the remittances made each month to the Treasurer.

1916	Rect. Nos.	Membership Dues			Proceedings				Convention	Remit to Treas.	Date
		Act. & Mun.	Assoc.	Affil.	Sold	Advts.	Reprints	Specif.			
Oct......	4115–4238	$512.50	$150.00	$5.00	$5.85	$35.00	....	$21.80	....	$730.15	11/9
Nov.....	4239–4257	55.00	....	5.00	....	8.55	$97.67	4.74	$101.43	272.39	12/7
Dec......	4258–4341	295.25	340.00	17.50	37.00	....	....	2.75	....	692.50	1/6
1917											
Jan......	4342–4431	320.00	310.00	5.00	7.00	24.00	34.60	7.50	....	708.10	2/6
Feb......	4432–4472	150.00	45.00	20.00	8.00	....	119.65	6.25	....	348.90	3/7
Mar.....	4473–4510	127.35	20.00	....	48.85	319.20	....	11.00	....	526.40	4/6
April...	4511–4555	67.50	....	....	62.00	216.50	66.90	13.50	....	426.40	5/4
May....	4556–4588	72.50	....	....	41.00	97.00	....	8.00	....	218.50	6/11
June.....	4589–4611	87.50	....	10.00	15.00	....	....	61.75	....	174.25	7/3
July-Aug.	4612–4642	107.50	20.00	7.50	9.00	....	....	12.88	....	156.88	9/10
Sept.....	4643–4661	60.00	35.00	15.00	2.00	30.00	....	0.50	....	142.50	10/2
Totals..	....	$1855.10	$920.00	$85.00	$235.70	$730.25	$318.82	$150.67	$101.43	$4396.97	

The expenditures during the year were as follows:

Office and Miscellaneous.

Printing and Stationery	$106.94
Telegrams and Exchange	1.93
Postage and Express	353.57
Clerical Aid	590.00
Copyright on Proceedings	1.00
Treasurer's Bond	7.50
Committee Expense	17.60
Traveling Expense of Secretary	63.70
Salary of Secretary	300.00
	$1,442.24

Proceedings.

Advance Papers	$91.50
Reprints	163.61
Proceedings	1,732.80
Specifications	120.42
	2,108.33

Convention.

Membership and Advertising Campaign	$402.50
Program	314.15
Stenographer	90.00
Local Convention Expense	104.77
	911.42
	$4,461.99

Both receipts and expenditures are larger than in preceding years. Due to the efforts prior to the Newark Convention, there was an increase in membership, including those admitted at and immediately after the Convention of about 28 per cent. There was a large increase in the receipts from advertising due to these efforts and to the admission of advertising to the program distributed in advance of the Convention and at the Convention. The cost of the program, which was the most elaborate the Society has had, was more than paid by the advertising obtained because of it.

The classification of expenditures is somewhat different from that of previous years, but by comparing items it will be seen that the office and miscellaneous expenses were about $275 less than in 1916. The expenditures for the proceedings, including reprints and specifications, were about $650 more than in 1916. This is accounted for, first by the greater number of pages in the 1917 proceedings, second by the greater number of cuts used in illustrations, third by the much higher price of paper in 1917, and fourth by the larger number and size of the reprints made. If the printing of the proceedings had been let by contract as in previous years, they would have cost still more. They were printed under the direct supervision of the Secretary's office, each part of the work being done where it could be done cheapest and at the same time well, and thus the overhead and the profit on materials was saved, except for the slight increase in the payment for clerical service.

The Convention expense was much greater than usual, due to the cost of the work done before the 1916 Convention and paid for this year in the campaign for membership and advertising, which was nearly all for printing and mailing; and for the higher cost of the more elaborate and extensive program booklet. The cost of both was justified by the increase in receipts, and the Society will receive the benefit this year, and possibly in future years, if the postponement of the Convention does not nullify the work done. There is but one advertising account unpaid and it will wipe out the deficit for the year, $65.02, when added to membership dues received in October.

Permission was given the following cities during the year 1916-1917 to use the standard specifications of the Society:

Boston, Mass., Elevated Railway.
Charleston, Mo.
Durham, N. C.
Pawtucket, R. I.

A vote of the Executive Committee by mail in June registered the decision to postpone the 1917 Convention on account of the suggestion of the local committee at New Orleans that the municipal offices were so much affected by the enlistments for the war, and similar experience in the offices of other members of the committee.

A meeting of the Executive Committee was held on call of the President at the house of the American Society of Civil Engineers in New York City, on July 18, 1917, to consider the program for the year without a Convention. After full discussion of plans and suggestions offered, it was decided to call for papers and committee reports as tho the Convention were to be held, and to publish them in three sections, in October, 1917, and in January and April, 1918. Written discussions of the same are requested, to be published in the next issue following the paper or report. The President was requested to notify all chairmen of committees that their committees are continued with the same membership for the year 1918, and should serve in preparing reports and securing papers for the publication. All committee reports not requiring executive action by the Convention will be published in the issue following their receipt by the Secretary. The Committee on Revision of the Constitution was instructed to have its report ready to be printed in the April issue. It was suggested that wherever possible local meetings be held to discuss papers, both papers and discussion being forwarded for publication. The decision as to the contents of the publications was placed in the hands of the President and Secretary.

In accordance with these general instructions, the Secretary reports that enough material has been received and promised for publication of the first issue soon after October 15, and that enough advertising contracts have been received to pay the expense of the publication for the year even if considerably larger than the estimated size.

Respectfully submitted,

CHARLES CARROLL BROWN, Secretary.

(Publications of names added and subtracted from list is postponed until January for lack of space.)

REPORT OF TREASURER

Fred. J. Cellarius, Dayton, Ohio.

RECEIPTS.

1916
Nov. 14	W. B. Howe	$1,605.76
Nov. 20	C. C. Brown	730.15
Dec. 18	C. C. Brown	272.39

1917
Jan. 11	C. C. Brown	692.50
Feb. 13	C. C. Brown	708.10
Mar. 9	C. C. Brown	348.90
Apr. 14	C. C. Brown	526.40
May 7	C. C. Brown	426.40
June 14	C. C. Brown	218.50
July 5	C. C. Brown	174.25
Sept. 18	C. C. Brown	156.88
Oct. 3	C. C. Brown	142.50

Total Receipts $6,002.73

DISBURSEMENTS.

1916
Nov. 8	W. K. Stewart & Co., env. for adv. papers	$ 6.90
Nov. 8	Miller & Mercer Co., pr. and fld. 800 inserts for adv. pprs.	5.00
Nov. 8	Unity Press, prtg. and binding adv. pprs. and reprints	100.00
Nov. 8	U. S. Photo Engrav. Co., cuts adv. pprs., pro and prog.	89.28
Nov. 8	Frank VanSickle, makeup and lockup, reprints and comp. adv. pprs.	34.00
Nov. 8	Thomas & Evans, composition on advance papers	104.79
Nov. 8	Bookwalter-Ball Printing Co., conv. prog. and ad. cut.	314.15
Nov. 8	Indiana Paper Co., paper for covers of adv. pprs. and reprint	9.63
Nov. 8	Chas. C. Brown, Secretary, office exp. month of Oct.	58.73
Nov. 8	Chas. C. Brown, Secretary, Convention expenses	104.77
Nov. 8	Engineering Publishing Co., paper for reprint adv. pprs.	5.04
Dec. 7	Franklin Press, Treasurer's check book	5.75
Dec. 7	Southern Surety Co., premium on bond for Treasurer	7.50
Dec. 7	U. S. Photo-Engraving Co., cuts for proceedings	139.80
Dec. 7	Oval & Koster, 900 lith. inserts for 1916 proceedings	35.00
Dec. 7	West Va. Pulp & Paper Co., paper for 1916 proceedings	186.24
Dec. 7	Central Law Reporting Co., reporting proceedings and 2 trans. Newark Convention	90.00
Dec. 7	Charles C. Brown, Secretary, office expenses for Nov.	68.88

1917

Jan.	6	Unity Press, proceedings and reprints 1916	127.75
Jan.	6	Appollo T. Gaumer, press work reprints and eng.	4.00
Jan.	6	Wm. W. Hampton, office supplies	1.35
Jan.	6	U. S. Photo-Engraving Co., cuts for 1916 proceedings	104.51
Jan.	6	Indiana Paper Co., stationery, officers and com. memb.	13.90
Jan.	6	Thomas & Evans, typesetting 1916 proceedings	252.63
Jan.	6	Frank VanSickle, comp., etc., reprints for Gran. Pav. Assn.	6.38
Jan.	6	Charles C. Brown, Secretary, exp. for Dec. (office)	70.00
Feb.	6	Indiana Paper Co., env. (Kashmir Bd.)	1.95
Feb.	6	Sewell-Clapp Envelopes	11.62
Feb.	6	U. S. Photo-Engraving Co., cuts for 1916 proceedings	2.50
Feb.	6	Bookwalter-Ball Printing Co., locking pages for fdy. and ads.	10.00
Feb.	6	Thomas & Evans, composition for 1916 proceedings	33.79
Feb.	6	Charles C. Brown, Secretary, office expenses for Jan.	75.00
Feb.	24	Bookwalter-Ball Printing Co., printing and serv. 1916 conv. pro.	402.50
Mch.	3	Unity Press, printing and gath. pro. and fld. inserts, printing and binding 4 reprints	199.50
Mch.	3	Thomas & Evans, comp. on pro., spec. and proceedings	54.10
Mch.	3	Indiana Paper Co., paper for P. S. & R. and boxes (shipping)	64.41
Mch.	3	Appollo T. Gaumer, comp. and press work on Secretary's stationery, also officers and comm. chairmen, cover for reprint, corrections for specifications	39.25
Mch.	3	Frank VanSickle, proceedings, specifications and reprints	137.63
Mch.	3	West Va. Pulp. & Paper Co., paper for proceedings	102.29
Mch.	3	Charles C. Brown, Secretary, office expenses for Feb.	60.51
Apr.	5	The Haverstick Co., bind., wrap. and mailing 1916 Pro.	248.14
Apr.	5	Thomas & Evans, comp. on reprints, Bit. Pav. Spec. St. and Grav. Rds.	25.14
Apr.	6	Charles C. Brown, Secretary, office expenses for March	200.35
May	4	Frank VanSickle, makeup and lockup Standard Spec. and comp.	10.00
May	4	Unity Press, press work on Standard Specifications	29.75
May	4	Indiana Paper Co., paper for Standard Specifications	13.20
May	4	W. K. Stewart, 250 col. clasp env.	4.00
May	4	Thomas & Evans, typesetting Standard Specifications	4.88
May	4	Charles C. Brown, secretary, office expenses for April	65.36
June	11	F. B. Neff Printing Co., bill heads	3.50
June	11	Charles C. Brown, Secretary, office expenses for May	70.40
July	3	A. P. Folwell, exp. Committee on Standard Forms	17.60
July	3	Charles C. Brown, Secretary, office expenses for June	68.05
Aug.	24	Indianapolis Mailing Co., letters to members, office exp.	4.75
Sept.	1	Charles C. Brown, Secretary, exp. N. Y. com. meet., etc.	181.80
Sept.	10	Charles C. Brown, Secretary, salary to Oct. 1, 1917	300.00
Sept.	29	Franklin Press, office exp. and printing	12.75
Sept.	29	Charles C. Brown, Secretary, office expenses	61.29

Total Disbursements $4,461.99

Total Disbursements $4,461.99
Balance October 10, 1917............ 1,540.74

Total Receipts $6,002.73

Respectfully submitted,

F. J. CELLARIUS,
Treasurer.

THE PRESSING OF SEWAGE SLUDGE

By Kenneth Allen.

DISCUSSION OF PAPER ON PAGE 1.

E. S. Dorr—I beg to submit the following discussion on Mr. Allen's statement of the Miles-acid process:

The time of settling was 4 hours instead of 8 hours as stated. Two tanks, in series, were used, and the time of detention of sewage was 4 hours in each tank. Ninety-eight per cent of the sludge collected was in the first tank.

Five tons instead of 4 tons of concentrated sludge were obtained by settling to 80% moisture.

The advantages claimed in the use of sulphur dioxide are:

1. Cheapness of the initial acidulation.

2. Separation of the grease from the alkaline constituent of soaps, so that about 40% more grease is obtainable than the ordinary ether test shows in the sewage.

3. Low moisture content in the sludge, as stated.

4. High bacterial removal, 99.99%.

5. Complete deodorization at all stages of the process, and absence of fly nuisance.

6. Availability of the effluent for broad irrigation in arid regions where conditions admit of it, due to the large amount of potash present, and also the freedom from clogging of the soil (a serious detriment to ordinary sewage farming) on account of the removal of the fat.

Recent tests of the Moon Island and North Metropolitan sewage (single samples of each) showed an average of 1,000 lb. of potash, 70 lb. of phosphate, and 120 lb. of organic nitrogen and 183 lb. of nitrogen as free ammonia per million gallons in the effluent after the acid treatment.

The only expense for preparation would be for lime enough to neutralize the excess of acid (about 20 p.p.m. SO_2) costing 35 cents per million gallons.

7. Economy of the process, due to low cost of installation, moderate cost of operation, and high value of recoverable products.

Cost of installing a plant on 100,000,000 gallon basis would not exceed $12,500 per million gallons per year.

Cost of operation, including interest and upkeep, should be between $15 and $18, while the value of the recovered products, grease and fertilizer, is $24 per million gallons treated, all on a pre-war basis.

This process shows an actual profit, with normal time values;

with war prices there can be no doubt that a large revenue can be derived.

This process has a distinct war phase which deserves mention.

The manufacture of explosives may require all the sulphur and pyrites available to be devoted to this purpose; but if so, there is a by-product of the manufacture of smokeless powder produced, called "nitre-cake," which is suitable for the acidulation of sewage, because it contains 30% to 40% excess sulphuric acid.

The more sulphur used, the more nitre-cake produced.

Its use would increase cost of acidulation about $10 per million gallons, but the increased value of the products would warrant it.

Cost of pyrites has also increased $9 to $10 per ton, which increases the cost of a ton of SO_2 by the same amount.

In short, the cost of acidulation, before the war, was $7 to $9 with pyrites; the value of the grease was $16, and of the fertilizer base $8; total $24; leaving a margin of $16 for drying and degreasing.

Now it will cost less than $20 to acidulate a million gallons with either pyrites or nitre-cake, the grease is worth $64.50 and the fertilizer $25.50, total, $90.00; margin $70.00 for drying and degreasing.

On the other hand, the effect of a large development of this process would be a factor in several ways in helping "win the war."

The products recovered from this vast unused waste are grease and an ammoniated fertilizer.

The grease contains 5% glycerine; production of glycerine from this source would help the munition manufacture, and also the food situation, by releasing for food, fats which would otherwise have to be taken for glycerine.

Munition manufacture will probably require all the ammonia, now available, leaving the fertilizer manufacturers, already deprived of potash, in bad straits.

The fertilizer from sewage, with its 4% to 5% ammonia, will help supply this deficiency and help the food situation.

While these sewage products from one city would not be large compared to the demand, the products from the large cities of the country would be a factor.

This process is really a new departure in the treatment of sewage. It is rational, because its object is conservation instead of destruction, which is the only object of the biologic processes.

It is, more specifically, a grease recovery process, which is the logical way to attack the problem, both because the grease is by far the more valuable product to recover, and because the numerous previous attempts at utilization have failed on just this point: The presence of grease has spoiled the sludge as a fertilizer.

EDITOR'S NOTE. It is stated that the treatment of the 93,000,-000 gallons of sewage produced by Boston would result in the saving of 68 tons of fertilizer and 40,000 lb. of grease per 24 hours, the grease yielding 2,000 lb. of glycerine and the fertilizer 6,800 lb. of ammonia for war purposes. If the same estimates are extended to the 97 cities of 50,000 or more population, the amounts of saving are as large as 4,869,684 tons of ammonia and 1,289,034 tons of glycerine a year. If it is possible to save only one-fourth of this estimate the effect upon munitions production would be most salutary.

C.-E. A. WINSLOW, PROFESSOR OF PUBLIC HEALTH, YALE SCHOOL OF MEDICINE.—All who are interested in the difficult problem of sludge handling will feel indebted to Mr. Allen for this most admirable review of the existing data in regard to sludge pressing. The material which he has brought together fills an important gap in the literature of sewage treatment and it should be of immediate practical value to designing engineers and a powerful stimulus to future improvements in the art of sewage treatment.

In spite of past failures I am inclined to agree with Mr. Allen, and Mr. Thompson whom he quotes, that in view of the intrinsic value of sewage sludge, its utilization without appreciable cost is ultimately certain. The problem of economic dewatering is year by year approaching nearer to a satisfactory solution.

Mr. Allen rightly emphasizes the fact that there is no universal method of sludge drying since the sludges derived from different processes vary so widely in their chemical and physical properties. At the Sewage Experiment Station of the City of New Haven we have been for the past year dealing with sludges of three types, produced respectively by the Imhoff Tank, the Activated-Sludge process, and the Miles Acid process. It seems quite possible that each one of these three may require a different method of dewatering.

The New Haven experiments are on too small a scale to warrant extensive studies of sludge treatment, but in view of the paucity of available data in regard to the handling of Miles acid sludge a few words about our experience with this process may be pertinent.

The New Haven sewage which we have been treating has an average alkalinity of only about 60 parts per million, so that we have found it necessary to add only 700 pounds of SO_2 per million gallons of sewage treated. This gives us an acidity of about 50 parts per million in the effluent and effects a removal of 55-60 per cent. of suspended solids with a high degree of bacterial purification.   The sludge obtained has, however, a much higher water content than that reported by Weston in Boston and that cited for Bradford, England, by Mr. Allen.   In the three runs we have made (of 25 days, 24 days, and 44 days respectively), the water content of the settled sludge has varied between 86 and 88 per cent.   On the other hand, the grease content of the sludge is most encouragingly high, ranging from 23 to 29 per cent. ether extract on a dry basis.

The sludge appears to dry well on drainage beds and it has the great advantage of a high relative stability.   In warm weather it would no doubt prove ultimately putrescible, but it may be allowed to stand for several days, even in summer, without becoming malodorous, a property which would prove of very great importance in practical operation.   This conclusion, of course, might not hold for all sewages.   Ours is peculiar in the fact that it contains a considerable amount of copper from industrial wastes and the antiseptic action of the acid may be superposed upon that of the copper.

Centrifugal treatment of the Miles sludge with a small machine of the imperforate bowl type has not been a success.   The dried sludge cake removed from the basket contained only 12.8 per cent. of ether extract and the effluent liquor, 45.0 per cent. Other types of centrifugal machines, might, of course, prove more efficient.

In view of the necessity for adding lime to ordinary sewage sludge before dewatering with sludge presses it might be surmised that this procedure would be unsuitable for acid sludge.   It may prove, however, that a strongly acid sludge can be pressed as successfully as a strongly limed one, and the experience of Bradford has, so far as I can gather, been favorable to this process.

Mr. Allen's paper should serve as a starting point for renewed activity in the study of all these problems.   The promise of actual financial return, primarily from the nitrogen in the activated sludge, and primarily from the grease in the Miles sludge, offers a powerful stimulus to find methods of dewatering which shall realize their potentialities.   Fundamental studies of the laws of colloid-chemistry involved may perhaps be necessary before the final goal is reached; but in the case of both these processes it seems to the writer that the possibility of recovering at least a large part of the cost of sludge disposal is already within our grasp.

ROBERT SPURR WESTON.*—The writer has read over Mr. Allen's paper with a great deal of interest.   It is full of well digested information and should prove of great value to the designer and operator of sewage disposal works.

*Of Weston & Sampson, Consulting Engineers, 14 Beacon St., Boston.

Mr. Allen gives the characteristics of the four common sewage sludges, namely, those from Imhoff tanks, plain subsidence tanks, chemical precipitation tanks and activated sludge tanks, respectively. He also mentions the sludge obtained by treating sewage with sulfur dioxide gas, the so-called Miles process.

These sludges make the real sewage disposal problem; the disposal of sludge is the most difficult part of the art. Many processes yield good effluents but offer troublesome sludge problems. The most representative of these is the activated sludge process, which produces an effluent of high quality and excellent appearance, but a very bulky, wet sludge, difficult to dewater. Opposed to this, is the Imhoff tank process, which yields only a partially purified effluent, one usually requiring further treatment, yet the sludge, while of low fat and fertilizer value, is disposed of with comparative ease. Under proper conditions and where no recoverable products are sought, the Imhoff tank offers a fairly satisfactory solution of the sludge problem.

The Miles process for producing sludge,—that is, by treatment with sulfur dioxide gas,—causes the rapid precipitation of the most of the suspended matter, decomposes the soaps, thereby increasing the recoverable fats in the sludge, and produces more sludge in a subsidence period of four hours than does plain subsidence in a period of eighteen hours. While acid treatment probably costs more than plain subsidence, it produces an effluent which is nearly sterile, requires about one-quarter of the tank capacity demanded for effective plain subsidence, and produces a sludge containing considerably less than 90 per cent. of water,—that is, its bulk is one-tenth that of activated sludge and half that of Imhoff-tank sludge.

Over 1,900 pounds of this sludge can be obtained from each of the hundred million gallons of the sewage discharged by the main discharge works in Boston,* and this amount of sludge contains 430 pounds of fat and considerable fertilizer nitrogen. Before the war, the cost of acid treatment was conservatively estimated to be less than $10.00 per million gallons; it would probably cost less than $20.00 a million gallons to apply this treatment at the present time. On the other hand, the value of the products recoverable from sewage has risen from about $22.00 to about $100.00 per million gallons. There remain, therefore, $80.00 per million gallons with which to dewater, dry and degrease something less than a ton of sludge, containing about 85 per cent. of water. Mr. Allen's paper confirms the writer's fixed belief that the chances of doing this are so good that some governmental or other authority ought to make a trial of the process on a large scale while the high prices obtain.

A simple computation will show what enormous amounts of

*Contributions from Sanitary Research Laboratory of Mass. Institute of Technology, Vol. X.

fats and fertilizer nitrogen are present in the total sewage sludges of our large cities, and every effort should be made to recover these products and the 5 per cent. of glycerine which may be derived from the fat, during the present period of high prices, even if at first glance the position has a "gold-in-sea-water" sound. When the figures are analyzed, however, the practicability of the process becomes more probable. For example, compared with the activated sludge process, it is very promising. It is claimed by eminent authorities that even the very bulky, wet sludge from this process can be dewatered, dried and degreased profitably. This sludge contains, if anything, less recoverable products than the denser sludge from the Miles process. Therefore, if, under present conditions, the activated sludge process can be worked profitably, surely the Miles process can be. Anyway, the process ought to be tried on a large scale to determine the costs, and in the writer's opinion, "the game is well worth the candle." Even if the process should prove only self-supporting, it would at least have the advantage of discharging a partially clarified and nearly sterile effluent into bodies of water now receiving nuisance-producing discharges of raw or roughly screened sewage, at a cost far below that of any process of equal bacteriological and nuisance-preventing efficiency.

TO MEMBERS.

NEXT CONVENTION. Will the members signify to the Secretary their desires regarding the holding of the next Convention in New Orleans early in November. Expressions for and against the holding of the Convention this year are equally strong altho the count of votes of the Executive Committee is in favor of holding the Convention this year at the time this number is sent to press. The Convention will be held at a date early in November to be fixed before the April number is issued, and at New Orleans, unless conditions change materially before that date or the expression of members and executive committee is strongly against it.

The executive committee has voted to remit the dues of members who enter the uniformed service of the United States. The list of members in the service as it is known at present is printed on another page. G. R. Tuska is Major and R. L. Morrison is Captain, E. O. R. C., unassigned; L. V. Sheridan is in the third Officers' Training Camp; Benj. Brooks was in first Officers' Training Camp, but present position is unknown. Full information regarding all members in uniformed or civilian service for the war is earnestly requested by the Secretary, that the list may be as complete and correct as possible.

ECONOMICAL BRICK PAVEMENT

By Maurice B. Greenough, Chief Engineer, National Paving Brick Manufacturers' Association.

Chief among the hindrances to advancing road improvement programs in 1917 were found labor and transportation shortage. A canvass of state highway departments showed that 42% and 38% respectively were the weights of these obstacles. Others mentioned were high prices of materials and no funds, but they were of little relative weight as compared with labor and transportation deficiencies.

Further inquiry by the National Paving Brick Manufacturers' Association in 700 cities of the United States of more than 5,000 inhabitants, assigned 30.7% and 21.6% of the hindrances to labor and transportation shortage respectively. High prices of material, no funds and war were given as other obstacles.

On the other hand, 93.5% of the states reported favorable or very favorable public sentiment towards carrying on road improvements. The cities reported somewhat less keen sentiment, as might be expected, but 62.1% were favorable or very favorable. Only 24.8% reported citizens opposed to carrying on street improvements, while the balance were non-committal.

These figures are cited to show the preponderance of appreciation in favor of developing our roads and streets for commercial transportation and as a basis of fact to learn what must be overcome if we are to meet this demand and provide the transportation relief so sorely needed by the country. It is the purpose of the writer to endeavor to point out briefly how these conditions affect the design and construction of brick pavements and what may be undertaken to minimize obstacles in the way of greater activity.

Machinery has played a slight part in building roads and streets as compared with developments in other engineering construction, and yet by its use is now presented the only compensation for labor shortage. There are relatively few instances in which brick and other materials may not be hauled from the switch to the work in motor trucks. Excavations may be made with steam shovels and the spoil hauled to the dump by trains of wagons drawn by small tractors. One small caterpillar tractor capable of negotiating almost any terrain will displace at least three team, driver and dump wagon units. Concrete mixers of course are common in building brick pavement bases, but small batch mixers in use for preparing or actually making grout applications are relatively few. Conveyors for handling brick from the roadside to the work generally permit of a reduction in man-power.

Attention may be called to the use of a mechanical tamping template illustrated in its use by the construction of a monolithic brick pavement on South Meridian Road, Indianapolis.* Not only in this one phase of construction, but universally in the use of well-adapted machinery designed to perform special functions, there is not only a saving in man-power, but also an increase in the effectiveness of the work. More perfect organization is effected as well as a saving in cost. These advantages, combined with more effective control of the various operations, suggest themselves as desirable, in what used to be normal times, in establishing efficiency. Under present circumstances, however, we are obliged to revise our point of view. They become necessities if work is to go on.

These are times in which to exercise increased study in determining the type of brick pavement to build in a given case. The high cost of cement has led engineers to thoughtful study of other types of bases which have shown or promised merit. Well-rolled stone, gravel and slag bases have demonstrated their worth for many years. Occasionally defects are reported, but very few that are not found to be the direct outcome of inadequate rolling during construction. With the added advantage of a sand-cement bed over the plain sand cushion, these bases become even more desirable.

In country road construction particularly, there are many times local deposits of stone which will suit base construction with a minimum crushing and hauling expense and would not serve as an aggregate for concrete. Or gravel banks may admit the use of bank-run material many times with no screening required. In the neighborhood of blast-furnaces slag becomes desirable. Durable and effective bases may be built of any of these materials and where the hauls are not too long, at a less cost than concrete.

Several writers have advocated a light bituminous penetration of rolled bases to waterproof them and add to their stability. Others have suggested the use of natural cement in the place of Portland cement, for bases only, of practically all types of pavements on concrete bases.

The value of sanitation in city streets renders those types of cement-grout-filled brick pavements most satisfactory for use. Such a pavement may be cleaned and kept clean.

For country roads, even of heavy traffic, the type employing a plain sand filler serves a wide usefulness. Sand was the filler most widely used in the early days of brick pavements. Even under the rigors of modern traffic there are a great many of these old sand-filled pavements which continue to provide satisfactory service. In combination with well-rolled stone bases, a sand filler affords a brick pavement costing as little as a brick pavement on

---

*See *Dependable Highways*, October, 1917.

a base may cost and at the same time supplies a type that can stand exeessive wear.

Highway engineers are more and more coming to the belief that every street, however small, furnishes opportunity for individual study if we are to secure the best work for the money spent. True as this stand may be on its merits, it is particularly important in these times that it should be followed. The blind use of any one type without careful study of all incurs the risk of wasting dollars.

MUNICIPAL ENGINEERING PRACTICE

Municipal Engineering Practice. By A. P. Folwell, editor of *Municipal Journal,* John Wiley & Sons, New York.

Professor Folwell has books on sewerage and on water-supply engineering, and there are many books on paving, so that his latest book is devoted to the other lines of municipal engineering practice, of which there are many; some in which the city engineer should be an expert and some of which he should have enough knowledge to determine at least what should be done and where he can get the special help which he needs in solving his local problems.

The subjects treated in this book are grouped under the titles fundamental data; city plan; street surface details; bridges and waterways; city surveying; street lights, signs and numbers; street cleaning and sprinkling; disposing of city wastes; markets, comfort stations and baths; parks, cemeteries and shade trees.

It is evident that such subjects as those treated in the last two or three chapters require not one but several books for complete treatment, but for the city engineer, who is not supposed to be an expert upon the details of these subjects, the treatment in the book is ample. The book might be more valuable to the engineer desiring to make himself fully conversant with one of these lines if a bibliography of the special books and the more valuable papers and articles in each of their fields were included.

In such subjects as street surface details, the treatment in the book is adequate to the needs of any engineer. In all the subjects treated it is adequate to the needs of the average city engineer, except, possibly, as to the bibliographies suggested.

OLD AND NEW BRICK PAVEMENT CONSTRUCTION
METHODS COMPARED AND CONTRASTED

By *Charles Carroll Brown.*

Possibly some valuable data on the economics of brick pavement construction can be gleaned from the following comparison of methods and costs of building brick pavements which will be worth considering when the design of brick pavements for light traffic under good conditions is in progress.

The first street described was constructed in Bloomington, Ill., in 1896, 3,205 feet long, 35 feet wide for 2,612 feet, where a single track street railway ran down the center, and 30 feet wide for 593 feet where the car line did not run. There were four 56 to 64-ft. street intersections and four 20-ft. alleys, and the sidewalk and lawn widths were 15.5 ft. each. There are 5,960 lin. ft. of Berea curb with 14 round corners.

The natural earth graded to a definite line and cross-section was rolled and some sand was used to "smooth up" the surface. Bloomington hard burned bricks, which are hardly tough enough for the wearing surface, were laid flat as a lower course, lengthwise of the street, with broken joints, filled with sand. A 1-in. sand cushion formed the bed for the wearing surface of Springfield wire-cut brick set on edge. This course was also sand-filled, the filler being applied during the process of rolling. The cost of the pavement proper was $1.42 a square yard for the portion assessed on the abutting property, $1.33 for the portion paid for by the street railway company and $1.34 for the street intersections paid for by the city, or an average of $1.40 for the whole 11,850 sq. yd. of pavement. These figures do not include $200.15 for drainage inlets to sewer and adjustments with adjoining pavements and structures or $118.80 for inspection, but do include the Berea stone curb.

The street is in a residence section with a small park on one side for 0.4 the length and is not on a line of thru travel. The gradient is light, but is ample for good drainage. The street is sewered and the pavement described is but a block or so from the summit of the street, so that there is no accumulation of water on or under it. In short, except that the sub-soil is retentive of water, rather than porous, the conditions are very nearly ideal for permanence in any sort of pavement. Since automobiles have so largely replaced wagons the wear on the pavement has become inappreciable. It has never been serious and aside from an occasional soft brick or shattered brittle brick, there are no breaks and comparatively few irregularities in the surface other than the slight rounding of the corners at all joints consequent on the use of the sand filler.

The street car track area has been relaid several times on account of reconstruction of track, new rails and new turnouts, as well as insufficient foundation for the heavier cars in use of late years, and many new bricks have been used, but the repairs on the street proper have been practically negligible and there is no record of their cost, nor do they show on the surface of the street.

This street was extended during the season just past and laid according to the latest specifications. This new portion of the street is comparable in every respect with the one above described. It was constructed as follows:

The sub-grade was excavated to proper cross-section within 2 in. of grade and rolled with an 8-ton roller until compressed to grade, any projections above grade of the thoroly compressed surface being removed with pick and shovel. On the sub-grade was laid 6 in. of 1:3:5 broken-stone concrete, followed after 7 days set by a 2-in. cushion of sand and Springfield plain wire-cut vitrified blocks with cement-grout filler. Abrasion loss of blocks was specified at 23 per cent or less and absorption of water by bricks, after 24 hours baking, to be not more than 4 per cent with one-third not exceeding 3 per cent.

Cement-grout filler was used except in the street car area, where asphalt filler was used. Berea stone curb was used on one block where there is a single street car track. Here the pavement is 30 ft. wide, 8 ft. being the width of the street car area. On the remainder of the street the brick pavement is 23 ft. wide and the concrete gutters are each 1.5 ft. wide, the curb and gutter being combined. Three street intersections and two alley wings were paved. Four other intersections were already paved, one with asphalt and three with brick, one asphalt filler and two cement filler.

The pavement laid is about 1,750 ft. long and its area is 5,963 sq. yd. The total cost was $14,454.83, including pavement and curb, the average cost being $2.42 a sq. yd. This does not include $308.60 for inlets and sewer connections. The average cost of the whole area of the old pavement first described is $1.40 a sq. yd. The new pavement should cost more by the difference between the cost of concrete and brick foundations and of asphalt and sand fillers. Eighty cents may not be too much to allow for these two differences, which would leave but 22 cents to be accounted for. This is but 15 per cent of the cost of the old pavement and the increase in cost of materials and labor in the past four or five years would equal this, leaving the increase in cost on account of more stringent specifications and inspection to be offset by reductions in cost of doing the work on account of the improvements in modern machinery and methods.

General view of construction of monolithic brick pavement with fine gravel and sand concrete base.

Altho the new pavement has not yet gone thru a whole year, each block shows two or three expansion cracks across the street. Since this portion of the street has been paved, some traffic over it to a freight depot has developed, as it is a good alternative route to the business section. Otherwise it is as quiet a residence section as the older one, whose pavement was laid in 1896. Concrete foundation and cement-grout filler are therefore justifiable.

The good state of preservation of the old, comparatively cheap pavement under its light traffic raises the question as to whether all of the 80 cents or so of increase in cost due to better foundation and filler is justified on lightly traveled streets, especially when the property on such streets is not able to stand an assessment for the best quality of brick pavement. While no one would go back to the old flat brick or board foundations of the early days of brick paving, the fact remains that some of those old pavements have existed for over 20 years and are now in good enough condition to last another 20 years. Light traffic and the change from solid steel tires to pneumatic or solid rubber tires are responsible for their continuance in good condition. But there are many such streets now awaiting improvement which would pay the cost if it were brought to a minimum by getting back toward the older and cheaper designs as far as the engineer's judgment will permit.

The monolithic brick pavement with thinner concrete base than 6 in. is such an approach to cheaper design without reverting to the older designs which have been discarded because insufficient when traffic becomes heavy or when foundations or drainage are poor. Engineers are quite prone to forget that the differences in amount and weight of traffic on different streets are very great and that it is good engineering economy to take account of these differences in making their designs. Indeed, on some streets the design should be made largely to produce a street surface which will not deteriorate under the action of the elements, supplying permanent materials so placed that water, heat, cold, frost, will have the least possible tendency to disturb them, these forces causing more deterioration than the traffic over the pavement.

Equalizing box and screed and tamping template making concrete surface ready for laying brick.

Well rolled broken stone or gravel for foundations, sometimes filled with grout or bitumen of some sort, may often be ample for foundations and produce a pavement medium in cost between the old and the new constructions above described. In these days of high cost of labor and materials it may be possible, *where such construction has ample strength for the traffic* expected, to keep the cost of pavement down to that with which the taxpayers are familiar and thus remove one of the great objections to street improvements at the present time.

The accompanying photographs from a recent number of *Municipal Journal* show a comparatively cheap construction of a monolithic brick pavement, which is sufficient for the conditions on some streets tho probably not on streets of heavy traffic. The foundation is of 5 in. of concrete of fine gravel, largely coarse sand and not perfectly clean, taken from a pit alongside the street. This concrete was so fine-grained that the templet screeded off the surface perfectly smooth and the bricks were laid directly on it without any cement-sand coat. The error in the construction of this pavement was in using the dirty, coarse sand for the cement-grout filler so that the bricks themselves were not safely enough joined to insure a monolithic pavement.

WAR MAPS.

In connection with the Encyclopedia Britannica are published three world's war maps, making it possible to compare the wars of 6000 years with the present world's war. The maps have on them the locations of the great battles of the past and much of the detail of the present war, showing the most important movements thus far and the location of the lines of the respective fronts at the beginning of this year. There are many historical notes of the most important points, located by corresponding numbers on the maps so that a vast amount of history is definitely located and referred to the present crisis.

The first of the set of three has been issued and covers the western front, covering the area from London to Berlin and from the Kiel canal to the Rhine-Rhone canal, the present location of the American forces. The second map, to be issued shortly, covers Eastern Europe and the eastern front, and the third the Italian, Roumanian, Salonican, Mesopotamian and Palestinian fronts.

The authority of the organization of the encyclopedia guarantees the quality of the maps and they are brought down to the present year. They are of wall-map size and cost for the set $2 on plain folded paper, $5.25 mounted on linen and $7.25 mounted with brass to hang on the wall, and are published by The Encyclopedia Britannica Corporation, 120 W. 32d St., New York City.

BRICK PAVEMENTS OF THE MONOLITHIC TYPE
(Brick Laid in Green Concrete)

By James C. Travilla, Consulting Engineer, The Dunn Wire-Cut Lug Brick Company, St. Louis, Mo.

The merits of vitrified brick as a paving material have been demonstrated by its long life under all kinds of vehicle traffic and extreme weather conditions. Its continued popularity with public officials and taxpayers for paving streets and highways is evidenced by the large yardage of brick pavements laid each year.

New values have been established for vitrified brick pavements by reason of improvement in the shape and texture of the brick, modern methods of construction and the new standard set for pavements due to the change in type of vehicle and motive power for same. The evolution in the method of manufacturing paving brick and in the design and construction of modern brick pavements, as compared with those used in the early stages of the paving industry, is attracting the attention of paving engineers and road builders everywhere. A pavement free from inherent defects in the material, due to the process of manufacture, manipulation or construction, is unknown. Brick pavements have failed, due partly to the quality of the brick and partly to weakness of foundation, but more often the failure may be attributed to the design of the pavement.

A study of brick pavements constructed with brick laid upon a sand cushion with the spaces between the brick filled with a cement-grout filler, has proven the sand cushion to be the direct cause of many of the failures. Engineers have been too ready to condemn the cement-grout filler without giving sufficient consideration to the sand cushion in connection with the failure. The writer has had experience in the construction of all types of brick pavements and is thoroly convinced that the sand cushion and not the brick or cement-grout filler, has been the direct cause of most of the failures, by reason of the cushion sand rolling up in the joints and preventing the filler from going the full depth of the brick. From this construction weakness, temperature strains in the wearing surface of the pavement are not uniformly distributed to the individual brick, thus causing them to chip and the pavement to break down in spots, making it rough and unsightly. Engineers, in their desire to overcome this weakness in design and construction have evolved a type of brick pavements which are rigid from the sub-grade to wearing surface. The brick are laid in the green concrete or upon an added foundation of cement-sand. The methods of construction, while dissimilar, attain the same end. The final result is a better built brick pavement as compared with the older type of construction.

The brick laid in green concrete, monolithic type, is now generally used for constructing pavements for highways and streets whose width does not exceed 24 ft. and where the cross-section is uniform. It is admitted for true monolithic construction, the brick should be laid directly in the green concrete, but the results obtained from a thin film of cement-sand, spread over the green concrete or the cement-sand added foundation, have proven that for all practical purposes, the desired result is obtained, i. e., a rigid beam from sub-grade to wearing surface.

A brick pavement with the brick laid in green concrete is constructed in the following manner, to-wit: The concrete is deposited on the sub-grade and spaded, tamped or floated to bring the mortar to the surface and to thoroly imbed the coarse aggregate. It is brought by means of a template or lute to a grade slightly in excess of the depth required. The concrete base is then cut to a true surface with a template. To provide for slight variation in the depth of the brick and any roughness due to "tearing" the concrete in the process of cutting, a thin film of dry mortar is spread over the base, leaving the surface of the concrete entirely smooth. Upon the prepared foundation the bricks are immediately laid and rolled with a hand roller. Cement grout is then applied to fill the joints in the brick. Before the grout is applied, the brick are thoroly wet by sprinkling. After sufficient time has elapsed for the cement to set, the surface is covered with earth or sand to prevent a rapid setting up of the cement. No traffic is allowed on the pavement for a period of at least fifteen days.

It is considered good engineering practice to specify 1:3:6 mix for cement base, 1:4 mix for dry mortar bed and 1:1½ mix for cement grout filler.

For paving country highways this type of pavement, either method of construction, has the special merit of not requiring concrete edging or curb. In green concrete construction, the completion of each day's work produces so many yards of finished pavement constructed and cured as a unit, which is an advantage to the engineer and contractor by reason of having the contractor's organization concentrated.

The depth of pavement for monolithic construction is a variable quantity. The engineer in designing same should give consideration to the following factors, to-wit: The sub-soil and its value as a natural foundation, drainage and topography, geographical location of work, traffic, kind of brick, available aggregate for concrete, etc.

Pavements built with the brick laid in green concrete, the combined depth of brick surface and foundation varying from 5 in. to 9 in., have proven satisfactory under modern vehicle traffic and in latitudes where frost action is encountered. The economic importance of correct design for the depth of pavement, is best expressed by assuming that each inch in depth of the concrete base adds 25 cents per square yard to the cost of the pavement. Sufficient importance is not always given to proper analysis of the above factors. Natural soils have different values in determining the depth of the pavement. Some soils crack badly in dry weather, others show an "affinity" for moisture and "lift" when frost action is encountered. Cracks in pavements are generally traceable to frost action, kind of soil for the natural foundation, or contraction due to temperature changes. The importance of ample drainage applies to all kinds of pavements. A traffic census of the class, tonnage and amount of traffic is of great value. The wide range of geographical locations in which vitrified brick are available, and the extreme changes in temperature incidental thereto, together with the above factors, make it necessary to design different depths of pavement.

Vitrified paving brick are classified as wire-cut lug brick, repressed brick and plain wire-cut brick. The standard size of paving brick is $3\frac{1}{2}$ in. wide, $8\frac{1}{2}$ in. long and 4 in. deep. There is a decided tendency among paving engineers to reduce the depth of the brick from 4 in. to 3 in. In the manufacture of 3-in. paving brick, there is little saving in cost at the plant. The big saving is in freight, haul, handling, filler, etc. The paving engineer in preparing his design, should investigate the saving in 1 in. of brick as compared with 1 in. of artificial foundation.

The commercial sizes and grading of aggregates vary in different localities. Local conditions should be considered. Different kinds of aggregate work differently in green concrete construction. In connection with this analysis, attention should be given to laboratory tests of the strength of monolithic brick slabs. (See published report—Brown & Edwards, College of Engineering, University of Illinois.)

The official report states, "With a sand-cushion-sand-filler pavement, it would take a trifle over $5\frac{1}{2}$ in. of concrete base alone to support the same load as a 5-in. monolithic brick pavement. The brick used would be the same in either case, and therefore it would save $4\frac{1}{2}$ in. of concrete to use 5-in. monolithic brick construction." The saving in excavation, material and labor, the economic importance of which at the present prices of labor and material is a factor in the cost of a pavement, is worthy of careful consideration. It is not unusual to find specifications calling for an 8-in. brick pavement, monolithic type, placed in a competing class with "soft top" pavements designed for a 2-in. wearing surface laid upon 4 in. of concrete. The comparative beam strength of the slabs is 64 for brick and 16 for the "soft top" or four times as great for the brick slab. The 2-in. "soft top" adds nothing whatever to the load-bearing strength of the concrete base. The economic design of pavements certainly offers a field for study and investigation.

The construction features of paving brick laid in green concrete, are comparatively new to many engineers and contractors. Where the engineer and contractor appreciate the importance of attention to detail in construction, there is no trouble in securing a smooth pavement. If the right consistency of the concrete and cement-grout filler is properly understood by them, a satisfactory job is assured. A contractor's organization large enough to construct from 500 to 700 sq. yd. of pavement per 10-hour day, the pavement designed for a 4-in. concrete foundation, ½-in. dry mortar bed, 4-in. paving brick, cement-grout filler, is made up as follows:

Organization.

> 2 Men—Form setting
> 8 Men—Concrete mixer
> 1 Man—Finishing concrete (float board or lute)
> 2 Men—Paving
> 12 Men—Carrying brick
> 2 Men—Rolling and culling
> 4 Men—Grouting

Additional men for covering pavement not necessary. Men are available at the beginning and end of period of work.

Approximate Labor Cost.

PAVING.

Concreting	$0.08	sq. yd.
Dry mortar bed	0.01	" "
Paving	0.08	" "
Rolling and culling	0.02	" "
Grouting	0.03	" "
Covering	0 01	"
	—	
Total	$0.23	" "

Common labor at $0.40 per hour.

INCIDENTALS.

Water pipe line	$0.03	sq. yd.

HAULING AND HANDLING.

Cement	$0.015	sq. yd.		
Brick	0.100	" "		
Incidental	0.010	" "	$0.125	sq. yd.
	—			
Total			$0.155	" "

Teams for hauling at $6.00 per day.

MATERIAL AND MIX.	PORTLAND CEMENT.

1:3:6 mix—4-in. concrete base
1:4 mix—¼-in. dry mortar bed
4-in. wire-cut lug brick
1:1½ mix cement grout

WATER

Per sq. yd.
Concrete base _____0.124 bbls.
Dry mortar bed____0.002 "
Grout filler _____0.025 "
                    ———
Total _____0.151 '

Wire-cut lug brick—40 to sq. yd. or 25 sq. yd. to the 1,000 brick.

Weight of brick, 9.3 lb.

The cost of brick, cement and aggregate depends upon the proximity of the supply and the local market quotations. For the year 1917, contract prices for the above type of pavement have ranged from $1.90 to $2.50 per square yard, depending on local conditions.

This type of pavement being comparatively new, it necessarily follows the details of construction must be worked out and be governed by local conditions. To obtain satisfactory results with a multiple template, the coarse aggregate should be gravel or small stone passing the one-inch ring. Oversized stone or gravel will cause the template to "tear" the concrete and produce a "pitted" surface. The use of the multiple template is recommended, but it should not be considered as one of the essentials. A single template is an essential. To overcome the difficulty in striking with a template, it is possible to imbed the stone in the concrete with a hand roller drawn over the surface, or at the time the concrete is being tamped and shaped to the approximate grade, to rake the surface of the concrete with a garden rake, the oversized aggregate being raked into the base of the concrete as it comes from the mixer. The concrete should be thoroly tamped along the side forms. Attention should be given to the method used for drawing the template along the side forms; "block and tackle" or "windlass" attached to the mixer, give the best results. To keep the template from "riding" the concrete, it is customary for men to stand upon it while in motion. After cutting concrete a lute is sometimes used, drawn at right angles to the axis of the road, for the purpose of removing "waves" in the surface, due to the template "riding."

The consistency of the concrete should produce a comparatively dry mix, otherwise depressions will appear in the wearing surface at the time the brick are rolled.

The importance of the cement-grout filler, and having the brick entirely free from dirt until the grouting is completed, cannot be overstated. The principle on which the strength of the slab is based, i. e., the rough contact sides of the brick providing a perfect union between the brick and the bond, is of no value if the brick are not free from dirt, or if the cement-grout filler is not of such consistency that there will be a free flow of material to the bottom of the brick and to all parts of the joints, and a flush-grouted joint at the wearing surface. Two applications of grout will be required to fill the joints. The second should not be made until after the first has subsided. Excess mortar on the surface of the pavement should be squeezed into the joints to bring them up flush and full. A small film of mortar on the surface of the pavement is not objectionable, but the cement grout should not be left in "ridges." A smooth finish is essential. To avoid the possibility of thickening of the cement grout during any part of the work, there should be a man with a sprinkling can or a hose with "spray nozzle" sprinkling the filler ahead of the sweepers and squeezers.

There is little definite information regarding the action of temperature stresses in brick pavements. The frequent "blow ups" in the old type of cement-grout-filled pavements created the impression that transverse expansion joints should be used in the monolithic type. Some engineers who have studied the subject from every angle do not consider them necessary for county highways. But for city streets they are recommended at selected places on account of street intersections and changes in the cross-section of pavement incident thereto. Expansion troubles in brick pavement may be attributed to imperfect construction and to unseasonable weather at the time paving work was completed. The writer has examined pavements which have shown the brick crushed or "blown up" in spots from temperature strains, but indirectly caused by the cement-grout filler not having penetrated the full depth of the joints between the brick. It has been demonstrated that the height of buildings, their continuity, and the size and placement of shade trees along highways or streets, had a direct bearing as to the effect of temperature stresses in pavements. The direction of a highway with reference to the cardinal points may be considered in this same connection.

Transverse joints develop a weakness in construction of slab pavements, they allow movement of slab, the inherent strength of which under tension will not prevent cracking of the slab. The cracks are not prevented by placing transverse joints at stated distances. Contraction cracks will appear in any type of rigid construction, but it is better to permit them to develop naturally than to provide contraction joints. In brick pavements they develop between the courses of brick. Longitudinal expansion joints about ½ inch in width and extending the full depth of the pavement, should be used for street work next to curbs. At street intersections, small transverse joints (¼-inch) are recommended to be placed at the prolongation of corner lot lines to make the intersection a separate unit, on account of the varying temperature stresses by reason of curb roundings, returns and cross-section.

In conclusion it may be stated that brick pavements, monolithic type, are regarded a success and a decided step forward in the science of constructing paved highways.

CITY PLANNING.

The Planning of the Modern City, by Nelson P. Lewis, Chief Engineer of the Board of Estimate and Apportionment of New York City. John Wiley & Sons, Publishers, New York City.

Mr. Lewis writes this book from the fullness of his own knowledge of city planning activities in the largest city in the world and with a breadth of view which is rather unusual, and shows the essential relations of the engineer to such work. His treatment of the fundamental principles is complete and thoro and furnishes a basis for the study of the books on specific problems of which there are so many. A thoro study of this book should give the student the balance and sense of comparative values which will keep him within reasonable bounds and prevent concentration on non-essentials to the detriment of work of real value, or attempts to put through plans too ambitious for the people to carry them out and therefore resulting in failure and abandonment without adequate results from the money actually expended.

The sketches of city planning movements in general and in the correction of earlier mistakes in the growth of cities form a good introduction to the discussion of the elements of a proper city plan, including the transportation system by water, rail, subway, surface and elevated, road, tunnel and bridge, and streets, park and recreation facilities, public buildings and civic centers, the treatment of the industrial town or district, street traffic regulation, street details for utility and adornment, restrictions of use of public and private property, the environs of the city, and garden cities. The economic value of a city plan, the legislation desirable as a basis, the progress of city planning and the various methods followed, the essential subject of financing a plan and the closely related subject of municipal land policies are fully and scientifically treated. The book closes with a brief outline of the opportunities of the municipal engineer in city planning, which should do much to awaken the engineer to his rights and duties in the matter as a first step toward securing the recognition in the field which should be his and will be if he does his part in showing that it would be worthily bestowed.

SECRETARY'S REPORT.

(Continued from page 55)

The active members added to the list since the Secretary's 1916 report are as follows:

Aldrich, Bruce, Baltimore, Md.
Allen, Henry C., Syracuse, Md.
Aloe, L. P., St. Louis, Mo.
Barrett, C. H., Gloucester, Mass.
Bastis, Albert, Minneapolis, Minn.
Berthe, L. T., Charleston, Mo.
Bourleau, Edward, Chicopee, Mass.
Brehm, G. C., Marlboro, Mass.
Cardwell, Wm., East Orange, N. J.
Carson, H. O., Butler, Pa.
Chase, Guy H., Fitchburg, Mass.
Chrisman, O. D., Springfield, Mo.
Christy, E. A., New Orleans, La.
Clark, Alexander, Orange, N. J.
Condon, P. P., Watertown, Mass.
Cozzens, A. B., Newark, N. J.
Crowley, J. W., Davenport, Iowa.
Currie, C. H., Webster City, Iowa.
Davis, C. O., Milwaukee, Wis.
Denison, H. S., Framingham, Mass.
Devlin, Harry, New York City.
Duchastel, J. A., Outremont, Que.
Durkin, Patrick, Danbury, Conn.
Eager, George, Millburn, N. J.
Ellingson, O. J. S., Sherman, Tex.
Emerson, C. A., Harrisburg, Pa.
Erwin, M. C., San Antonio, Tex.
Estler, C. E., Boonton, N. J.
Evers, H. A., Cranston, R. I.
Fisher, E. A., Lakewood, O.
Fisk, G. F., Buffalo, N. Y.
Gault, Matthew, Worcester, Mass.
Goff, E. E., Cranston, R. I.
Hall, Wm. H., New Britain, Conn.
Halsey, Edmund R., S. Orange, N. J.
Hamley, S. J., Cleveland, O.
Hardee, W. J., New Orleans, La.
Harrison, A. W., Livingston, N. J.
Harrison, E. M., Montclair, N. J.
Hawley, J. B., Boonton, N. J.
Heilman, H. W., Newark, N. J.
Helland, Hans, San Antonio, Tex.
Hoover, Clarence B., Columbus, O.
Johnson, G. A., New York City.
Jones, R. A., Waltham, Mass.
Kappele, A. P., Hamilton, Ont.
Kemper, Joseph, Utica, N. Y.
Kennedy, W. E., Waterbury, Conn.
Kistlet, J. M., Minneapolis, Minn.
Knapp, N. A., Greenwich, Conn.
Kneale, R. D., Atlanta, Ga.
Knott, F. B., Newark, N. J.
Kraus, Jaros, Flushing, N. Y.
Lacombe, A. L., Irvington, N. J.
Lafaye, E. E., New Orleans, La.
Lamb, Richard, New York City.

MacDonald, G. E., Gloucester, Mass.
Mahnken, A. J., Weehawken, N. J.
Marchant, K. I., Gloucester, Mass.
Mattia, R. F., Newark, N. J.
May, E. A., Patchogue, N. Y.
McCandless, Robert, New Rochelle, N. Y.
McCarthy, J. J., Brooklyn, N. Y.
McCarthy, P. A., Lufkin, Tex.
McClelland, R. J., Kingston, Ont.
McComb, D. Q., Miami, Fla.
McCoubry, Thomas, Chicopee, Mass.
McMahon, P. F., Brockton, Mass.
Meigs, J. V., Boston, Mass.
Moorehouse, W. B., Tarrytown, N. Y.
Morales, Louis, Havana, Cuba.
Mumm, Jr., Hans, Everett, Wash.
Newton, S. D., Cleveland, Tenn.
Noble, O. E., Manhattan, Kan.
Olroyd, Foster, New Orleans, La.
Parker, E. E., Madison, Wis.
Pennington, William, Newark, N. J.
Pickersgill, H. M., Elmira, N. Y.
Plunkette, J. L., Rome, N. Y.
Ramsey, J. E., Salisbury, N. C.
Rolfe, Wm. E., St. Louis, Mo.
Rowland, H. A., McPherson, Kan.
Ryman, E. R., Newark, N. J.
Schmieder, Chas., New York City.
Sheaf, F. W., Rutherford, N. J.
Sherron, G. A., Los Angeles, Cal.
Simmons, F. G., Milwaukee, Wis.
Simons, F. F., Carteret, N. J.
Sloman, A. L., Albion, Mich.
Smith, A. P., Boonton, N. J.
Smith, F. E., Rockport, Mass.
Smith, T. W., Newark, N. J.
Snow, Hubert A., Brockton, Mass.
Starks, W. F., Glen Cove, N. Y.
Swan, Jr., Abram, Trenton, N. J.
Taplin, Arthur E., High Point, N. C.
Taylor, W. H., Norfolk, Va.
Terry, A. H., Bridgeport, Conn.
Thayer, J. A., Taunton, Mass.
Thier, J. E., Montvale, N. J.
Truss, J. D., Birmingham, Ala.
Uhler, W. D., Harrisburg, Pa.
Upington, S. F., New Rochelle, N. Y.
Ward, Kenneth B., Durham, N. C.
Warman, H. S., Boonton, N. J.
Waterman, F. V., E. Providence, R. I.
Weber, B. B., Oil City, Pa.
White, H. H., Muskogee, Okla.
Willis, T. L., New Orleans, La.
Wulff, E. J., Tarrytown, N. Y.

Those added to the list of affiliated members are:

C. J. Kopf, Boonton, N. J.
A. F. Masury, New York City.

J. W. Routh, Rochester, N. Y.
H. A. Wise, Kansas City, Mo.

Five members were re-classified and transferred from the list of active members to that of affiliated members, viz.:

R. DeL. French, Montreal, Que.
J. G. Shakman, Chicago, Ill.
L. V. Sheridan, Cambridge, Mass.

F. J. Soutar, Sioux City, Iowa.
E. R. Webster, Chicago, Ill.

The following were added to the list of associate members, persons or firms in capitals being members, and names in lower case being representatives of firms as indicated:

AMERICAN CAR SPRINKLER CO., Worcester, Mass., E. D. Perry, representative.

ARABIA GRANITE CO., Atlanta, Ga., F. C. Mason, representative.

ASPHALT AND SUPPLY CO., Montreal, Que., W. A. Morris, representative.

Bayliss, C. W., Philadelphia, Pa., representative Barber Asphalt Paving Co.

Beistle, M. J., Cleveland, O., representative The Barrett Co.

BOOTH BROS. & HURRICANE ISLE GRANITE CO., New York City, Charles Mitchell, representative.

DUSTOLINE FOR ROADS CO., Summit, N. J., E. R. Lawson, representative.

Eades, C. V., Chicago, Ill., representative Standard Asphalt and Refining Co.

JAMES FERRY & SONS, Atlantic City, N. J., J. V. Ferry, representative.

Gartland, J. J., Richmond, Va., representative John Baker, Jr.

Hepburn, C. F., Chicago, Ill., representative John Baker, Jr.

Hess, L. E., Indianapolis, Ind., representative Republic Creosoting Co.

HVASS, B. CHARLES, New York City.

IMPERIAL OIL CO., Toronto, Ont., E. D. Gray, representative.

Larkin, A. E., Minneapolis, Minn., representative Republic Creosoting Co.

Lersch, H. E., New Orleans, La., representative John Baker, Jr.

Lippincott, J. H., Newark, N. J., representative Warren Bros. Co.

March, G. R., Philadelphia, Pa., representative Barber Asphalt Paving Co.

MORGAN, H. A., New York City.

NORTH CAROLINA GRANITE CORPORATION, Mt. Airy, N. C., Thomas Woodroffe, representative.

Reed, T. H., Birmingham, Ala., representative John Baker, Jr.

SEWER PIPE MANUFACTURERS' ASSOCIATION, Akron, O., John L. Rice, representative.

WATER WORKS EQUIPMENT CO., New York City, W. H. Van Winkle, Jr., representative.

WESTPORT PAVING BRICK CO., Baltimore, Md., J. W. Hall, representative.

The names dropped from the list of active members were as follows, classified as to reasons:

Resigned.

Andrews, Horace, Albany, N. Y.
Ashley, C. S., New Bedford, Mass.
Garland, E. A., Santa Barbara, Cal.
Gavett, A. J., Plainfield, N. J.
Lindsley, H. D., Dallas, Tex.
Macartney, M., Spokane, Wash.
McCullough, E., Chicago, Ill.
Mitchell, K. M., Sherman, Tex.

Parsons, M. G., Pasadena, Cal.
Rich, E. D., Lansing, Mich.
Sharp, J. C., Portland, Ore.
Smith, J. E., Urbana, Ill.
Taylor, A. J., Wilmington, Del.
Wertheim, L. J., Berlin, N. H.
Whipple, G. C., Cambridge, Mass.

Deceased.

Coombs, P. H., Bangor, Me.
Elwood, F. T., Rochester, N. Y.

Semple, W. J. C., Boston, Mass.

Not Re-appointed as Delegates.

Bow, D. C., Minneapolis, Minn.
Christy, L. V., Wilmington, Del.
Datesman, G. E., Philadelphia, Pa.
Hohenstein, August, St. Paul, Minn.

Sweeney, E. J., Minneapolis, Minn.
Uhler, W. D., Philadelphia, Pa.
Wait, H. O., Buffalo, N. Y.

Mail Returned.

Hawkins, A. J., Bartow, Fla.
Lykken, H. G., Minneapolis, Minn.

Smith, F. L., Rochester, N. Y.

Dropped.

Adam, W. A., Lethbridge, Alta.
Anschutz, H. E., Clearwater, Fla.
Campbell, W. C., Columbus, Ga.
Crook, J. W., Paris, Tex.
Danford, W. P., Oklahoma City, Okla.
Dickey, A. T., Galveston, Tex.
Emerson, R. W., Pittsfield, Mass.
Gardiner, W. H. R., W. Calgary, Alta.
Gregory, A. C., Trenton, N. J.
Hoff, C. P., St. Joseph, Mo.
Horrigan, W. J., Wilmington, Del.
Hughes, T. C., Tulsa, Okla.

Lewis, J. E., Dallas, Tex.
Lynch, F. G., Erie, Pa.
Mesiroff, J. A., Milwaukee, Wis.
Nicol, W. H., Tuscaloosa, Ala.
O'Hara, M. J., Hudson, N. Y.
Parkes, W. J., Pine Bluff, Ark.
Pealer, Thos., Indiana, Pa.
Peterson, E. F., Muskogee, Okla.
Pierce, J. I., Jackson, Miss.
Reed, M. H., Ft. Smith, Ark.
Taylor, C. F., Pittsburg, Pa.

The following names have been dropped from the list of affiliated members:

Hamilton, F. P., New Orleans, La., resigned.

Wise, Henry A., Kansas City, deceased.

Slifer, Wm., Pittsburg, Pa., dropped.

The following names have been dropped from the list of associate members:

Resigned.

ARABIA GRANITE CO., Atlanta, Ga., F. C. Mason, representative.
BESSEMER LIMESTONE CO., Youngstown, O.
EQUITABLE ASPHALT MAINTENANCE CO., Kansas City, Mo., F. H. and J. M. Moore, representatives.
KING, C. F. & CO., Wilmington, Del., C. B. King, representative.

Levering, W. A., Chicago, Ill., representative Standard Asphalt and Refining Co.
PRUDENTIAL OIL CORPORATION, New York, S. J. Dalzell and R. W. Sanders, representatives.
ROBESON PROCESS CO., New York City, G. I. Lindsley, representative.

Deceased.

Smith, W. Stuart, Rochester, N. Y., representative Warren Bros. Co.

Not Re-appointed as Representatives.

Brehm, H. L., Cincinnati, O., representative Warren Bros. Co.
Forester. J. D., Kansas City, Mo., representative John Baker Co.
Gay, L. W., Buffalo, N. Y., representative John Baker Co.
Hess, L. E., Indianapolis, Ind., representative Republic Creosoting Co.

Murray, S. R., Indianapolis, Ind., representative John Baker, Jr.
Myers, Geo. W., Columbus, O., representative Portland Cement Assn.
Patterson, F. W., Cleveland, O., representative Cleveland Trinidad Paving Co.

Mail Returned.

CREOSOTED WOOD BLOCK PAVING BUREAU, Chicago, Ill.
Curless, Will A., Los Angeles, Cal., representative Thomas - Hammond Co.
MUSSENS, Montreal, Que., in liquidation, W. H. C. Mussens, representative.

RIDLON CO., FRANK, Boston, Mass., J. J. M. Smith, representative.
WERN STONE PAVING CO., New York City, F. M. Crossett, representative.

Dropped.

HORTON, D. C., Jacksboro, Tex.
HYAMS, R. M., New Orleans, La.

OKLAHOMA GLAZED CEMENT PIPE CO., Tulsa, Okla., G. M. Wright, representative.

REPORT OF FINANCE COMMITTEE.

PAWTUCKET, R. I., Oct. 31, 1917.

To the Members of the American Society of Municipal Improvements:

GENTLEMEN—Your Committee on Finance has examined the receipts and petty cash books kept by the Secretary, together with the "Orders" issued to the Treasurer and the cancelled checks filed by said Treasurer as vouchers for payment of all bills. With the exception of certain minor typographical errors, which have been corrected, your committee has found these accounts agree.

The reports of said Secretary and Treasurer show as follows:

Balance from year 1915-16 _____$1,605.76
Receipts for 1916-17 (Nos. 4115 to 4661 inc.) _____ 4,396.97

Total receipts _____$6,002.73
Total disbursements (Orders No. 1 to No. 58 inc.) _____ 4,461.99

Balance on hand October 10, 1917_____$1,540.74

Respectfully submitted,

GEO. A. CARPENTER, Chairman.
FREDERICK A. REIMER.

THE PRESSING OF SEWAGE SLUDGE

By Kenneth Allen

DISCUSSION OF PAPER ON PAGE 1

G. BERTRAM KERSHAW, M. Am. Soc. C. E. (Westminster)—Mr. Kenneth Allen's paper on *"The Pressing of Sewage Sludge"* is a valuable contribution to the technical literature treating of sewage treatment and disposal.

The Aylesbury plant mentioned by the author seems to have been about the first in the country; very probably the filter press was, like so many other devices, then first adapted to sewage work, after having been used for many years for other somewhat similar purposes, e. g. in sugar refineries.

Concerning the production of sewage sludge by various processes, it may be of interest to supplement the author's table of sludge data with somewhat similar particulars prepared by the writer in conjunction with his chemical colleagues for the English Sewage Commission some years ago. Although hypothetical, these figures were arrived at after a very careful comparison of a very large number of examples, and subsequent experience has showed them to be very fairly accurate.

Amount of Sludge from Sewage Treatments

Derived From	Moisture, %.	Tons Per M. G.
1. Quiescent chemical precipitation	90	17
2. Continuous flow chemical precipitation	90	16
3. Quiescent settlement	90	12
4. Continuous flow settlement	90	11
5. Open septic tanks	90	6.5

The figures refer to sludge produced per million gallons dry weather flow of domestic sewage of average strength, and they do not include the heavy increases in suspended matter, such as would result during storms, especially when the sewerage system is combined and the bulk of the streets are macadamized.

The following figures relating to Heywood and Sheffield show how very greatly the suspended solids may be increased in rain time, especially during the earlier stages of the rainfall.

Effect of Rain on Sewage Sludge

Name of Place.	Time of Taking Sample.	Total Suspended Solids (Parts Per 100,000).
Heywood (4 hours "heavy" rain).	First part of storm	238
	After 1 hour	110
	" 2 hours	69
	" 3 "	50
	" 4 "	38
Sheffield (Rainfall 0.11 inch).	10.50	59.24
	11.50	60.24
	12.50	67.12
	1.50	170.07
	2.50	125.93
	3.50	133.46
	4.50	101.20
	5.50	100.60
	6.50	97.93
	7.50	41.73

Mr. Allen does well to lay some stress upon the very variable characters of different sludges, as regards their amenability to pressing; frequently sanguine estimates of cost of pressing have not been realized by actual results.

With regard to the composition of sewage sludge, it is not, perhaps, generally remembered, when using sludge (either pressed cake or wet sludge) for fertilizer, that the inorganic or mineral matter, forming say 50 per cent. of the sludge, must exercise a marked physical effect upon some of the soils to which it is applied. In this country, various road metallings, from which the bulk of the mineral matter in sewage sludge is derived, are often obtained from geological formations quite dissimilar to those from which the surface soil has been weathered, in the locality where the sludge is applied as fertilizer, and the subject would appear worthy of investigation by physicists and agricultural chemists.

In this country, in the near future, sewage sludge will probably be taken much more freely by farmers, both in cake form and as "spadeable" sludge; owing to its cheapness, it can be applied in heavy dressings per acre, and its manurial effects, tho much lower and less stimulating than, say, sulphate of ammonia, are spread over a longer period than the "artificial," whose effect is somewhat transitory, and generally limited to the season of application.

War-time conditions have had their effect upon sewage treatment, and several precipitants formerly in use can now hardly be obtained, whilst even the price of lime is high. Alumino-ferric has been practically unobtainable for some time past, since its manufacture involves the use of sulphuric acid, and "nitre-cake," or acid sulphate of sodium, a by-product from the manufacture of nitric acid, has been largely used as a substitute. The writer has recommended its use for neutralizing a very refractory alkaline waste resulting from the production of hydrogen for airships.

Regarding the pressing of sludges which have been treated with sulphuric acid, Mr. Allen cites the well-known case of Bradford. It might be thought that the pressing of acid "magma," resulting from the "cracking" of wool-scouring liquors, would involve a high cost for press cloths owing to the action of the sulphuric acid; a well-known English firm, however, who for years have used pressing (the old-fashioned vertical type of press) for abstracting grease from acid magma, stated a few years ago that the average cost for press cloths per ton of grease produced was 5s 1d. Another firm gave the average cost over a period of five years as 4s 8d per ton of grease. Pre-war prices for the pressed cake were 3s 6d to 7s 6d per ton (2,240 pounds).

The process of recovery of fat from woolsuds very generally used in this country consists in "cracking" the suds in tanks holding about 4,000 to 5,000 gallons each, a slight excess of acid— some 100-200 parts per 105 parts of suds—being used, the fat separating at the top and bottom of the tank. The acid liquor is run to waste, and the fatty "magma" made into "puddings" with sacking, and hot-pressed.

At Huddersfield, as a result of considerable research and specially designed plant, grease is successfully recovered from dried press cake by means of benzine, the grease being afterwards purified, and commanding a price of about £20 per ton. This is an interesting case since, until recently, the use of solvents was deemed impracticable, largely owing to the difficulty of recovering the solvent.

So far as the writer is aware, lime is universally employed in this country for pressing purposes, altho there would appear to be no very valid reasons against using other materials, such as fine ashes, sawdust, etc., where circumstances warranted their use; further, the nonuse of lime would result in saving the ammonia otherwise set free. As the author points out, the main function of the lime is to give "body" and to produce better drainage. At Hanley, in Staffordshire, it may be noted, the milk of lime is added hot.

Analyses of press liquor derived from domestic sewage sludge have shown it to be practically free from bacteria when any large quantity of lime is used; this was found to be the case at Wimbledon. Probably, however, the more resistant spores would persist, almost certainly those of anthrax.

The quantity of lime required for pressing varies somewhat, as one would expect, according to the time of year. Quite broadly speaking, the average quantity of lime used for sludges produced by precipitation processes is about 1 per cent. dry lime on the weight of the sludge. The limed sludge is usually left to settle for about twelve hours in a sludge settling tank, after which the top water is drawn off and the sludge pressed. Properly limed and settled precipitation sludge should be pressed into good firm cakes in from sixty to ninety minutes. Fine "silty" sludges, e. g. septic sludges and the like, are found to require a very large quantity of lime; they also take much longer to press into a firm cake.

Mr. Allen's observations upon conveying sludge by channels and pipes are very useful. Trouble frequently arises from sludge pipes with slack gradients, and these often result in a large amount of tank liquor being used to flush thru the pipes, thereby materially increasing the percentage of moisture in the sludge. As the author points out, unless the sludge coating in the pipes is kept moist, it will partially dry and shrink from the pipes, often causing a blockage, and therefore the outlet valve should be closed after use. Sludges derived from fellmongers' yards and tannneries are very prone to cause trouble in sludge mains by reason of the lime and hair they contain. It may be of interest to add that at Bradford the sludge, containing about 84 per cent. of moisture, is fed into the 8-inch sludge main with compressed air at an initial pressure of 30-40 lb. per sq. in. The fall from the inlet to the outlet of the sludge main is about 70 feet.

Concerning the lifting of sludge to the presses, rams and compressed air are most commonly used, altho ejectors are also employed. For raising sludge from a sludge pump and forcing it thru sludge mains, and also for lifting unscreened sewage, the Stereophagus centrifugal pump has received marked attention of late years. This pump is provided with cutters which chop up any pieces of wood, etc., which would otherwise tend to choke the pump.

Most of the sewage sludge presses used in this country are made by Johnson, Manlove Alliott, or Goddard, Massey & Warner. The 72-chamber "Pyramid" Johnson press has a filtering area of 2,400 sq. ft., the capacity of the chambers being 144 cu. ft. The weight of pressed sludge per charge is 100.8 cwt., the thickness of the cake being 1½ in.

Mr. Allen does well to point out that the moisture in sludge cake is by no means uniform, being greatest where admitted at the center of the press. Indifference to this fact has proved a stumbling block to several distillation processes.

An average proportion of moisture in pressed cake is about

60 per cent. In certain cases, however, as for example where the cake is tipped and used to fill up disused brickyards and the like, there would seemingly be no necessity to reduce the moisture much below 65-70 per cent., thereby saving time in the production of the cake.

. I note that the author queries the number of presses at the Glasgow (Dalmarnock) sewage works. There are, I am informed by the manager, Mr. Thomas Melvin (Jan. 17, 1918) 19 presses, 7 of which have 38 cells, and the remainder 41. With regard to the press plates, the design of the grooves in these is highly important, otherwise the press cloths are soon cut thru.

Respecting the disposal of sludge cake; when sold to farmers it is usually broken up into fragments of about 1 or 2 cubic inches.

Coming to the cost of pressing sludge, particulars of cost relating to Rochdale and York may be of interest, altho the figures are now some years old. The Rochdale sewage it may be noted contains much grease, and sulphuric acid is used as a precipitant.

ROCHDALE

Cost of Pressing Sludge for the Years Ending March 31, 1904-5

Particulars.	1904.			1905.		
	£	s	d	£	s	d
Press men and labor......................	235	19	0	235	19	0
Engine drivers, coal, coke and water, proportion of oil, waste, repairs, etc..................	324	19	6	305	10	8
Lime..	123	9	1	118	2	4
Press cloths................................	73	9	11	58	3	6
Press plates................................	25	8	0	19	9	0
Totals........................	£783	5	6	£736	4	6

The actual weight of pressed sludge (60% moisture) during 1904 was 4,048 tons ($1_0 n_0$), the weekly average being 82 tons, and the cost of pressing 3s 10½d per ton. For the year 1905, the weight of pressed sludge (60% moisture) was 4,147 tons, the weekly output averaging 82.5 tons, whilst the cost of pressing per ton was 3s 6½d.

The cost of disposal was 7d per ton of pressed cake (both years).

At York, the cost of pressing for the year ending March 31, 1905, was as follows:

York

Cost of Pressing Sludge, 1905

Total Quantity Treated, 1,456,708,216 Gallons. [Imperial? Ed.]	Total Cost.			Cost per M. G.		
	£	s	d	£	s	d
Wages—						
Engineers and stokers.................	171	12	10	2		4.28
Lime mixing	68	11	2			11.29
Pressing	307	19	10	4		2.74
Maintenance of machinery, cleaning presses and press house, making press cloths, etc.	46	17	3			7.72
Materials—						
Coal, 582 tons @ 10s 1d, discharging, 17£ 12s 4d......................	311	0	10	4		3.25
Oil and packing.....................	21	12	7			3.57
Lime 492 tons @ 13s 9d............	338	5	0	4		7.73
Press cloths, etc...................	146	6	3	2		0.11
Maintenance of plant and machinery.......	20	5	2	0		3.38
Totals....................	£1,432	10	11	£0	10	8.02

The Wimbledon sewage, to which details given by Mr. Allen refer, may be termed a suburban sewage, containing rather a large amount of laundry wastes. Up to the commencement of the war the sewage had probably altered but little since Santo Crimp's time.

The writer is of the opinion that chemical precipitation may very possibly have an increase in vogue after the war, owing to increased demands for more efficient removal of suspended solids, thereby permitting an increased rate of filtration, and it is therefore quite probable that where the treatment works are restricted as regards extensions, pressing will come to the fore again. With many industrial wastes having no outlet to a sewer available, the use of precipitants will be almost imperative during the preliminary stages of treatment.

As Mr. Allen remarks, the de-watering of activated sludge may give a considerable stimulus to sludge pressing during the next few years. As yet, however, we have no large sewage works in this country where the entire sewage flow, including storm water, is dealt with by this process, altho it must be remembered that the war has greatly interfered with progress in sewage treatment, and the activated sludge process would seem to possess decided advantages, if and when sundry details have been carefully worked out and met.

If the recommendations of a recent committee on electrical power are carried into effect, power may soon be available all over the country at a far cheaper rate than is at present the case.

It is quite possible that a revival of interest in agriculture, following a successful termination to the war, may lead to attention being focused upon a more extended use of sewage sludge as a fertilizer. As regards storage of sludge in large heaps, it is perhaps well to remember that a very considerable amount of heat is generated by so doing, and it is not perhaps very accurately known how far this may reduce the value of sludge cake as fertilizer by eliminating certain bacteria. As a general proposition, one would infer that heat would destroy the nitro and nitroso bacteria and protozoa, whilst leaving the ammonia-forming sporing bacteria, and that the soil would contain the necessary nitrifying microbes, but this may not be invariably the case, especially where barren sandy soils are concerned.

With reference to sludge cake from tanneries or derived from sewages containing tannery wastes, the sludge is almost certain to contain spores of anthrax, and these persist almost indefinitely; such sludge should therefore not be used for grass or meadow land to which cattle are likely to have access.

RUDOLPH HERING, D. Sc.—Mr. Allen has given us a very comprehensive paper. The disposal of sewage sludge, for over half a century, was the most troublesome part of sewage treatment, and England, which was the most active of all countries in developing such treatment, had granted, as I was informed, over fifty different patents to remedy some or all of the sludge troubles.

The most hopeful treatment was derived from sewage precipitation; the sludge, usually having a percentage of water exceeding 90, was given its artificial drying by pressing. Mr. Allen has collated practically all of the best data available on the subject. He discusses them in general for all of these four now most used processes: Plain sedimentation, chemical precipitation, Imhoff tanks and activated sludge process. He gives us the fundamental data, methods of computation, in short a present-day complete collection of facts, most useful to the designing and operating engineer.

The main part of the paper is confined to sludge filter pressing, not only because it is most used, but also because it presents the most difficulties, if full satisfaction is desired.

Mr. Allen's past experience, his personal observations both of actual large plants and experimental devices, has enabled him to give us an unusually fair and full statement of the essential points that we must consider.

Another merit of the paper is that in liberal foot-notes Mr. Allen gives his authorities so that we can study the particular statements in more detail, thus much increasing the value of the paper.

Conveying and pumping sludge have generally not been described with sufficient detail, so that the results could be directly applied elsewhere. But Mr. Allen has conveniently collated the information from the most different conditions so that it becomes very helpful.

More information might perhaps have been given under the heading of sludge cake, in view of the completeness found under other headings, especially covering our American experiences. Our cake differs, sometimes substantially, from the European cake, due not only to the different manufacturing waste, but to our usually dirtier street wash water, to our greater dilution of the solid sewage matter and the greater solution of organic matter contained therein when the delivery is at a great distance.

It would be interesting and perhaps of some value to have analyses of the liquor issuing from filter presses. The writer does not remember seeing such analyses. The interest would lie chiefly in the changed composition from that of the original sewage, after a long contact with the sludge in its pores.

A number of cost data are given. The writer desires to repeat a suggestion, which is especially apropos at the present time when war has so largely affected money values, and refers to the unsatisfactory cost statements of engineering structures and operations during abnormal times, when they are based on wages. Wages have always differed materially in different countries and parts of the same country. At present the war has doubled them in some places over what they were before the war.

There is a much less variable unit basis of cost than wages. It is the time which is required to do a certain kind of work. Over a score of years ago I contributed an article to the Engineering Record on The Street Cleaning of the City of Berlin. From the data there given it was practical to fix the number of hours required for all the different processes connected with street cleaning labor, entirely independent of the wages. To ascertain the cost of the same kind of work in our country, we would simply have to multiply the time data with the respective wage per hour and get a fairly good estimate for our conditions, because a laboring man and a mechanic will do about as much work of a certain kind per hour the world over.

It must at once be admitted that the original data required must be compiled with care. But once ascertained, they would hold good as long as the work is done in the same manner. It was once my intention, should the opportunity be favorable, to have respective tabular matter of this kind prepared. But it never appeared.

The advantage of this method of cost estimating first came to my notice at college over fifty years ago in the architectural lessons. Our text-book gave the man-hours for doing every part of practical work required in the construction and finishing of a building, divided, if I remember rightly, into superintendent, mechanics and laborers. From such time or work data, the measured quantities and the current raw material price lists, we made our cost estimates.

Whatever new difficulties might arise by using the man-hour basis in preparing cost estimates for new work, there has never been any doubt in my mind that, to compile such information, would at least be a useful step ahead in our engineering practice. It would be particularly helpful at present when the wage basis is so distorted, changeable and unreliable. The time basis can never be much changed. An estimate of the time required to do each kind of work, and which would be fairly constant and permanent, would then, in its various items, simply be multiplied by the current wage rate in the particular country, now, next year, or any year when the work is to be done.

KENNETH ALLEN (Closure)—The author notes the interest taken in the Miles process, to which the discussions of Messrs. Dorr, Winslow and Weston are mainly confined. Since writing the paper some rough estimates have been made for the application of this mode of treatment to a large volume of New York's sewage and the results appear to confirm Prof. Weston's statement that it could be adopted "at a cost far below that of any process of equal bacteriological and nuisance-preventing efficiency" provided the assumption as to costs and the revenue from products can be relied upon. Operating costs are for well-known processes and it would seem that the nub of the whole matter lies in the revenue from sales. The price of grease was about 4 cents per lb. before the war and according to Mr. H. H. Bighouse, New York manager of the C. O. Bartlett & Snow Co., the acidulated product is worth 12 cents today. The price of ammonia in tankage was about $2 per (short) ton unit before the war and is now about $5.50. In the estimate referred to, grease was assumed at 6 cents per lb. and ammonia in the dried sludge at $4.50 per ton unit. The result in round numbers was as follows:

Per million gallons of sewage per day—

Total annual charges for operation, maintenance, renewals and interest...$ 8,100

Total annual revenue from sales... 14,600

Net annual profit...$ 6,500

On the other hand, a letter recently received from Mr. G. L. Noble, Assistant Superintendent, Armour & Co., states, with reference to a sample of "Miles" sludge obtained from Dr. Mohlman, "that on account of the large proportion of volatile matter, unsaponifiable material and insoluble impurities, we consider it practically worthless for the manufacture of soap or glycerine."

The analysis of this sample was as follows:

Moisture and volatile matter, i. e., loss on drying.............. 32.86%
Total mineral matter... 7.1%
Unsaponifiable 19.6%
Free fatty acids (as oleic)... 18.3%

"Insoluble impurities could not be determined. As a matter of fact the 'grease' behaved as if it were quite insoluble in the fat solvents employed, namely, kerosene and light gasoline."

These contending opinions bring the matter to a point where the only thing to do is to wait for the results of further investigation, such as that now being carried out at New Haven under the direction of Prof. Winslow.

Ignoring any return from grease or fertilizer, the friends of acidulation claim advantages in its use as an inodorous disinfecting agent and in furnishing an effluent high in fertilizing properties—that at Moon Island (Boston) being worth $175 per million gallons if land were available for its utilization (Weston and Sampson) ; also, a sludge that is relatively stable.

Prof. Winslow has brought up the question of the pressability of acid sludge without the addition of lime. There seems to be no difficulty in accomplishing this at Bradford, but this might not hold good with all sewages. In that case it is a question whether the addition of some inert powder, such as fine ashes, suggested by Mr. Kershaw, or lignite, as at Spandau, would not secure the same result.

Mr. Kershaw's discussion contains much information regarding experience in England.

In the tables giving *Amount of Sludge from Sewage Treatment* the tons are of 2,240 lbs. and the gallons British, and in view of the note given at the beginning of the original paper it may not be amiss to state that by applying a factor of 0.93 the figures in the last column may be converted to short ton and U. S. gallons. Also the costs for pressing sludge at York should be multiplied by 0.83 to give results per million U. S. gallons.

To the ordinary person sludge is sludge; but Mr. Kershaw brings out the great variation in quantity, due to wash from rains, and in the fertilizing value, depending upon the origin of the mineral as well as the organic constituents, matters which should be duly considered in planning new work. Wet sludge has been used in England as well as Germany for irrigating crops, but the grease tends to clog the soil if overloaded. At Bradford this is partially removed from the cake by heating the presses, but there is sufficient remaining, as the author was told by Mr. Joseph Garfield, the engineer, to cause the sludge to heat up during the voyage to America, where a limited amount was sold prior to the war. The possible loss in fertilizing value by this increased temperature is mentioned by Mr. Kershaw. In this connection, it is believed that the more complete removal of grease by SO_2 and percolation with benzine would avoid this trouble and result in a larger return than by precipitation with H_2SO_4 and filter-pressing. Otherwise the grease may be eliminated by burning the sludge, as has been done at Leeds and Stoke-on-Trent. The fine red ash, one-third the bulk of the cake, when used on a stiff clay soil, has given good results with crops altho this is probably due to the contained lime rather than to any true fertilizing ingredient.

Percolation of cake dried to 15% moisture with benzine was not found profitable at Cassel, however, as already mentioned, and also proved offensive by the dissemination of odor from the solvent. The latter objection would probably be met by the use of the enclosed percolating tanks and connections used by the C. O. Bartlett & Snow Co. in the Cobwell process for garbage reduction.

To produce an equivalent of sludge cake without the cost of pressing, Dr. Grossman of Manchester suggests precipitation with H_2SO_4, concentration by gravity for several days, and then mixing cinders with the sludge, now 80% moisture, producing "a resultant mass equal to the average filter-pressed sludge cake at about one-third the cost.*

Mr. Kershaw mentions the comparative sterility of a well-limed press liquor. An acid effluent will also be well sterilized, as already pointed out, but with this difference: that the subsequent development of bacteria after discharge will be retarded, whereas with an alkaline effluent it will sometimes be accelerated.

Referring to the large amount of laundry wastes at Wimbledon, referred to by Mr. Kershaw, it may be of interest to mention some experiments made by Mr. Copeland for the Metropolitan Sewerage Commission on the effect of soaps in aiding the precipitation of solids, following the discharge of sewage into salt water. In his report he says that "Whereas, in the absence of other coagulants, from 20 to 25 per cent. of sea water must be added to sewage in order to coagulate the solids and secure a clear, liquor, when castile soap is added to the sewage in the proportion of 270 p.p.m. (or 15 grains per gallon) 5 per cent. sea water coagulates the solids and 10 per cent. of sea water precipitates all of the solids, leaving a clear supernatant liquor." Without considering the use of pure castile soap pending a peace settlement, might not chemical precipitation of laundry wastes by sea water be a reasonable proposition under certain situations?

The danger to be apprehended from the dissemination of anthrax spores from tannery wastes should not be ignored. At Ballstôn-Spa, N. Y., Dr. D. D. Jackson has provided for sterilization of the effluent after passage thru Riensch-Wurl screens having 5/16" and 1/32" slots. By a removal of 4 to 6 bbl. of matted hair, fleshings, etc., from a flow of 500,000 gal. per day of wastes

*Surveyor, Jan. 30, 1914.

by the screens, most of the spores are also removed. The screened effluent is then treated with 50 p.p.m. of liquid chlorine, and at no time in the ten months "since the installation was complete was anthrax found in the treated sewage" altho found on four occasions in the raw sewage.*

Experiments indicated that neither sulphur dioxide nor bleaching powder would give satisfactory results.

The author agrees with Mr. Kershaw in believing that under special conditions or with special sewages chemical precipitation is likely to find a greater field of usefulness than in the past, one important consideration being the removal of the colloids. Now, according to Dr. J. H. Johnson,† "about one-half the organic matter in sewage is in colloidal solution," and Purvis and Coleman refer to this as consisting of "highly complex nitrogenous compounds." These statements coincide with the results of experiments by Lederer** in which he found that "on removal of 63% of the total suspended matter, or 54% of the suspended volatile matter, the actual improvement in the sewage from the standpoint of prospective nuisance is but 31%"; from which he concludes that "the finely divided slowly settling suspended matter and pseudo-colloidal matter not capable of settling make up the greater part of the putrescibility due to the suspended and colloidal matter." Now with a well-operated chemical precipitation plant the putrescible matter represented by colloids is pretty well eliminated, leaving only that in solution to be further dealt with by nitrifying organisms. This lightens the load on filter beds or the oxidizing capacity of the stream receiving the effluent altho, it is true, at the expense of disposing of a large volume of sludge. Every economy in this process, therefore, improves the outlook for sewage precipitation.

Mr. Hering calls attention to the lack of analyses of the press liquor and as yet the author has been unable to find any on record altho Mr. Kershaw's reference to the bacterial contents of such liquor would indicate that such have been made.

Every designing engineer will appreciate the force of Mr. Hering's remarks regarding the difficulty in preparing estimates that are reasonably reliable under these disturbing war conditions, based upon the usual unit cost data which are almost always expressed in dollars and cents. Time or work data are only occasionally published altho a large fund must exist in the hands of contractors. It is well to bring out the importance of collating information of this kind as Mr. Hering has done and to urge contractors as well as engineers to place it on record for the benefit of the community.

*Engineering & Contracting, Jan. 10, 1917.
†E. Kuichling. Transcript of Record. People State of N. Y. vs. State of N. J. and Passaic Valley Sewerage Commrs. Vol. III, p. 2712.
**The Relation of the Putrescibility of the Settling and Non-Settling Suspended Matter in Sewage. Dr. A. Lederer, Am. Jour. Pub. Health, Feb., '13.

F. A. DALLYN, C. E., Assoc. M. Can. Soc. C. E. (Toronto), Chairman Committee on Sewerage and Sanitation (Closure)— Mr. Kenneth Allen's paper on "The Pressing of Sewage Sludge" and the splendid discussion which it has evoked makes a satisfactory contribution to our technical literature and the Society may well be proud of it. As Chairman of the Committee I wish personally to thank Mr. Allen for his paper and Mr. E. S. Dorr, Dr. C. E. A. Winslow, Mr. G. B. Kershaw and Mr. Rudolph Hering for the discussion which so splendidly supplements it.

The Society might well make Mr. Allen's paper the first of a series dealing with the particular question "Can Sewage Sludge Be Utilized?" The two recoveries which have attracted most attention in the discussion of Mr. Allen's paper are the manurial value and the value of the grease. With reference to the former agriculture has made giant strides.

Sewage sludge is now recognized as having a value, mainly for its nitrogen content and for the mineral salts present, together with the general improvement in humus following its introduction. The results of experiments, especially those in which its usefulness was condemned and reported in the transactions of the Royal Commission on Sewage Disposal, should not discourage us in this country from further effort. The soil conditions are materially different in this country, as well as the methods of agriculture. With us the great cost of transportation of prepared fertilizers should tend to encourage the use of sewage sludge locally.

If the sludge is to be dried to the 10% basis now commonly required for fertilizer compounds, or as a filler for fertilizer repacing the abattoir tankage, which is fast disappearing owing to the development of prepared stock foods, it will require drying in a temperature sufficient to sterilize all bacterial organisms. Where this has not been done the material in fine powder form has been shown to have an injurious effect upon workmen handling it, in some instances occasioning violent skin eruptions after its inhalation in large quantities.

The sludge containing over 3% nitrogen on a dry basis may be said to be marketable and the difficulty is merely to determine the particular point where it can be used with greatest advantage. In England the export of sewage sludge has largely been to France, Germany and the States. The markets were fairly good. The American market, however, was shut off owing to the fact that sludge with a higher moisture content than 10% gave a good deal of trouble from heating during the voyage and this more than anything else was responsible for the discontinuance of shipments. The grease recovery from sludge, introduced in this country by Mr. Dorr, supported by his experiments at Boston, has attracted a good deal of attention. Too little attention, however, seems to have been paid to the quality of grease and to the effects of extraction.

Grease in sewage divides, naturally, into two classes, mineral oils and fatty oils. In the latter the percentage of animal fats is somewhat higher than that of vegetable oils. It is unreasonable to expect to be able to discover grease in a sewage sludge which has not been introduced directly to the sewers, either by domestic wastes, abattoirs, manufacturing or wool-washing industries, and the success of municipal recovery will depend largely upon the fact that the manufacturers and abattoirs are dilatory in practicing the art of local recovery. A local census of the industries discharging to any given sewerage system and an inventory of the proportion of their material which reaches the sewers should be undertaken before attempting a report upon the advisability of grease recovery on a municipal scale at sewage disposal works. Generally speaking, there would not be a sufficient amount of grease in sewage sludge to make recovery a paying proposition or to interfere with its fertilizer value if the manufacturers were alert and recovered grease locally.

The presence of considerable quantities of grease interferes very materially with the pressing operations, and the use of neither acid nor lime removes this handicap. The action of lime is to saponify the grease and to form an insoluble lime soap. Treatment of alkaline sewage with acid occasions a very similar reaction, the acid saponification yielding 55 to 63 per cent. fatty acid, as against 45 to 47 per cent. by the lime process.

The advantage which has been observed in the Miles process lies not so much in the greater effectiveness of the acid process, but almost solely to the fact that with the acid the molecular weight of the fatty acid is increased, the tri-stearate being formed instead of the stearate. The acid process in the soap is not generally used commercially except for the manufacture of fatty acids from inferior fats, such as those obtained from garbage, putrid bones, etc.

Mr. Allen appears to have overlooked a very important matter in connection with the pressing of sewage sludge, and that is that the soaps and greases present in sludge are frozen or solidified at the ordinary sewage temperatures and in this condition are capable of clogging the filter cloths.

The following table gives the melting and solidification points of a few of the fatty acids from various oils and fats which may be encountered in sewage sludge and you will note that temperatures in excess of 69° C. are necessary to melt this material:

SOLIDIFICATION POINTS, DEGREES CENTIGRADE

Beef tallow	38–46	Palm oil	36–45
Mutton tallow	41–48	Cocoanut oil	20–25
Lard	34–42	Palm-nut oil	20–25
Horse fat	33.7	Japan wax	59
Neatsfoot oil	26.5	Vegetable tallow	45–53

Linseed oil	13.17	Olive	17–26
Tung oil	37	Arachis	23–29
Hemp oil	14–16	Cod-liver	18–24
Poppy-seed	16.5	Whale	24
Cotton-seed	32–36	Japanese sardine	28
Rape	12–18		

MELTING POINTS, DEGREES CENTIGRADE

Oleic	4	Elaidic	51
Oxystearic	84–86	Stearic	69
Iso-oleic	44–45	Palmitic	62

This would readily account for the success of Mr. Garfield in his sludge-pressing and de-greasing work at Bradford. The acid treatment which is in use there, and which I had the pleasure of inquiring into a year ago, is introduced mainly to promote precipitation, the sewage being quite alkaline at the works. Precipitation starts when the sewage is about 8 grains alkaline to methylorange. The cost of heating the presses is not so material as one might generally be led to believe, in view of the fact that no evaporation takes place and it is only the specific heat and the temperature range which has to be taken into count. My recollection is that in Mr. Garfield's plant the total operation of the works required about one ton of coal to forty tons of wet sludge, that is, sludge containing about 82% moisture. It works out to about one ton of coal to a ton of sludge as it comes from the presses with about 25% to 28% moisture, and which is further reduced by the heat of the mass to about 15% or 16% moisture by simply piling in the storage yards. This further improvement is assisted by the fact that after coming from the presses the sludge is made into egg-shaped briquets, as has been indicated by Mr. Allen, which leave plenty of voids for the circulation of air. The introduction of heat has a further benefit in the fact that the viscosity of the water and of the melted fats is very much improved and they escape readily from smaller openings or with higher velocities from the same opening.

As to the market for grease recovered from sludge, as far as I have been able to determine, there is but one considerable market and that is for the manufacture of textile soaps. Some years ago it would probably also have been introduced into lubricants, but with our present knowledge of the behavior of the fatty oils in the presence of oxygen, which tends to liberate free fatty acids which have a corrosion action, it would appear that for the future the mineral oils will be used exclusively for that purpose.

The mineral oils do not materially interfere with pressing operations. Lubricating oils and greases which escape to the sewers will not tend to clog the press cloths. They are mainly manufactured from mineral oils and seldom solidify above 15° C. in winter, 5° C. in summer, different classes of oil being thus permitted at different seasons. Their viscosity, however, may be markedly improved by increasing the temperature of the sludge.

It is worth noting that the glycerol content of grease extracted from sewage will be low in view of the fact that fats in the presence of nitrogenous animal or vegetable impurities decompose readily into free fatty acids and glycerol by enzyme hydrolysis. The acids will, in some of the processes, absorb oxygen and form the oxyacetic. The glycerol is also partially destroyed.

Grease extracted by solvent processes, which is about the only process left when the grease content is not in excess of 20%, limits the market to its use in the soap industry or as adulterant to lubricating oils. The wool-washing industries should advance the art of local recovery and this type of grease, largely composed of lanolin, cannot be hoped for in our sewage sludges. Lanolin recovered without the use of solvents, as is the practice in all the newer apparatuses, for this purpose has a very high market value. Hitherto it has proven impossible to remove the final traces of solvents which give it odor and preclude its use for certain purposes.

Nothing has been introduced into the paper suggesting the advantages of centrifuging sewage sludge. This should be a fertile field for experimental work in the near future. The type of centrifuge which I expect to see developed will be quite different from the earlier machines, principally introduced in Germany, in which the water was thrown thru the sludge, the sludge being held on canvas or metal gauze somewhat similar to the arrangement in the ordinary laundry drier.

Dr. Bartow's experiments at Champaign with a very small centrifuge have shown very good results. The main disadvantage of centrifuges for sludge recovery or dewatering lies in the time required for cleaning operations.

In conclusion it would seem practicable to group our incinerator and sludge pressing plants and take some advantage of the heat usually available at such plants, for the English experiments have shown that there is no difficulty in conveying sludge long distances thru pipes. The combination of the two will work just as well if centrifuges are introduced and low pressure steam with vacuum condensers used for motive power.

It is the writer's confident opinion that the utilization of sewage sludge is not by any means a remote possibility and that we may expect satisfactory returns from its manurial values as soon as we determine its limitations and make its application coincide more closely with soil requirements.

MINNEAPOLIS CITY WATERWORKS, DEPARTMENT OF PURIFICATION

By F. W. Cappelen, City Engineer

FILTRATION DATA

The purification plant for the Minneapolis Water Department was put in operation January 10, 1913. The plant consisted of twelve filter beds, each of four million gallons maximum capacity, with two coagulation chambers, each of 1,300,000 gallons capacity.

During the year it was found that the coagulation basins were not large enough, and also that the filter capacity had to be increased.

This work was completed, in 1915, by adding four filters, each of four million gallons maximum capacity, and two coagulation basins, each of 1,500,000 gallons capacity.

In 1917 we again commenced construction of eight filters, giving us a total of ninety-six million gallons which will be in operation this fall. But the complete report for 1917 is not yet out, so the complete laboratory, operation, and cost data for the four years that the filtration plant has been in service will be found in the following tables, making the comparison possible for 1913, 1914, 1915 and 1916, at a glance.

Table No. 1—Shows amount of water filtered; rate of filtration; wash water; chemicals used; fuel and electric energy used.

Table No. 2—Cost data.

Table No. 3—New construction cost, not chargeable to operation.

Table No. 4—Routine chemical laboratory tests; odor; turbidity; color; alkalinity, etc.

Table No. 5—Sanitary chemical data.

Table No. 6—Analysis of mineral residues.

Table No. 7—Bacteriological data.

Table No. 8—Bacteriological data; B coli determinations.

Table No. 9—Microscopical examinations.

Table No. 10—Typhoid fever statistics.

Table No. 11—Comparison of color in river water with precipitation data.

Table No. 12—Relation of amount of water filtered to precipitation and temperature data.

Table No. 13—Reduction in color per grain of alum.

Chart No. 1—Typhoid fever chart.

TABLE I. FILTRATION DATA.

	Rate of filtration 24 hours Mill. gals.	Number of filters in service	Period between washings Hours	Number of filters washed	Loss of Head Feet	Water Filtered Gallons Total	Water Filtered Gallons Net	Wash Water Gallons	Wash Water Per Cent	Coagulant Pounds	Coagulant Grains per gallon	Lime Pounds	Lime Grains per gallon	Chlorine Pounds	Chlorine Parts per million	Fuel used Pounds	Electric Energy used K.W.H.
1913																	
Max. daily						4,581,000	4,452,000	1,218,000	6.3	34,417	8.11						
Min. daily						14,704,000	14,192,000	170,000	0.7	1,396	0.39						
Aver. daily	3¾	9	13¾			25,869,000	25,114,000	775,000	3.0	12,820	3.47						
Total						9,294,198,000	9,015,907,000	278,291,000		4,602,577				b.210,652		625,610	266,362
1914																	
Max. daily						44,949,000	42,942,000	2,860,000	9.8	39,750	9.36						
Min. daily						10,256,000	9,682,000	0	0.0	1,400	0.60						
Aver. daily	3¾	9	24¾			25,739,000	24,129,000	1,010,000	4.0	11,176	3.11						
Total						9,175,840,000	8,806,943,000	368,898,000		2,078,783				b.199,549		734,621	245,210
1915																	
Max. daily						36,806,000	35,939,000	1,728,000	7.1	24,700	5.70						
Min. daily						17,800,000	17,254,000	186,000	0.8	2,200	0.64						
Aver. daily	2¾	13	37½			25,667,000	24,743,000	944,000	3.7	9,664	2.63				0.3		
Total						9,375,681,000	9,031,060,000	344,621,000		3,518,974		4,239,658		a.190 C.62 b.204,818 C.1,608		870,769	268,180
1916																	
Max. daily						58,929,000	57,237,000	2,208,000	6.1	37,200	5.81						
Min. daily						19,827,000	18,608,000	0	0.0	2,850	0.80						
Aver. daily	2¾	15	44¾			29,289,900	28,319,800	969,700	3.9	10,636	2.54				0.32		
Total						10,703,959,000	10,365,036,000	354,923,000		3,892,780				c.75½ b.27,541		1,010,930	295,940

Notes: a. Lime used in water softening experiments. b. Hypochlorite of lime. C. Liquid chlorine. 2. High wash-water due to micro-organisms.

TABLE 2. COST DATA.

	Coagulant	Lime	Chlorine	Fuel	Electric energy	Wash Water	Supervision and Office Wages	Supervision and Office Supplies	Laboratory Wages	Laboratory Supplies	Operation Wages	Operation Supplies	New machinery and equipment Wages	New machinery and equipment Supplies	Total purification cost Wages	Total purification cost Supplies	Maintenance and repairs Wages	Maintenance and repairs Supplies	Total Cost Wages	Total Cost Supplies	Credits	Interest and depreciation	Total net cost
1913																							
Total	122186.5		3382.84	1597.26	3170.14	5966.65	2960.00		3480.00		17098.04	4024							23036.54				41536.28
per mill. gals.	4.66		0.36	0.17	0.34	0.60	0.32		0.38		1.84	0.53							2.53	6.65			9.18
1914																							
Total	52744.52		3455.87	1635.86	3060.85	7317.96	3426.64	122.23	3460.00	1067.49	18125.59	1734.56	126.13	1876.68	25310.57	1794.32	1011.75	252.84	27108.87		64.65		86207.38
per mill. gals.	7.11		0.35	0.20	0.33	0.80	0.40	0.01	0.38	0.12	1.98	0.14	0.01	0.20	2.76	6.26	0.20	0.25	2.96	6.51	0.07		9.40
1915																							
Total	52504.02	913.14	1922.38	1934.10	3006.56	6832.52	3960.00	83.16	3480.00	935.76	17646.52	998.60	1162	752.06	4509.44	9090.57	2348.11	123.68	21442.22		0.00		78649.50
per mill. gals.	3.97	0.10	0.21	0.21	0.32	0.74	0.42	0.01	0.37	0.10	1.88	0.11	0.00	0.08	2.68	5.32	0.25	0.14	2.92	5.46	0.00		8.38
1916																							
Total	16594.52		2946.00	2432.99	3109.44	7098.69	3964.00	219.75	3605.57	1009.04	16082.77	1152.02	82.50	4906.25	14190.05	4950.05	4446.05	1677.23	18090.05		0.00		83971.05
per mill. gals.	4.25		0.27	0.23	0.29	0.66	0.37	0.02	0.34	0.09	1.69	0.11	0.01	0.05	2.90	5.97	0.39	0.15	2.79	6.12	0.00		

TABLE 3. NEW CONSTRUCTION COST.

	Filtration Plant Railway						New Construction		Reservoir Boulevard		Old Reservoir Expense		Public Safety		Total Cost		Credits	Total Net Cost
	Construction		Maintenance	Operation		Int. and Deprec.	Total Cost											
	Wages	Supplies	Supplies	Wages	Supplies			Wages	Supplies	Wages	Supplies	Wages	Supplies	Wages	Wages	Supplies		
1913																		
1914								84.80	1028.58						84.80	1028.58		1113.38
1915								972.75	2252.50	621.51	449.19	67.50	22.50		1061.76	2724.19		3785.95
1916	42.50	0.00								738.44	726.53				800.94	726.53		

TABLE 4. Summary of Routine Chemical Laboratory Tests.
Parts per million.

Descriptive / stat	Odor		Temp.°		Turbidity			Color			Alkalinity as CaCO₃ — Phenolphthalein			Alkalinity as CaCO₃ — Erythrosine			Incrustants as CaCO₃			Total Hardness as CaCO₃			Magnesium as CaCO₃			Carbonic Acid as CO₂			Residual Chlorine	
	S.B.	C.E.	S.B.	C.E.	R.W.	S.B.	C.E.	R.W.	S.B.	C.E.	R.W.	S.B.	C.E.	R.W.	S.B.	C.E.	R.W.	S.B.	C.E.	R.W.	S.B.	C.E.	R.W.	S.B.	C.E.	R.W.	S.B.	C.E.	C.E.	D.M.
1913 Max daily	M.		27.5	27.5	30	20	0	108	102	49				198	224	229				208	248	252				5	9.5	36.	.180	—
Min daily	0	0	0.8	1.0	10	10	0	38	11	4				129	106	76				135	118	114				0	0	1.5	.000	—
Aver daily	0	0	11.0	11.4	18	8	0	59	45	18				153	163	137				161	172	179				0	1.5	13	.030	—
No. of samples	346	346	344	346	194	345	354	193	351	471				195	340	347				41	57	63				182	314	323	350	0
1914 Max daily	F.M.		27.5	26.	90	30	0	130	118	48				222	220	214				235	232	233				8	8	39	.095	.028
Min daily	0	0	0.5	1.	3	2	0	19	19	11				100	111	61				107	115	84				0	0	4	Tr.	.000
Aver daily	0	0	10.6	11.	17	10	0	49	46	17				162	162	140				169	169	169				1.3	1.3	13	.033	.004
No. of samples	365	365	364	362	322	364	720	322	364	365				322	364	364				61	63	69				322	364	364	732	339
1915 Max daily	0	0	25	24	55	20	0	86	79	28				207	217	210				218	229	230				6	9	30	.071	.022
Min daily	0	0	1	1.5	2	2	0	22	20	9				120	123	69				127	130	103				0	0	24	.000	.000
Aver daily	0	0	10	10.4	17	9	0	47	43	14				155	161	140				167	173	171				0	2	12	.017	.000
No. of samples	365	365	365	365	373	365	1078	273	365	1076				273	365	365				43	69	70				274	365	368	718	241
1916 Max daily	0	0	28	28	150	55	0	84	78	27				202	199	190				217	214	216				7	7	20	.025	.019
Min daily	0	0	1	1	1	1	0	21	21	9				77	80	52				82	85	79				0	0	4	.000	.000
Aver daily	0	0	10	10	18	11	0	41	40	12				153	154	134				165	166	167				2	2	10	.002	.004
No. of samples	366	366	366	366	359	366	1098	359	367	1100				359	366	366				61	61	61				359	366	367	701	283

NOTE: S.B. = Sedimentation Basin. R.W. = River Water from force Main. C.E. = Combined Filter effluent. D.M. = Filtered Water from distribution main. M. = Marshy. F.M. = Faint Marshy. T.R. = Trace only.

TABLE 5. Summary of Sanitary Chemical Data (Parts per million)

| | Mineral Residue | | | | | | Chlorides | | | Nitrogen as free ammonia | | Nitrogen as albuminoid ammonia | | Nitrogen as nitrites | | Nitrogen as nitrates | | Oxygen Consumed | | Dissolved Oxygen | |
	Total		Non Volatile		Volatile																	
	S.B.	C.E.	S.B.	C.E.	S.B.	C.E.	R.W.	S.B.	C.E.	S.B.	C.E.	S.B.	C.E.	S.B.	C.E.	S.B.	C.E.	S.B.	C.E.	S.B.	C.E.
1913																					
Max.	246	251	144	145	102	106	2.8	—	2.9	.098	.060	.900	.296	Tr.	Tr.	.360	.257	21.1	9.1	—	—
Min.	189	194	97	109	82	71	0.9	—	1.6	.033	.019	.175	.115	Tr.	Tr.	.110	.075	3.5	2.7	—	—
Aver.	208	210	115	128	91	80	1.5	—	2.1	.058	.032	.292	.193	Tr.	Tr.	.223	.159	11.4	5.3	—	—
No. of samples	16	13	16	13	16	13	17	0	17	16	16	9	9	16	16	16	16	16	16	0	0
1914																					
Max	240	240	139	141	103	105	2.5	—	3.8	.115	.108	.359	.205	Tr.	Tr.	.292	.276	17.5	7.3	—	—
Min	187	191	99	115	82	71	1.5	—	2.5	.011	.015	.214	.152	.00	.00	.107	.083	4.9	3.6	—	—
Aver.	204	211	118	127	92	84	2.0	—	3.2	.043	.041	.270	.186	Tr.	.00	.192	.152	9.6	5.2	—	—
No. of samples	29	29	29	29	29	29	30	0	30	30	30	30	30	30	30	30	30	29	29	0	0
1915																					
Max.	241	241	141	141	100	100	3.0	3.0	4.0	.156	.133	.335	.226	.003	.002	.281	.251	12.0	4.9	10.6	11.2
Min.	180	183	100	107	80	66	2.0	2.0	2.5	.006	.006	.139	.116	.000	.000	.070	.062	4.8	3.2	7.7	8.0
Aver.	210	212	121	132	89	80	2.4	2.4	3.3	.041	.035	.222	.143	Tr.	Tr.	.129	.109	7.9	4.3	9.6	9.8
No. of samples	20	20	20	20	20	20	19	19	19	19	19	19	19	17	17	18	18	19	19	15	15
1916																					
Max.	220	220	130	133	95	89	—	2.6	3.0	.244	.161	.308	.170	.004	.003	.252	.190	15.1	4.8	10.3	10.3
Min.	140	137	78	93	62	44	—	1.5	1.8	.007	.008	.135	.073	.000	.000	.036	.030	7.4	2.8	9.4	9.5
Aver.	192	192	110	119	82	73	—	1.8	2.1	.064	.044	.228	.137	Tr.	0	.118	.091	8.3	3.6	9.8	9.9
No. of samples	12	12	12	12	12	12	0	12	12	12	12	12	12	12	12	12	12	12	12	12	12

NOTE   R.W.=River Water from force main.   S.B.=Sedimentation basin.   C.E.=Combined filter effluent.   Tr.=Trace only.

Typhoid fever statistics for Minneapolis for the years 1900 to 1916, inclusive, will be found in Table No. 10, while the accompanying Chart No. 1 shows diagrammatically the typhoid death rate per 100,000 for the same period. It is interesting to note that the typhoid death rate has remained practically the same since 1911, the year following the installation of the hypochlorite of lime treatment of the city water supply, until the year 1915, when it dropped to 7 per 100,000. In 1916 there was a further drop in the typhoid death rate to 4.7 per 100,000, the lowest for Minneapolis of which there is any record, and one of the lowest of any city in the United States.

The relation between the rainfall on the Mississippi watershed above Minneapolis, and the color of the river water at Minneapolis, is shown in Table No. 11. This relation is masked somewhat by the storage of the flood waters in the large reservoirs controlled by the U. S. Government, and also influenced by the intensity of the precipitation during short intervals of time. It may be stated in general, from the data at hand, that the cumulative effect of the rainfall upon the color for the succeeding months is apparent and that a decided increase in color of the river water at Minneapolis follows in from fifteen to thirty days a heavy precipitation on the Mississippi watershed above Minneapolis.

Table No. 12 shows the relation of the amount of water filtered each month of the years 1913, 1914, 1915 and 1916, to the total monthly precipitation and average temperature data in Minneapolis for each month as supplied by the U. S. Weather Bureau.

Table No. 13 indicates the added efficiency of the two additional coagulation basins in reducing the amount of alum used. The parts per million of color removed by one grain of alum is shown for each month of the four years, as compared with the number of coagulation basins in service.

OPERATION AND COST DATA

Filters

Table 1 shows that the greatest total amount of water filtered during any one year was in 1916, with a total of 10,719,959,000 gallons, an increase of 1,344,278,000 gallons over 1915. The average daily amount of water filtered during 1916 was 29,289,500 gallons, an increase of 3,602,500 gallons per day over the 1915 average. The maximum amount of water filtered during any one month was in July, 1916, with 1,203,628,000 gallons, and the maximum amount filtered during a twenty-four-hour day was on July 28, 1916, when 58,929,000 gallons were put through the filters.

TABLE 6. Summary of Analyses of Mineral Residues (Parts per million)

Sedimentation Basin

	K+Na	NH₄	Mg	Ca	Fe	Al	HCO₃	NO₃	Cl	SO₄	SiO₂
	Potass. Soda	Ammon. Hyper.	Magnes.	Calc.	Iron	Alu.	Bicarb Without Chlor.		Chlorid	Sulphat	Sulphat Silica
1913					Fe₂O₃+Al₂O₃						
Max.	5.9	0.11	18.6	55.7	12.6		266	1.59	2.0	8.4	18.5
Min.	1.9	0.04	6.1	34.5	1.7		166	0.49	1.0	6.6	11.5
Aver.	3.0	0.07	11.7	39.4	5.2		189	0.88	1.4	7.4	14.5
No. of samples	10	10	10	10	10		10	10	10	10	10
1914											
Max.	7.7	0.15	17.1	52.7	0.99	3.64	249	1.29	2.5	9.2	17.6
Min.	3.4	0.01	9.9	34.3	0.14	0.46	146	0.47	1.5	4.7	10.1
Aver.	5.2	0.06	13.7	42.4	0.45	1.16	200	0.84	2.0	6.6	13.6
No. of samples	12	12	12	12	12	12	12	12	12	12	12
1915											
Max.	7.7	0.20	17.1	51.4	0.58	1.01	247	1.28	3.0	10.7	15.2
Min.	5.1	0.01	10.7	34.7	0.18	0.13	157	0.31	2.0	4.6	9.8
Aver.	6.4	0.05	13.9	42.0	0.35	0.51	198	0.59	2.4	8.0	11.7
No. of samples	12	12	12	12	12	12	12	12	12	12	12
1916											
Max.	9.9	0.31	16.0	51.7	0.66	1.03	231	1.14	2.8	8.7	16.8
Min.	5.5	0.01	8.3	25.7	0.11	0.24	116	0.16	1.5	5.1	8.6
Aver.	7.4	0.09	12.8	40.1	0.33	0.46	189	0.46	1.9	6.5	12.0
No. of samples	12	12	12	12	12	12	12	12	12	12	12

Combined Filter Effluent

	K+Na	NH₄	Mg	Ca	Fe	Al	HCO₃	NO₃	Cl	SO₄	SiO₂
	Potass. Soda	Ammon. Hyper.	Magnes.	Calc.	Iron	Alu.	Bicarb Without Chlor.		Chlorid	Sulphat	Sulphat Silica
1913					Fe₂O₃+Al₂O₃						
Max.	6.3	0.08	18.3	55.7	13.4		260	1.14	2.8	56.5	17.6
Min.	2.0	0.02	2.8	35.9	1.5		114	0.33	1.6	37.5	8.5
Aver.	3.9	0.05	9.6	40.0	6.6		155	0.44	2.0	40.4	10.9
No. of samples	6	6	6	6	6		6	6	6	6	6
1914											
Max.	7.4	0.14	16.7	52.3	0.29	4.13	249	1.22	3.5	53.9	13.5
Min.	3.1	0.02	8.5	34.5	0.01	0.52	78	0.57	2.7	10.7	5.8
Aver.	5.0	0.06	13.1	42.1	0.09	1.40	174	0.79	3.2	27.5	9.7
No. of samples	12	12	12	12	12	12	12	12	12	12	12
1915											
Max.	7.6	0.17	17.1	51.8	0.06	1.6	235	1.16	4.0	50.6	12.2
Min.	5.2	0.01	10.2	35.2	0.01	0.4	104	0.26	2.5	13.6	6.3
Aver.	6.5	0.05	13.6	42.0	0.05	0.8	173	0.47	3.2	28.4	8.5
No. of samples	12	12	12	12	12	12	12	12	12	12	12
1916											
Max.	9.6	0.26	16.0	51.1	0.07	1.12	219	0.86	3.1	45.4	11.9
Min.	5.4	0.01	8.2	26.1	0.03	0.33	85	0.13	1.8	13.6	5.9
Aver.	7.3	0.06	12.7	39.9	0.05	0.63	164	0.36	2.2	26.7	8.9
No. of samples	12	12	12	12	12	12	12	12	12	12	12

TABLE 7. Bacteriological Data.
Colony Counts on Agar at 37° and Gelatine at 20°C.

	Raw Water Agar	Raw Water Gel.	Settling Basin Agar	Settling Basin Gel.	Coag. Basin Agar	Coag. Basin Gel.	Infl. to filters Agar	Infl. to filters Gel.	Effl. from filters Agar	Effl. from filters Gel.	Effl. from plant Agar	Effl. from plant Gel.	Distribution Main Agar	Distribution Main Gel.	City Taps Agar	City Taps Gel.
1913																
Max.	2300	10000	1200	5400	900		650				130	150	11	210	800	4500
Min.	70	125	5	120	3		2				0	1	1	3	0	1
Aver.	645	1665	240	395	155		85				7	11	4	24	80	215
No. of Samples	196	194	599	381	599		337				599	380	36	95	341	339
1914																
Max.	2700	5300	1000	8800	1500		1700		2200		155	160	170	13500	150	11000
Min.	55	250	40	150	20		4		3		0	1	0	1	2	2
Aver.	510	1000	255	790	155		120		195		12	11	14	200	16	310
No. of Samples	322	322	730	365	728		566		542		730	365	337	337	87	83
1915																
Max.	2600	12,700	1700	10400	1100		1400		2100		210	160	160	1100	215	400
Min.	40	120	38	110	14		10		2		0	1	1	1	1	1
Aver.	1710	1720	395	860	152		195		70		8	6	7	24	14	98
No. of Samples	274	274	729	364	729		720		744		728	364	241	241	97	97
1916																
Max.	33,500	42,000	7300	52,000	2200		2000		800	65	800	2000	50	475	500	475
Min.	30	120	30	110	20		10		1	10	1	1	1	1	1	2
Aver.	775	2250	390	1345	160		165		90	35	13	27	7	24	18	25
No. of Samples	959	958	732	364	731		696		599	17	840	727	259	252	142	142

A. Aftergrowths in clear water reservoir

TABLE 8. Bacteriological Data

B. Coli Determination (Percentage of total number of tests positive)

	River Water			Settling Basin			Coag. Basins			Influent to filters			Effl. from filters			C.E.			D.M.
	10 C.C.	1 C.C.	1/10 C.C.	10 C.C.	1 C.C.	1/10 C.C.	10 C.C.	1 C.C.	1/10 C.C.	10 C.C.	1 C.C.	1/10 C.C.	10 C.C.	1 C.C.	1/10 C.C.	10 C.C.	1 C.C.	1/10 C.C.	
1913																			
Max. Monthly	100	96		100	63		98	72		69	30					20	0		17
Min. Monthly	93	40		48	3		72	0		2	0					0	0		0
Aver.	99	74		86	38		66	23		36	13					2	0		5
No. of samples	198	198		596	595		595	595		337	250					597	36		341
1914																			
Max. Monthly	100	100	84	100	100	92	100	97	74	98	92	33				64	3	4	50
Min. Monthly	100	86	12	96	73	8	93	30	3	47	10	0				13	0	0	0
Aver.	100	97	50	90	68	45	97	68	33	60	39	9				39	1	1	13
No. of samples	79	317	263	211	178	728	612	429	727	299	428	507	534	330	279	542	728	949	87
1915																			
Max. Monthly	100	77	13	100	62	21	93	47	11	90	36	11	72	21		7	3		60
Min. Monthly	44	6	0	42	10	0	3	2	0	3	2	0	3	0		0	0		0
Aver.	92	49	6	79	34	8	55	19	4	55	18	4	33	.7		4	0		12
No. of samples	274	274	274	729	729	729	729	729	729	720	720	720	744	744		728	224		98
1916																			
Max. Monthly	100	67	37	98	76	98	85	32	19	83	46	12	95	62		37	10		43
Min. Monthly	75	9	0	46	11	0	20	2	0	19	3	0	19	0		0	0		0
Aver.	89	42	10	78	29	9	47	11	3	45	15	3	66	16		11	2		6
No. of samples	959	359	359	791	791	791	791	791	791	727	727	727	730	727		861	252		144

Notes: "City tap samples largely from dead ends." C.E.= Filter Plant Effluent. D.M.= Distribution Main.

The average number of filters in service during 1916 was 15, as compared with 13 in 1915. The rate of filtration was reduced to an average of 2.1 million gallons per day in 1916 for each filter, or in other words, to a rate of 80 million gallons per acre of sand surface per day. This would be 64 per cent. of the normal rate of filtration for which the filters were constructed, namely 125 million gallons per acre per day. The additional filters in service during 1916 also caused an increase of 20 per cent. in the length of filter runs and a decrease of 10 per cent. in the amount of wash water used for 1915.

Coagulant

The amount of alum used in 1916, while greater in total amount because of the greater amount of water filtered, was 3.4 per cent. less than the amount used in 1915, if we consider the number of grains of alum per gallon of water treated. The cost of alum per million gallons of water for each of the four years was as follows: 1913, $4.66; 1914, $4.11; 1915, $3.47, and 1916, $4.25. The increase in cost for alum in 1916 was due to the European war, the price of alum having advanced approximately 37 per cent. A large stock of alum carried over from 1915 helped to keep down the alum cost for 1916.

Sterilization

Hypochlorite of lime had been used for sterilization from the time the filtration plant was put in operation until December 6, 1915. At that time it was replaced by liquid chlorine, due to the scarcity and high price of hypochlorite, caused by the war.

The cost for sterilization in 1916 was $0.27 per million gallons, as compared with $0.21 in 1915. If hypochlorite had been used in 1916 the cost would have been fully 1000 per cent. greater for sterilization, the price of hypochlorite having advanced from $0.015 to $0.20 maximum per pound in 1916. A stock of 5,640 pounds of hypochlorite of lime which was left over when the liquid chlorine treatment was begun was sold by the Purchasing Department at an average price of $0.112 per pound, a net gain to the city of approximately $0.09 per pound.

There have been no complaints of odors or tastes in the filtered water due to the sterilizing agent since the liquid chlorine treatment was installed. The Wallace & Tiernan chlorine machines have given very satisfactory service. Table 2.

Total Cost of Operation

The total cost per million gallons for purification of the water was $9.18 in 1913; $9.40 in 1914; $8.38 in 1915, and $8.90 in 1916. The cost for 1916 shows an increase of 6.2 per cent. over that for 1915, the chief increase in unit costs being for coagulant

TABLE 9. Summary of Microscopical Examinations.

	Diatomaceae											Chlorophyceae					Cyanophyceae		Protozoa			Various			Total	
1913																										
Max.	214	1285	473	56	42	82	18	46	14	8	2	50	98	22	36	12	4	5		15		Pr.	38	340		340
Min.	120	40	0	12	8	0	0	2	0	0	0	0	0	0	0	0	0	0		0			0	170		170
Aver.	176	691	240	99	28	32	10	15	4	4		13	19	3	10	2	1	2		10		12	266	1297	640	
Present in samples	10	10	9	10	10	8	10	10	9	6	3	8	8	4	8	2	7	4	0	8	1	8	10	10		
1914																										
Max.	198	2479	459	58	39	85	12	24	15	31	5	35	18	36	18	14	5	12	2	31	2	26	620			
Min.	40	40	6	4	7	0	0	0	0	0	0	0	0	0	0	0	0	0	0	0	0	0	100			
Aver.	104	695	101	23	20	16	6	8	6	8	2	14	6	9	7	3	1	4	1	9	1	10	290	1070	402	
Present in samples	35	36	34	35	33	94	94	94	33	19	99	33	24	31	20	10	27	10	29	13	12	33	36	35		
1915																										
Max.	298	2480	386	62	90	125	9	23	26	26	1	29	7	10	8	4	2	4	1	22	2	27	388			
Min.	69	48	5	7	6	0	0	4	1	3	0	1	0	0	0	0	0	0	0	0	0	9	98			
Aver.	127	317	65	21	18	20	4	11	10	11	1	11	2	4	9	1	1	1	1	7	1	9	237	506	920	
Present in Samples	43	43	43	43	34	40	43	43	43	25	43	31	39	26	29	24	8	33	4	14	43	43	43			
1916																										
Max.	116	490	174	9	23	55	9	17	37	37	4	19	10	9	8	4	6		11	4	32	875				
Min.	57	21	2	2	5	0	0	4	0	2	0	1	0	0	0	0	0	0	0	0	9	70				
Aver.	86	156	41	11	10	9	3	10	10	16	1	8	2	4	2	2	1	3	1	3	1	11	271	374	265	
Present in samples	39	99	39	39	27	36	36	39	39	39	12	39	19	33	23	23	6	26	14	39	39	39				

and sterilizing agent, which advanced in price in 1916. There were decreases in several of the other unit costs for 1916 as compared with 1915.

Laboratory Data

The average turbidity of the river water as it is received in the sedimentation basin at the Filtration Plant has remained practically the same for each of the four years that the plant has been in operation, the maximum of 150 parts per million occurring in 1916.

The average yearly color of the river water has decreased steadily from year to year as may be seen in Table 11. The reason may possibly be found in the decrease in the logging industry along the Mississippi river above Minneapolis, and also in the increasing demand for agricultural lands with the consequent draining of swampy areas. A maximum color of 130 parts per million occurred in the river water in 1914, as compared with 86 parts in 1915, and 84 parts in 1916. The average color of the filtered water was 18 parts per million in 1913; 17 parts in 1914; 14 parts in 1915, and 12 parts in 1916.

The average alkalinity of the river water has remained practically the same from year to year. It varies during the year from a maximum of 224 parts per million to a minimum of 80 parts.

The average total hardness also has remained practically the same. It varies from 248 parts per million to 82 parts during the year and averages 165 parts per million for 1916.

Free carbonic acid in the filtered water showed an average of 10 parts per million in 1916 as compared with 12 parts in 1915

TABLE 10. Typhoid Fever Statistics.
Supplied by Minneapolis Health Department.

	Number of Typhoid Cases	Number of Typhoid Deaths	Death rate per 100,000 pop.	Remarks.
1900	876	79	38	
1901	630	121	58	
1902	320	66	29	
1903	720	95	39	
1904	738	103	41	
1905	269	62	23	
1906	252	97	34	
1907	181	77	26	
1908	104	51	17	
1909	95	59	19	
1910	1252	173	57	Chlorination Began Feb. 1910
1911	299	36	11	
1912	186	37	11	
1913	136	41	12	Filter Plant in operation Jan. 1913
1914	278	38	12	Pop. 343,460
1915	166	25	7	Pop. 353,460
1916	181	21	5.8	Pop. 363,460

and 13 parts in 1914 and 1913. Free carbonic acid in the filtered water is due chiefly to decomposition of the bicarbonates of calcium and magnesium by the aluminum sulphate added and is chiefly of interest because of its corrosive action on the iron pipes in hot water systems thereby causing "red water."

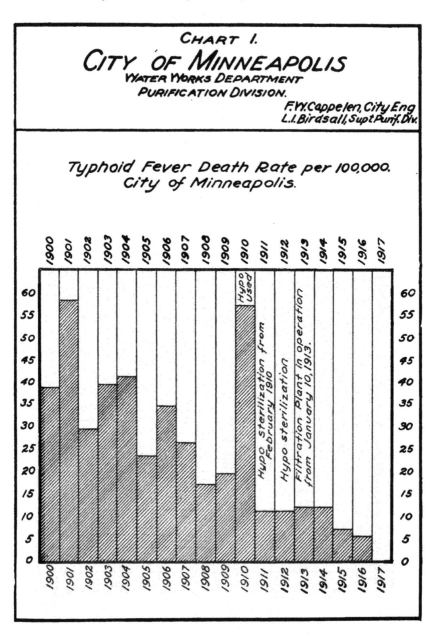

TABLE II. Comparison of Color in River Water at Minneapolis with Average Monthly Precipitation on Mississippi River Watershed above Minneapolis.

	Jan.	Feb.	Mar.	April	May	June	July	Aug.	Sep.	Oct.	Nov.	Dec.	Summary
1913													
Average Precipitation	0.32	0.96	1.11	2.00	3.07	3.03	7.18	1.57	3.63	3.12	0.48	0.02	25.89
Max.	17	17	38	41	51	59	108	93	71	61	50	42	108
Color Min.	11	14	17	28	29	50	48	55	48	49	38	38	11
Aver.	14	16	25	39	43	55	76	74	58	63	45	40	47
1914													
Average Precipitation	0.74	0.43	1.14	2.45	2.43	8.36	2.56	5.51	3.67	1.81	0.41	0.18	29.71
Max.	38	23	26	42	81	1.90	124	75	60	55	40	30	130
Color Min.	23	19	20	37	42	58	75	40	32	38	31	25	19
Aver.	29	20	22	39	64	99	91	53	42	45	34	27	49
1915													
Average Precipitation	0.67	1.20	0.42	1.73	4.00	8.54	3.64	1.53	2.87	2.13	1.89	0.73	29.35
Max.	25	23	72	42	77	75	86	55	29	47	79	60	86
Color Min.	22	20	27	30	40	46	57	32	24	22	35	30	20
Aver.	23	21	38	36	53	63	75	43	27	37	54	42	44
1916													
Average Precipitation	2.05	0.38	1.63	2.06	4.94	5.14	2.47	5.23	3.89	1.42	0.16	0.79	29.57
Max.	30	25	50	75	84	72	82	50	46	57	28	26	84
Color Min.	24	21	24	49	68	51	39	90	39	27	25	21	21
Aver.	27	23	19	64	75	60	60	96	39	31	26	23	41

Note: Precipitation data from U.S. Weather Bureau for stations at Bemidji, Cass Lake, Brainard, St.Cloud and Minneapolis.

TABLE 12. Relation of Amount of Water Filtered (Million Gallons) to Precipitation and Temperature Data at Minneapolis.

	Jan.	Feb.	Mar	Apr.	May	June	July	Aug.	Sep.	Oct.	Nov.	Dec.	Summary
Normal Precipitation	0.69	0.76	1.65	2.44	3.92	4.01	3.81	3.69	3.66	2.58	1.18	0.95	28.34
Normal Temperature	13.7	15.1	29.4	46.6	57.3	67.2	72.1	69.6	62.0	49.7	33.0	20.1	44.6
1913													
Precip.	0.42	0.74	1.65	1.86	2.86	2.21	7.75	1.40	4.12	2.55	0.48	0.05	26.09
Temp.f.	13.0	12.7	25.7	49.0	55.8	70.5	70.4	72.8	64.4	46.4	40.2	30.4	45.7
Total	568.585	674.858	679.159	679.199	703.525	1072.735	887.488	1,007.002	829.899	786.337	681.982	649.429	9,294.198
Daily Aver.	23.691	24.102	21.908	22.440	25.275	35.758	28.626	32.485	27.669	25.366	22.799	20.949	26.218
Max. Daily	25.821	26.125	25.916	25.146	30.479	45.817	39.069	41.766	37.506	31.490	24.770	29.266	45.817
1914													
Precip.	0.83	0.95	0.98	3.69	1.80	8.63	1.17	8.70	2.76	1.58	0.15	0.37	31.15
Temp.f.	21.4	7.6	30.6	44.7	64.4	66.8	75.1	69.2	62.4	55.4	36.0	12.2	45.2
Total	656.574	610.644	705.849	678.582	846.267	772.499	1052.907	879.975	769.077	763.172	721.946	754.948	9,175.840
Daily Aver.	21.148	21.809	22.770	22.620	26.331	25.750	33.965	28.173	25.636	24.619	24.065	24.353	25.413
Max. Daily	23.290	26.033	26.706	26.824	33.059	34.779	44.949	38.557	29.622	30.138	26.770	28.759	44.949
1915													
Precip.	1.97	2.01	0.93	1.87	3.98	4.91	6.92	3.49	2.57	2.59	3.62	0.46	33.72
Temp.f.	12.6	25.4	27.8	56.0	52.2	62.5	67.2	65.4	60.6	51.4	35.4	22.6	44.9
Total	761.226	658.648	720.465	739.168	780.158	790.606	843.216	875.435	871.765	813.626	750.997	770.477	9,375.681
Daily Aver.	24.556	23.529	23.242	24.699	25.166	26.353	27.200	28.240	29.059	26.243	25.033	24.854	25.687
Max. Daily	27.443	26.314	26.047	30.659	32.908	33.299	33.038	32.017	36.806	30.437	27.647	28.802	36.806
1916													
Precip.	2.88	0.32	1.19	3.07	6.97	4.54	1.27	1.66	2.42	1.60	0.58	0.98	27.48
Temp.f.	10.0	11.0	26.0	43.6	56.9	62.9	79.0	72.0	69.8	46.9	34.6	12.1	42.9
Total	791.914	739.577	791.961	791.147	864.922	883.770	1203.628	1140.035	941.466	899.210	836.735	888.095	10,719.969
Daily Aver.	25.546	25.503	25.528	26.372	27.901	27.726	38.827	36.779	31.382	29.007	27.891	28.645	29.290
Max. Daily	28.570	28.460	28.728	27.970	35.880	35.202	68.929	52.348	40.269	34.014	32.958	33.922	58.929

TABLE 13 Reduction in Color per grain of Alum

	Alum Grains per Gallon	Color Settling Basin p.p.mil.	Color Clear Well p.p.mil	Reduction in color parts per million	Reduction in color per grain of alum	Number of Coagulation Basins in service
1913						
Max.	5.52	70	29	46	14	2
Min.	0.68	14	6	8	7	2
Aver.	3.47	45	18	27	8	2
1914						
Max.	6.63	91	26	65	13	4
Min.	0.70	20	14	6	7	2
Aver.	3.11	46	17	29	9	3
1915						
Max.	5.20	72	16	56	14	4
Min.	0.86	21	10	10	9	4
Aver.	2.63	43	14	29	11	4
1916						
Max.	4.60	75	15	61	15	4
Min.	0.90	22	10	9	7	4
Aver.	2.54	40	12	28	11	4

The average mineral content of the river water and filtered water has remained fairly constant during the past four years. It is interesting, however, to note that the average sodium and potassium content in the river water has been increasing gradually from year to year. This fact may possibly be accounted for by the sodium sulphate waste from paper mills on the upper Mississippi, although there are no data to prove this statement. The chlorine content of the river water decreased in 1916 and has not followed proportionately with the rise in the alkali metals. It would seem, therefore, that the steady increase in the sodium and potassium is not due to increasing amounts of common salt caused by sewage contamination of the river water above Minneapolis.

The bacteriological data are shown in Tables 7 and 8. It will be observed that there has been a considerable increase each year in the bacterial content of the river water and the water from the settling basin. This increase may be expected to continue as the watershed above Minneapolis becomes more densely populated.

The bacterial content of the filtered water has been uniformly low. It is gratifying to note a continued drop from year to year in the bacterial content of the water from city taps. This shows that the flushing of the city mains, carried out consistently, and the sterilization of new pipe lines before they are used, is having the desired effect. The city water supply has been uniformly safe and wholesome. The remarkably low typhoid death rate is added testimony that the typhoid fever attributed to city water previous to 1910 has been entirely eliminated and the residuum of typhoid in Minneapolis is due to causes other than city water. Dr. H. M. Guilford, City Health Commissioner, has stated in a letter to me recently that no case of typhoid fever in Minneapolis has been traced to city water since the Filtration Plant was put in operation.

CONCRETE PAVEMENTS

By Murray A. Stewart, Assistant Engineer in Charge of Roadway Section, Toronto, Ont.

It is not the intention in this article to institute any comparison between the usefulness of concrete and other materials for pavement purposes, as it is merely a recital of what might be called experimental work undertaken in order to ascertain the respective merits of different classes of concrete, and different methods of construction adopted in connection therewith.

For many years a highway known as the Lake Shore Road has existed between the cities of Toronto and Hamilton in the Province of Ontario. Its name is significant of its location, which is generally in close touch with the shore line of Lake Ontario between the two cities. The eastern end of the road for a distance of slightly over a mile lies within the city limits of Toronto, and it has been, and is now the duty of that municipality to maintain this portion of the road in a good state of repair. On this section the road lay at the time of the construction pavement closer to the lake than at any other point thruout its entire length, its proximity to the water being merely a matter of a few feet, as is indicated on the accompanying sketch. An examination of the cross-section will indicate also the very slight difference between the water level and the road level.

In 1911 the Toronto Harbor Board was constituted with powers to formulate a comprehensive scheme for the improvement of the water front of the city. Part of the subsequent development included extensive filling along the shore, opposite the Lake Shore Road, and drastic alteration, both as to level and location of the road itself. The shore line when the work is completed will be several hundred feet farther out into the lake, and while a considerable portion of filling has already been done, no alteration has yet been made to the road. This filling has been placed at a higher level than the road, and consequently a great deal of difficulty is experienced in getting rid of water during certain seasons of the year, particularly as the drainage facilities on the road are inadequate to meet the demands. The cross-section shown indicates generally the condition brought about by the filling.

For a great many years a macadam road existed on the highway and owing to the great amount of traffic which passes over it, particularly during the summer season, and its close proximity to the water, which renders the sub-soil somewhat unstable, a great deal of difficulty has been experienced in the past in maintaining the surface in a satisfactory state of repair. The work also has been of a somewhat costly character.

There has been, during recent years, a considerable amount of argument as to the most suitable mixture for use in concrete pavements, and the most satisfactory type of construction. In view, therefore, of the necessity which arose in 1914, of expending a large amount of money on the reconstruction of the macadam road existing at that time, it was thought that a good opportunity was presented to construct what might be called an experimental concrete pavement, particularly as it would be wiped out in the course of a few years as the harbor work developed, and failure of some of the sections would then not be a matter of great moment. An amount of money was, therefore, appropriated by the city council for the construction of a concrete pavement, and the work was divided into seven sections, each approximately 700 feet in length. The general details of these different sections are best set out in tabulated form as follows, and their relative positions on the road are clearly indicated on the sketch, viz.:

Section No. 1. Plain concrete, 1:2:5.

Location—Station 42 + 33.8 to 49 + 00.
Length—666.2 feet.
Width—Average 25.2 feet.
Type—Monolithic, 6″ in depth.
Proportions—1 cement, 2 screened sand, 5 stone.
Stone—1″ trap rock.

Expansion Joints.

Intervals—Every 25 feet.
Width—½″.
Depth—Thruout pavement.
Direction—Across pavement at right angles to sides.
Material—Baker steel bars, with ½″ elastite strips in some joints, and ½″ thickness of Samson ready roofing in others.

Section No. 2. Two-course concrete (reinforced).

Location—Station 49 + 00 to 56 + 00.
Length—700 feet.
Width—Average 23.3 feet.
Type—Two-course (reinforced).
First course 4″ in depth.
Proportions—1 cement, 2 screened sand, 5 screened gravel.
Stone—Screened gravel.

Reinforcing—Triangle mesh.
Second course 2″ in depth.
Proportions—1 cement, 1½ screened sand, 3 stone.
Stone—⅜″ trap.

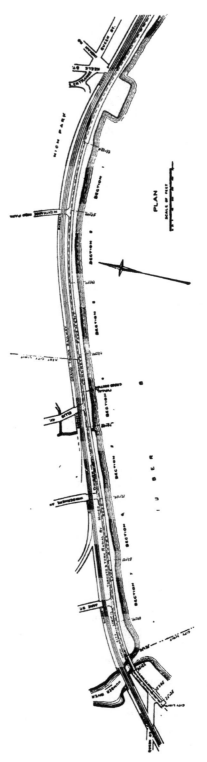

THE LAKE SHORE ROAD IN TORONTO

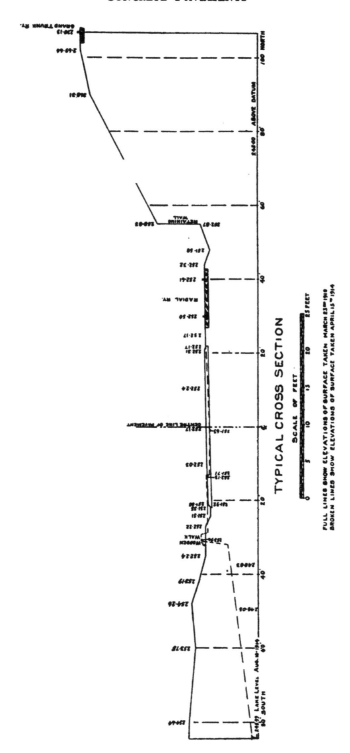

TYPICAL CROSS SECTION

SCALE OF FEET

FULL LINES SHOW ELEVATIONS OF SURFACE TAKEN MARCH 23RD 1912
BROKEN LINES SHOW ELEVATIONS OF SURFACE TAKEN APRIL 15TH 1914

Expansion Joints.
Intervals—Every 25 feet.
Width—½".
Depth—Thruout pavement.
Direction—Across pavement at right angles to sides.
Material—Baker bars, 49 + 00 to 49 + 75.
             Trussed Kahn bars, 50 + 00 to 56 + 00.
Filler—½" elastite strips.

Section No. 3.   Plain concrete, 1 :1½ :3.

Location—Station 56 + 00 to 63 + 00.
Length—700 feet.
Width—Average 21.3 feet.
Type—Monolithic, 6" in depth.
Proportions—1 cement, 1½ screened sand, 3 stone.
Stone—1" trap rock.

Expansion Joints.
Intervals—Every 25 feet.
Width—½".
Depth—Thruout pavement.
Direction—Across pavement at right angles to sides.
Material—½" genasco strips.

Section No. 4.   Two-course concrete (reinforced).

Location—Station 63 + 00 to 70 + 00.
Length—700 feet.
Width—Average 21.6 feet.
Type—Two-course (reinforced).
    First course 4" in depth.
    Proportions—1 cement, 2 screened sand, 5 gravel.
    Stone—Screened gravel.
Reinforcing—Expanded metal.
    Second course 2" in depth.
    Proportions—1 cement, 1½ screened sand, 3 stone.
    Stone—⅜" trap.

Expansion Joints.
Intervals—Every 25 feet.
Width—½".
Depth—Thruout pavement.
Direction—Across pavement at right angles to sides.
Material—Several Baker bars which were left over from
    section No. 2 were laid in this section.
Filler—½" elastite filler.

Section No. 5.   Plain concrete.

Location—Station 70 + 00 to 77 + 00.
Length—700 feet.

Width—Average 23.7 feet.
Type—Monolithic, 6" in depth.
Proportions—1 cement, 2 screened sand, 4 trap.
Stone—1" trap.

Expansion Joints.

Intervals—Every 25 feet.
Width—½".
Depth—Thruout pavement.
Direction—Across pavement at right angles to sides.
Material—½" genasco strips.

Surfacing.

Dolarway with stone screenings.

Section No. 6. Plain concrete.

Location—Station 77 + 00 to 83 + 00.
Length—600 feet.
Width—Average 23.9 feet.
Type—Monolithic, 6" in depth.
Proportions—1 cement, 2 screened sand, 4 stone.
Stone—1" trap.

Expansion Joints.

Intervals—Every 25 feet.
Width—½".
Depth—Thruout pavement.
Direction—Across pavement at right angles to sides.
Material—½" elastite; 12 joints were pitched.

Section No. 7. Two-course concrete.

Location—Station 83 + 00 to 89 + 00.
Length—600 feet.
Width—Average 20.9 feet.
Type—Two courses.
First course 4" in depth.
Proportions—1 cement, 2 screened sand, 5 screened gravel.
Stone—2" screened gravel.
Second course 2" in depth.
Proportions—1 cement, 1 screened gravel, 3 stone.
Stone—⅜" trap.

Expansion Joints.

Intervals—Every 25 feet.
Width—½".
Depth—Thruout pavement.
Direction—Across pavement at right angles to sides.
Material—½" genasco strips.

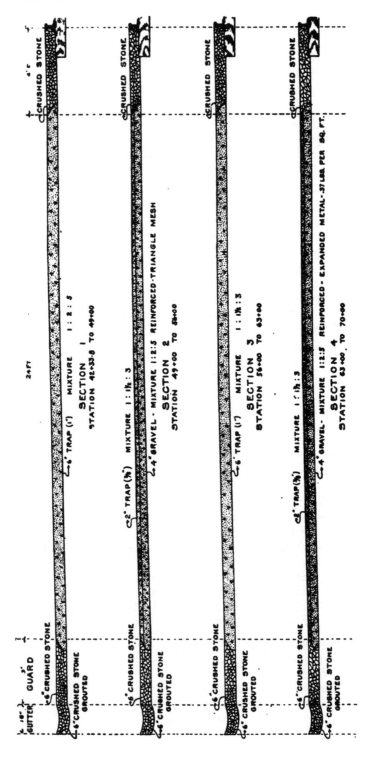

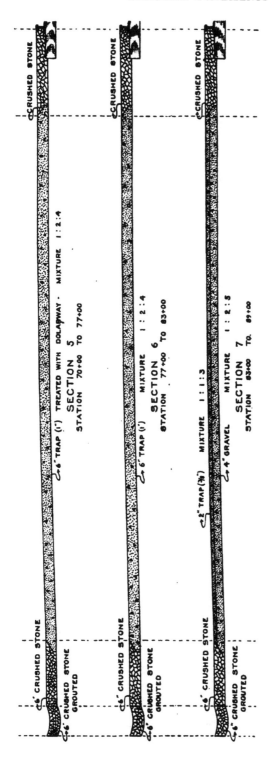

CROSS SECTIONS OF CONCRETE PAVEMENTS

LAKE SHORE ROAD

SCALE

6" CRUSHED STONE
6" CRUSHED STONE GROUTED

6" TRAP (1") TREATED WITH DOLARWAY - MIXTURE 1 : 2 : 4
SECTION 5
STATION 70+00 TO 77+00

6" CRUSHED STONE
6" CRUSHED STONE GROUTED

6" TRAP (1") MIXTURE 1 : 2 : 4
SECTION 6
STATION 77+00 TO 83+00

6" CRUSHED STONE
6" CRUSHED STONE GROUTED

2½" TRAP (¾") MIXTURE 1 : 1 : 3
4" GRAVEL MIXTURE 1 : 2 : 5
SECTION 7
STATION 83+00 TO. 89+00

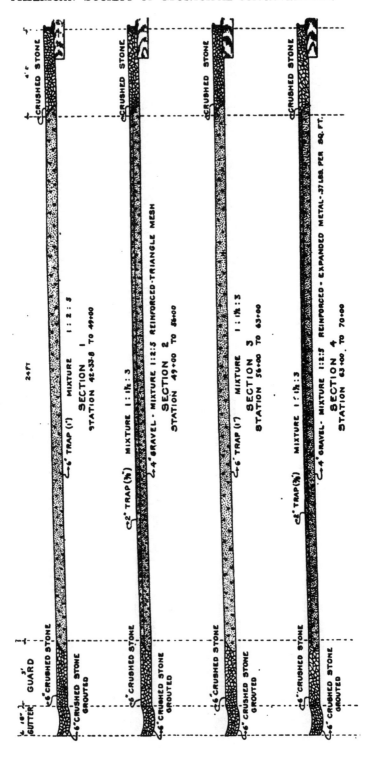

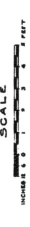

CROSS SECTIONS OF CONCRETE PAVEMENTS
LAKE SHORE ROAD

SCALE

The accompanying set of cross sections, together with the above details, show clearly the various types of work constructed.

The work was commenced on May 29, 1914, and completed September 17, 1914, being finally opened for traffic shortly afterwards. A good deal of difficulty was experienced, owing to the narrowness of the road, in keeping ways open for traffic during the progress of the work, and for this reason the length of time occupied in actual construction was greater than it would otherwise have been.

A traffic census was taken at various points upon the road from September 5 to September 11 (inclusive), 1915, and it was found that for twelve hours each day, from 7 a. m. to 7 p. m., an average of 1,809 vehicles passed a given point. This count included all classes of vehicles and during certain hours of the day the traffic was, of course, heavier than at others. The evening traffic, of which there is a considerable volume during the summer months, was not taken. The traffic for the last year or two has increased very materially, and the result has been to bring out certain sections in strong relief as compared to others.

The mixture which seems to have given the most satisfactory result consists of 1 part cement, 1½ of sand and 3 of 1″ trap rock. Certain sections also which were reinforced have shown up to great advantage compared to those which contained no reinforcing material, the latter, in some cases being badly cracked, owing to the unstable base and aggravated surface water conditions.

In 1912 the town of North Toronto was annexed to the city, and as very few pavements existed there at that time, the necessity for the construction of many works of this character was strongly urged. The sewerage system in the annexed district being inadequate for future needs, it was felt by the administration that it would be inadvisable to lay permanent pavements until a new system had been installed. The demand, however, for pavement accommodation was insistent, and in June, 1914, a number of concrete pavements were recommended as a temporary measure. Five of these pavements were laid in 1915 at such a grade that they could be used as part of the foundation for a future pavement of a better type.

While the information which we hoped to obtain from the construction of the pavement on the Lake Shore Road was not in any way complete, it was apparent that probably the most satisfactory mixture was 1 part of cement, 1½ of sand and 3 of stone (1″ trap), and the work was carried out to these specifications, no reinforcing being used. All of these pavements showed longitudinal cracking the following spring, and as the reinforced portions of the Lake Shore Road showed at that time to advantage over the others, the further work done in 1916 consisted of concrete of the same mixture with the introduction of reinforcing.

These pavements have now come thru the winters of 1916-1917 and 1917-1918 without developing any cracks. While it is not argued that reinforcing will entirely eliminate cracking, the results clearly indicate the wisdom of placing it in these later pavements. It might be added that the surface of all of these pavements up to the present time shows no sign of wear.

It is perhaps worthy of mention that several types of joints, other than the patented metal type alluded to in the Lake Shore, were tried in these pavements, and from observation of them it is evident that the most satisfactory form consists of the introduction of the ½" strip of manufactured filler, so placed as to permit of a small projection above the surface to allow for protection of the edges.

The information, therefore, which it was desired to gain in laying the experimental road on the Lake Shore Road, has established two very definite points in connection with the laying of concrete pavements in a climate such as that of Toronto, where the temperature has a range of 130°.

They are mainly the character of mixture, and the necessity for the use of reinforcement, and in future in any case where concrete pavements are to be laid, they will follow the specifications adopted for the last mentioned work in the northern part of the city, and will provide in addition to the necessary drainage facilities, etc., for a 1:1½:3 mixture of 1" trap rock and some form of reinforcement.

ROADS AND PAVEMENTS

Professor Baker's book on Roads and Pavements has been a standard authority on that subject since the appearance of the first edition in 1903. The present rewritten and enlarged edition brings it down to date and includes the marked advancements which have been made in street and road paving, notably in monolithic brick, concrete, creosoted wood block and stone block paving and bituminous-surface roads and streets. Very properly Professor Baker has devoted a large share of his book, nearly half in this edition, to roads and one-third to the country roads, earth, sand, sand-clay, gravel and macadam, including treatment with oil and tar. Free quotations are made from the Standard Specifications of the American Society of Municipal Improvements. A tabulation is made of the specifications for the kinds of asphalts specified for binders for asphaltic macadams, and bituminous concrete and seal coat, showing the difference between their specifications and giving their names. The same is done for the kinds of tar specified for bituminous macadams.

As a record of good practice down to the present year, the book fully sustains the reputation of the earlier editions.

CONTRACT FOR MUNICIPAL PURCHASE OF COMPETING ELECTRIC DISTRIBUTION SYSTEM

By C. W. Koiner, General Manager of Municipal Lighting Department, Pasadena, California

---

The proposed contract for the purchase by the city of Pasadena of the electric distribution system of the Southern California Edison Company within the city has been printed for distribution and discussion.

The gist of the whole matter is this: After ten years' fighting the company has agreed to sell to the city and turn over its system and the business. It has about 5,000 meters as compared with the city's 10,000, and its gross receipts amount to approximately $143,000 a year. This added to our income will enable the city to make an excellent showing and effect considerable economy after the consolidation.

The company gives up thirty years of its franchise and the city will agree to take current for fifteen years from the company, after which the company will have no further rights in the city of Pasadena. It is an excellent proposition from the standpoint of the city and, as a matter of course, it is a good proposition for the company because it can make more money selling us electrical energy at wholesale price than it can make in competition with the city.

Following is an abstract of the more important features of the document, whose object is the elimination of the city's competitor in the light and power business, resulting in the transfer of distribution systems so that the city will own all of its distribution system and none outside. The city will purchase from the company for a term of years the current necessary to serve the customers taken over by it in the transfer of distribution systems.

The first section sets forth in some detail the agreed valuations of various classes of property involved from poles to buildings and land and an agreed addition of 15 per cent. for overhead and contingencies during construction, amounting in all to $503,038.65 as the value on January 1, 1917, with $12,387.32 more for additions since that date, which the city agrees to lease, together with any additions which may be made hereafter.

By the second section the city agrees to pay an annual rental of 8 per cent. on this valuation of $515,425.97, with additions as they may be made, divided as nearly as possible into twelve monthly instalments.

In the third section the city agrees to accumulate a depreciation reserve fund of 3.36 per cent. of $445,168.02, the valuation of the depreciable property, with such additions as may be made, also to be divided into approximately equal instalments and paid monthly to the company, to be held in trust for the purposes of the operating board in paying for any replacements necessary to keep the property in its present state of usefulness, the city to make the replacements under the supervision of the board. If the city exercises its option to purchase the property the balance of the fund with accumulated interest becomes the property of the city and is transferred to it. If the city does not purchase, the fund becomes the property of the company.

The fourth section fixes the rates which the city shall pay the company for electricity furnished, and if the supply is adequate the city agrees to receive electricity from no other source. Two schedules of rates are provided. The first is as follows:

First 250,000 kw. hr. per month, $0.0095 per kw. hr.

Next 500,000 kw. hr. per month, 0.009 per kw. hr.

All over 750,000 kw. hr. per month, 0.0075 per kw. hr.

On thirty days notice the city may elect to use the following schedule:

Annual Load Factor	Rate per kw. hr.
Less than 44%	$0.00875
44 to 46%	0.0085
46 to 48%	0.0084
48 to 50%	0.0082
50 to 52%	0.0079
52 to 54%	0.0077
54 or over	0.0075

The maximum yearly peak demand is defined as the average of the three maximum peak loads of not less than 15 min. duration each, occuring during the year, no two peaks to be in the same month. The load factor for the year is the ratio between the average load and this maximum peak demand. The two parties agree to the establishment of these rates by the state railroad commission and that neither party shall ask for a change of rates. Should the rates be raised by competent authority the city may terminate the contract and should they be lowered the company may do so.

Electrical energy from the company's outside lines shall be 3-phase alternating current with frequency of 50 cycles a second, delivered at the present company sub-station at approximately 15,000 volts, suitable for transformation to 2,400 volts and measured there. Energy delivered from the company's steam plant within the city shall be measured there at about 2,400 volts by poly-phase recording watt meters of the company. Transformers are furnished and maintained by the city and shall have an efficiency not less than 98%. Meters may be tested at any time, the expense to be paid, if accurate, by the party demanding the test, if more than ½% slow by the city, if more than ½% fast by the company.

The fifth section fixes the present percentage of the total business of the city as 56.2 on the city's lines and 43.8 on the company's lines. It is provided that new additions, extensions and business shall be made proportionally to these percentages as determined by the operating board, city uses, such as street lighting, schools, pumping plants, etc., not being included. The company agrees to pay each month the reasonable cost of such additions to its property within ten days after bill, certified by the operating board, is presented.

The sixth section provides for the continued segregation of the company's lines so that they can be separated in operation from the city's lines easily at any time. The city keeps the company's property in good order, at its own expense, reasonable wear and tear and damage by the elements excepted. Repair of such damage or orders from state authority requiring reconstruction are to be paid for out of the depreciation reserve fund of the third section.

The seventh section provides for the operation of the city's steam plant to maintain continuous service on due notice to the dispatcher of the company, five minutes interruption in the company's current without reasonable assurance of resumption within another fifteen minutes justifying preparation for such use. The company must pay the cost of such preparation and operation and in addition at the rate of 12 per cent. per annum on the depreciated value of the plant as shown on the books, for the period of operation. Payments of such costs are to be made monthly on presentation of bills for the same.

The eighth section grants the city an option to purchase the entire property leased to it, with two or three very small exceptions, for $497,609.70 plus whatever costs for extensions may have been made in the meantime.

The ninth section provides for like lease of city lines outside its limits to the company, with exceptions noted.

The tenth section fixes the rental to be paid by the company at 8 per cent. on the agreed valuation of $27,928.81 plus any additions on terms the same as stated in the second section for the city's rental payments.

The eleventh section duplicates the provision in the third section of 3.36 per cent. on the agreed valuation of depreciable city lines of $24,285.92, plus additions made from time to time and for replacements paid for out of this fund, under direction of the operating board.

The twelfth section provides that additions shall be made in the outside territory in the same proportion as city and company lines now exist in the same territory, agreed upon as 67.06% to the city and 32.94% to the company, other provisions being the same as in the fifth section.

The thirteenth section is the reciprocal of the sixth section.

The fourteenth section gives the company the option to purchase the city lines outside the city at the date of purchase for $35,174.38, plus any additions and minus any lines taken into the city by extensions of territory.

The fifteenth section creates the operating board referred to, which consists of the general manager of the municipal lighting works department of the city, or other person selected by the Pasadena city commission, and a representative of the company, to pass upon and approve expenses for replacement and the distribution of additions, extensions and new business. Should these two not agree they may designate an arbiter to become a member of the board and vote on all questions. The cost of such arbitration is divided between city and company.

The city is made by the sixteenth section the preferred community in case the company cannot supply all its customers.

The company is required by the seventeenth section to loan the city power transformers to step down to 2,400 volts, in addition to those leased, for the period of the lease and after purchase until others can be purchased.

By the eighteenth section the parties are restrained from selling electric energy to any one, that may be used in the other's territory, except for certain public uses and outside territory covered by the leases.

Section nineteen provides for the continuance of the agreement for two years from date it becomes effective, and at the option of either party, until four months after the end of the war. If bonds are voted and there is litigation over their validity, the city may extend its option of purchase until three months beyond the close of such litigation. The city does not lose its rights for non-payment of bills unless the company gives the city 5 days written notice of declaration of termination of contract and the city still fails to pay.

In section twenty the company agrees to pay damages resulting from defective construction of its leased property but disclaims responsibility for negligence of the city in making repairs. Negligence of the operating board is not negligence of the city.

Section twenty-one provides for adding to the city's lease any company property in territory hereafter annexed to the city.

The contract is made subject to the approval of the California railroad commission by section twenty-two and the obligations of the parties thereto are declared concurrent and not independent by the last section.

The contract is accompanied by the proposed grant of the property by the company to the city, to be made on payment of the agreed sum therefor, when voted by the taxpayers, the terms of which are concurrent with the terms set forth in the contract.

EARTH PRESSURES

By Leo Hudson, Consulting Engineer, Pittsburg, Pa.

INTRODUCTION.

The purpose of this paper is the epitomizing of the voluminous literature reviewed on the subject of "Earth Pressures" with the hope that it will fill the same purpose in other offices which it has served to fill in my office. In offering this addition to the already extensive literature we hope to establish that rule which will be of the easiest application, which may be acceptable to the busy engineer and at the same time be of value to the young engineer thru the light of his own understanding.

The fundamentals underlying this work are not new. The wedge theory is that of Coulomb. We have tried to make the application prove in mathematical agreement with Rankine's formula. From this we have derived a formula which seems to be of easier application, and also a graphical solution. We have proven our formula both analytically and graphically. We have used freely the work of J. Romilly Allen, A. I. C. E. as published in Van Nostrand's Magazine, Vol. XVII, p. 155. Also we have used certain features of the notes as prepared by M. Monduit and taught in the Ecole des Beaux Arts, Paris. We have purposely kept away from the refinements of later writers because we would find the maximum conditions and design to meet them.

Behind each linear foot of wall holding an earth fill there are many sliding wedges which may be assumed, but there is only one wedge which will produce the maximum force and it is this wedge and its force for which the wall must be designed. In turn, this maximum resultant force may be assumed to act in many directions and at many points, but it is the direction and point of application producing the maximum force in which we are especially interested. These functions of the resultant force, namely, its magnitude, direction and point of application are sought out in terms of their maximum effects and the formulae are based on these limits.

We have left the question of the friction of the earth on the back of the wall and the friction of the bottom of the wall on the ground to the design of the wall to meet the conditions. Also, in gravity walls with the back making an angle of greater than ninety degrees with the horizontal, instead of adding the weight of the materials between the back of the wall and a vertical line we might step the wall so that this would become an aid instead of an extra weight. In a smooth-backed reinforced wall, however, this additional weight must be added as indicated in the work to follow.

DISCUSSION.

To determine the effect of earth thrust against the back of a wall it is necessary to determine:

(1) The magnitude of the pressure.
(2) The point of application.
(3) The line of action.

These elements may vary greatly but there is a time when their action amounts to a maximum. It is this maximum condition against which we should design. It is best to neglect the cohesion of the earth particles to each other except in as much as this cohesion affects the "angle of friction," as cohesion of earth might be rendered ineffective by shock, and to consider it away from the line of rupture would be giving to the earth a slight tensile strength which might not, under certain conditions, exist.

It is at once apparent that in a mass of earth behind a wall there is one wedge which will cause the maximum thrust against the wall. One feature of our problem is the determination of this wedge. After this wedge which exerts (1) the maximum pressure is determined, we are confronted with the problem of (2) the point of application of its resultant force. Opinion differs widely as to this; some engineers taking one-third up the wall from the base, some taking four-tenths up from the base, and others points between these two points. If the material behind the wall were liquid then the resultant pressure would be one-third up from the base; if the material were solid then the resultant pressure would be one-half way up from the bottom. For earth, which is never either liquid or solid, it would seem that one-half the difference between one-third and one-half should be added to one-third, making the point of application at .415 up from the base or practically four-tenths up. (.50—.33= .17; .17÷2=.085; .085+.33=.415). As to (3) the direction of the line of action, the direction may be horizontal or make an angle with the horizontal. For an horizontal surface we would take the direction of the resultant as horizontal and for sloping surfaces we would still take it as horizontal and add the weight of the material above the horizontal top as surcharge (see figure 11). Anyway, the horizontal direction requires the heavier wall and as the material might produce a resultant which would act horizontally we would take that direction. Then, there is a wedge which will exert a maximum resultant pressure, said resultant acting at a point four-tenths of the height of the wall up from its base, and acting in a horizontal direction.

Now the problem is to determine this wedge which will exert the maximum pressure. All earthy material, if poured vertically on a horizontal plane, will form a surface slope making an angle with the horizontal. This angle is called the "angle of repose." Each particle on the slope is held in equilibrium by the force of gravity, due to its weight, and by friction. The tangent of the angle of repose is the "coefficient of friction" of the material. We all have noticed in a bank about to cave, that there first becomes a large crack near the edge of the bank and sometimes this crack partially develops before the cave takes place. Then back of this large crack there is a smaller one, then behind this still a smaller one, and so on until finally there is a mere "hair crack" almost twice as far back from the edge of the bank as the first large crack. This material between the first large crack and the edge of the bank is known as "the sliding wedge." And it is this wedge which we will undertake to prove, of all wedges, will exert the maximum thrust against the wall. The plane of the first large crack is called the "plane of rupture."

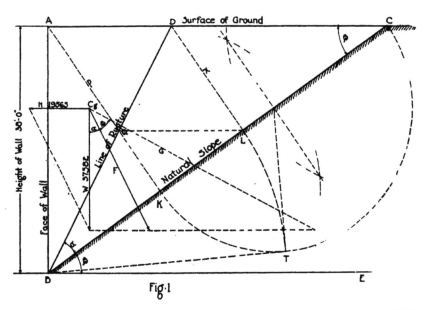

Fig. 1

Take Fig. 1. Let AB be the face of a vertical wall, let BE be the horizontal, let AC be the surface of an earth fill placed behind the wall. Then let BC be the line of repose of the material making the angle b with the horizontal. The angle b is the "angle of repose." The line BD lies somewhere between the face of the wall and the line of repose. It is our purpose to determine where the "line of rupture" BD will be, which will form a sliding wedge which will exert the maximum pressure against the wall. The resultant pressure of the sliding wedge ABD on BD makes an angle to the normal to BD equal to the coefficient of friction of the material, which angle is called the "angle of internal friction" and may differ materially from the "angle of repose." The friction of the "sliding wedge" is a different friction force from the surface-forming friction, one being due to a sliding action, the other being due to a rolling action. For loose, earthy material, it is safer and at the same time not too safe to assume that the "angle of internal friction" is equal to the angle of repose and therefore to take the resultant of the "sliding wedge" as acting with the normal to the line BD decreased by the "angle of repose." (For a liquid there would be no angle of repose and no line of rupture, and if W is the weight of a cubic foot of the liquid, h is the height at any point on the wall, and P is the horizontal pressure, then $P = \frac{1}{2} Wh^2$.)

To Determine the Line of Rupture

Again in Fig. 1 let AB be the back of a retaining wall, BE the horizontal, BC the line of repose making the angle b with the horizontal.

Then, from A, draw AK perpendicular to BC; bisect KC; with the center point of CK as center draw a semi-circle through K and C; from B draw a line tangent to the semi-circle; then let T be the point of tangency; with B as a center and BT as radius, describe arc TL cutting BC at L; from L draw LD perpendicular to BC, cutting AC at D; connect D and B. The line BD is the "line of rupture" and divides ABC into ABD and DBC. The wedge ABD is the "sliding wedge" which will exert the maximum pressure against the wall AB.

To Determine the Pressure Which ABD Would Exert Against AB.

The sliding wedge is held in equilibrium by gravity (due to its weight), friction which it makes on the line BD, and the wall. To determine the pressure against the wall, exerted by the wedge ABD, consider said wedge acting on one linear foot of wall; find center of gravity of wedge. (The center of gravity is at the intersection of lines drawn from any two angles to the center of the opposite sides.) From the center of gravity drop a line which represents the weight of the wedge one foot thick, W; from the center of gravity draw a line normal to BD; set off from this line the angle of internal friction b; which gives the line F; divide W into its two components, one acting on BD along the line F; and acting horizontally against the wall as H. By drawing W to scale and measuring H to the same scale, we find the magnitude of the force H against the wall which acts at a point 0.4 of the height of the wall up from the base. It is apparent that the angle which W makes with F is equal to a.

Then: $H = W \tan a$.   (I)

Then again: H attains its maximum value when Area ABD. tan a is greatest.

To Investigate

Let $p=AK$; $q=BC$; $b=$ angle ACB; which quantities are constant.
$x=DL$; $a=$ angle DBC; which quantities are variables.
Now: Area ABD tan $a=(\tfrac{1}{2}pq-\tfrac{1}{2}xq)$ tan a.

$$=\tfrac{1}{2}q(p-x)\left(\frac{x}{q-x\cot b}\right)$$

$$=\tfrac{1}{2}q\left(\frac{px-x^2}{q-x\cot b}\right)$$

Differentiating the quantity $\dfrac{px-x^2}{q-x\cot b}$ and putting the value obtained equal to o for a maximum, there results the following equation:

$$(q-x\cot B)\ (p-2x)-(px-x^2)\ (-\cot b)=o.$$
$$\text{or } x^2\cot b-2qx=-pq \qquad (II)$$

Putting this equation into another form

$$pq-qx= qx-x^2\cot b$$
$$= x(q-x\cot b)$$
$$= x.BL$$

Area ABC—Area DBC=Area DBL

Area ABD=Area DBL   (III)

which equality expresses the only condition necessary in order that ABD may be the "Prism of Maximum Earth Thrust," and BD the "Plane of Rupture."

The actual amount of earth thrust is found thus:

From Eq. I; $H=$ (weight of Prism ABD) tan. a
$=$ (weight of Prism DBL) tan. a

$$=w.\tfrac{1}{2}DL.\ BL.\ \frac{DL}{BL}$$

$$H=\tfrac{1}{2}wx^2 \qquad\qquad (IV)$$

Where: $H=$ maximum horizontal earth thrust per ft. forward;

$W=$ weight of one cu. ft. earth; $x=DL$; x may either be found by solving equation (II) or may thus be expressed in terms of known quantities.

$$x=DL=LC\tan b=(BC-BL)\tan b$$

$$x=(BC-\sqrt{BC.\ BK})\tan. b. \qquad (V)$$

The above formula applies equally well whether the surface behind the wall be horizontal or not, when the back of the wall is vertical of height h, and the surface of the bank horizontal.

$$H=\tfrac{1}{2}wh^2\frac{1-\sin b}{1+\sin b} \quad (VI) \text{ which is Rankine's formula.}$$

In addition to the above mathmatical proof that H is the maximum for the wedge formed by the line BD we give the following graphical demonstration:

Let Figs. 2 to 7 represent a wall, the same as in Fig. 1, where the natural slope makes an angle of 35° with the horizontal. In Fig. 2 assume a line $B_1\ D_1$ as the line of rupture; in Fig. 3 assume a line $B_2\ D_2$ as the line of rupture; in Fig. 4 make BD the line of

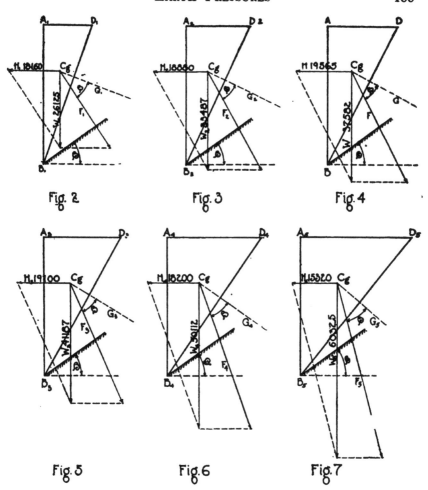

Fig. 2   Fig. 3   Fig. 4

Fig. 5   Fig. 6   Fig. 7

rupture, the same as in Fig. 1; in Fig. 5 assume a line $B_3 D_3$ as the line of rupture; and so on. In each case these figures show H as graphically determined, to be greatest in Fig. 4 which is the H we are seeking.

From the above discussion we draw the following general conclusions:

First: For a vertical backed wall and horizontal surface on fill, as in Fig. 8, the line of rupture bisects the angle between the back of the wall and the line of natural slope. The resultant pressure H against the wall is the weight of the triangle of earth so obtained multiplied by the tangent of one-half the angle between the back of the wall and the line of natural slope, which is the angle between the line of rupture and the line of natural slope.

Second: For a wall, the back of which makes an angle of less than 90 degrees with the horizontal and the surface of the fill horizontal, the same rule applies as in the first case. See Fig. 9.

Third: For a wall, the back of which makes an angle of more than 90 degrees with the horizontal and the surface of the fill horizontal, proceed exactly as in the first case and add to the force H obtained the weight of the prism of earth between the back of the wall and the vertical line passing thru the base. See Fig. 10.

Fourth: For a wall holding a fill with a sloping surface, as in Fig. 11, proceed as in Fig 8 and continue the line to the surface. Then find the center of gravity of the entire wedge between the wall and BD and divide into its two components as in all other cases.

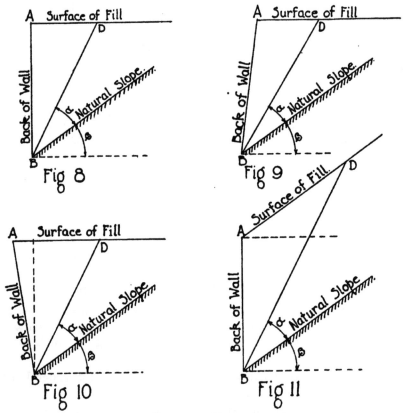

GENERAL RULE.

When back of wall is vertical and surface of fill horizontal, weight of fill taken at the usual figure of 100 pounds per cu. ft., then H is equal in pounds to the height of the wall times tan. a, times one-half height, times 100, times tan. a;

$$\text{or. } H = [(h. \tan a)\tfrac{1}{2}h. \ 100] \tan. a$$
$$\text{or } H = (\tfrac{1}{2}h^2 \tan.^2 a) 100$$

Angle a, being equal to 90 degrees less angle of repose divided by 2.

Value of Angle α For Different Angles of Repose β			
β	α	tan α	tan² α
10°	40°	0.83910	0.70409
15°	37½°	0.76733	0.58879
20°	35°	0.70021	0.49029
25°	32½°	0.63707	0.40586
30°	30°	0.57735	0.33333
35°	27½°	0.52057	0.27099
40°	25°	0.46631	0.21743
45°	22½°	0.41421	0.17157
50°	20°	0.36397	0.13348

Table No 1

Weight of Sliding Wedge Behind Vertical Wall When Surface is Horizontal. Angle of Repose 35° Weight of Material 100# per cu.ft.		
Height of Wall	Distance of lined Rupture from Top of Wall	Weight of Sliding Wedge.
5'	2.6'	650#
10'	5.2'	2600#
15'	7.8'	5850#
20'	10.4'	10400#
25'	13.0'	16250#
30'	15.6'	23400#
35'	18.2'	31850#
40'	20.8'	41600#
45'	23.4'	52650#
50'	26.0'	65000#

Table No 2

Value of H for Given Heights Where Earth Weight is 100# Angle of Repose 35° Angle of Internal Friction 35°	
Height of Wall	Value of H
5'	333#
10'	1353#
15'	3045#
20'	5414#
25'	8459#
30'	12181#
35'	16580#
40'	21655#
45'	27405#
50'	33857#

Table No 3

WORKING DATA

Weight of earthy materials in pounds per cu. ft.; sand, 105; gravel, 135; gravelly clay, 130; ordinary earth, 100; hard pan, 130.

Angles of repose degrees; coal, 54; bank sand, 54; earth, 35 to 48; quick sand, 37; clay, 42; cinders, 25; gravel, ½-in., 25; gravel, ¼-in., 19; fine sand, 10.

Ordinary Conditions: We take earth at 100 lb. per cu. ft. with angle of repose of 35 degrees and angle of internal friction of 35 degrees.

EXAMPLE

The following example will demonstrate the above principles in terms of the working data given:

What is the earth pressure behind a vertical wall which has a height of 38 feet, the surface of the fill horizontal, angle of repose 35 degrees, weight of fill 100 pounds per cu. ft?

Answer: Here a=90 degrees less 35 degrees, divided by 2 or 27½ degrees. Then tan² a=0.27099 (see table 1). Now H= (½h² tan² a) 100=(722 × 0.27099) 100=19,565 pounds.

Problem: Under the above conditions with a wall 25 feet high, what would be the resultant pressure in pounds?

Answer: See table No. 3—8,459 pounds.

CITY PLANNING IN AMERICAN CITIES

By Nelson P. Lewis, Chairman of Committee on City Planning

The following is not intended as a report of the Committee on City Planning of the American Society of Municipal Improvements, but is a preliminary statement by the chairman of the committee, giving the results of letters of inquiry addressed by him to a number of cities represented in the Society, which information, it is hoped, may furnish a starting point for a subsequent report of the committee.

The cities to which these inquiries were addressed were taken at random, but are believed to be typical. The following tabular statement will show the general location of the cities, the number of inquiries and the number of responses.

Cities.	Inquiries.	Replies.
Cities in northeastern states	20	13
Cities in central states	6	4
Cities in southern states	14	10
Cities in western states	5	....
Totals	45	27

To representatives of these cities were addressed the following eight questions:

1. Has your city established a city plan commission? If so, will you indicate how it is constituted and what powers it has, whether these powers are simply advisory, whether it has the power of veto, either absolute or suspensive, or the power of initiating city planning improvements?

2. If you have such a commission, will you please indicate the authority for its creation, giving the law or ordinance providing for it?

3. What city officer has jurisdiction over city planning matters?

4. Has your city undertaken any comprehensive planning, and, if so, what has been accomplished?

5. Have you any control over the platting of private property in a manner inconsistent with an adopted plan and can you control in any way the development of territory outside of the city boundary but contiguous to it?

6. Have you adopted or do you contemplate the adoption of a zoning system fixing for certain districts limitations as to building heights, the proportion of plots which may be built upon or the use to which property may be put?

7. Do you lay down or have you the authority to establish building lines in addition to street lines and, if so, does your city

acquire title to the spaces between the street lines and the building lines at the time of the acquisition of streets?

8. Have you a standard street width for streets of different kinds? If so, what are these widths and what are the proportions of roadway and sidewalks on such streets?

The information secured was quite full in some instances and very meager in others, and to avoid unnecessary repetition, the information elicited by the inquiries will be presented under the names of the cities furnishing the information, and not grouped under the several questions.

Albany, N. Y.

No city plan commission has been created, but all matters of city planning are handled by the Commissioner of Public Works and the City Engineer, who have the benefit of the advice and suggestions of a city planning expert retained by the city. The Commissioner of Public Works and the City Engineer have simply the general powers which usually go with their offices.

The following constructive work has been undertaken and partially carried out:

The city has acquired title to all docks and wharfage rights within the limits of the river-front improvement, and has also acquired a marginal street along the water-front. It has constructed and leased to the various steamboat companies suitable buildings and offices on the docks, has constructed a recreation pier with appropriate structures and landings and a reinforced concrete bridge of good design leading to the recreation pier. The sewer outlets have been submerged and the city has co-operated with the railroad companies in obtaining or planning for proper terminal facilities. It has created a plaza immediately back of this part of the water-front in what was formerly a congested district, has arranged for the construction of a monumental office building at the foot of Main street, has replanned and improved an old open space called "Steamboat Square" by parking the same, and has performed other work to make a complete improvement.

The city has entered into and practically completed a comprehensive plan for the repaving of streets in the business sections of the city, for the removal of sidewalk encroachments, the removal of poles and overhead wires, the attachment to buildings of span wires for trolley lines, has widened carriageways and narrowed sidewalks, or the reverse, depending upon traffic needs, has widened some streets by the acquisition of additional property, has parked open spaces where opportunity offered, and has done much other work to make the city better, cleaner and more attractive.

It has adopted the policy of planting trees on all new residential streets and on old streets wherever they are being improved; has planned, and in some cases already made, street extensions to provide more direct traffic routes; has formulated a program for the proper development of present park areas and the acquisition of additional parks and for the provision of recreational facilities.

The city has assumed control over the plotting of new streets by providing that no plan for such streets can be filed unless approved by the City Engineer. In one case where an existing rectangular street system on vacant property was not suited to the topography, the city, through the cooperation of the property owners, has entirely replanned the district with a new system of streets, which have been dedicated to public use.

The city can exercise no control over the plotting of streets outside its corporate limits, and has adopted no zoning system and has no authority to establish building lines back of the street lines. No new streets less than sixty feet in width will be accepted by the city, but no attempt has been made to standardize street widths, although on main traffic arteries an effort is made to secure widths of from seventy-five to one hundred feet.

Baltimore, Md.

This city, under authority of a law passed in 1910, created a Commission on City Plan. This Commission has, from time to time, passed upon various municipal improvements, principally the opening of extraordinary highways and the establishment of a civic center. It has not initiated any new improvements, but has acted in an advisory capacity on matters submitted to it by the Mayor.

In 1893 the Topographical Survey Commission was created by ordinance, and provision was made for a complete topographical survey of the city and the preparation of a topographical map. Upon the completion of this work, the Commission was directed to prepare a street plan for the development of the territory annexed in 1888, which plan was adopted in 1898 and is now in force. The Topographical Survey Commission is in reality the body which has jurisdiction over city planning.

While the Commission has no specific authority, it is often called upon to study and suggest means for the improvement of conditions in the older part of the city and is always asked for its opinion as to the advisability of any proposed changes. The Commission also takes the initiative in recommending such changes.

In the development of private properties, the Topographical Survey Commission has endeavored to gain the confidence of the land owners in order that developments may be carried out to the mutual advantage both of such owners and the city. A law enacted in 1906 prohibits the city from accepting streets which do not conform to the adopted street plan, but it has often been found that by slight modifications in some of the minor streets it will be possible to acquire such streets without resorting to condemnation proceedings.

The city can exercise no control over the mapping of territory outside its corporate limits. The height of buildings on Mount Vernon Place and Washington Place is limited by statute, but there is no general plan for limitations by districts.

The standard width for the average street is sixty-six feet, of which three-fifths is devoted to roadway. The principal thoroughfares range from eighty to 100 feet in width, while in the suburbs the street widths range from fifty to sixty feet with roadways of from twenty-four to forty feet, while parkways and boulevards are usually from one hundred and twenty to one hundred and fifty feet in width.

Birmingham, Ala.

The city has no planning commission. Several years ago an expert was retained to make some preliminary studies and reports, but owing to lack of finances, none of the plans has been carried out. The city has no control over the plotting of lands outside the city limits and has never attempted to exercise any control over the height or use of buildings. While there are no standard street widths, most of the important streets are from eighty to one hundred feet in width, while some minor streets are as narrow as forty feet. As a general rule, three-fifths of the street width is devoted to roadway.

Bridgeport, Conn.

A City Plan Commission, consisting of six members, has been appointed by the Mayor, two members of the Commission being appointed annually to serve for three years without compensation. The Commission has no actual powers, but was originally created to prepare a plan, to meet the expense of which five thousand dollars was appropriated by the city and an equal sum contributed by citizens. A report was prepared under the direction of this Commission in 1916, but no action has been taken by the municipal authorities to carry out this plan. The city has the right to establish building lines back of the street lines, title to the space between the two lines remaining in the owner of the abutting property. There is no standard street width except that a minimum of fifty feet has been fixed.

Buffalo, N. Y.

No city plan commission has been created unless the five City Commissioners, holding office under the commission form of government lately adopted, can be so considered. The city charter provides that the city "may acquire land by purchase, gift or eminent domain for any municipal purpose and erect buildings and other structures, including one or more buildings to be used for public assembly, and do anything necessary to beautify the city or preserve or add to the safety, intelligence, comfort and well-being of the city and its inhabitants. It may do everything necessary to carry into effect the powers granted to it and the duties imposed upon it, except as may be otherwise provided by law."

There is a general law in New York state authorizing the creation of city planning commissions and the appropriation of funds for the same, but this right has not been exercised by the city of Buffalo.

In 1913 the City Engineer's office, of its own initiative, prepared quite a comprehensive plan for the downtown district with a civic center and parkways, but this plan has not been officially adopted by the city.

Control of private developments is secured by the charter requirement that the plan of any proposed new street must be filed with the City Engineer and approved by him and the Superintendent of Public Works, and only after such approval can such street be accepted as a public street. The city has no control of the development of property outside the corporate limits, and while a zoning system limiting the height of buildings and the percentage of lands which may be covered by buildings has been recommended, no action has been taken.

Charleston, S. C.

No city plan commission has been established, and no action in that direction has been taken. There is a requirement that new streets shall not be less than sixty feet in width and that if extended from east to west, they shall be planned to run continuously from r.ver to river. There is no provision for establishing building lines back of the street lines.

Cleveland, Ohio

This city established a City Planning Commission by an ordinance adopted in 1914 and amended in the two subsequent years.

As originally provided, the Commission was to consist of seven members appointed by the Mayor, all of whom should be persons having knowledge and large experience in respect to one or more of the following subjects: Finance, commerce, industry, transportation, architecture, landscape architecture, real estate, engineering, building, painting, sculpture, social welfare, civic administration and law. This ordinance was amended the following year by increasing the number of the Commission to eleven, six of whom might be directors of departments, the other five being persons having knowledge or experience in the subjects named in the original ordinance. It was provided that no public building, harbor, bridge, street fixture or other structure should be located or constructed until the design should have been submitted to and approved by the Commission. No street could be extended, widened or opened unless the plan and location were first submitted to and approved by the Commission, but when such plans are referred to the Commission, if no report is submitted within twenty days, the Commission shall be deemed to have approved the ordinance or resolution providing for the laying out, extension or widening of such street.

All plans for new streets must conform to rules and regulations laid down by the Commission for the control of such areas before plans may be recorded, and it is made unlawful to receive or record such plans without such approval. The Commission is authorized to prepare and submit to the Council and Board of Control comprehensive plans for the future physical development and improvement of the city. Questions of zoning and the establishment of building lines back of the street lines are now under consideration by the City Planning Commission.

Dallas, Texas

This city has no city planning commission, although several civic organizations, such as the Chamber of Commerce and the University Club, have city planning committees which are quite active, although without any authority. All city planning matters are referred to the Commissioner of Public Streets and Public Property and the City Engineer.

In 1911 a report on a comprehensive plan for the city was made to the Park Board and considerable work in the way of construction of boulevards and the widening of streets has been accomplished in accordance with this plan, while some of the improvements recommended have been gradually accomplished by conforming new improvements to the plan.

The plotting of private property within the city limits or within territory to be annexed thereto must be approved by the Board of Commissioners.

Nothing has been done toward establishing a zoning system, although new buildings, including business buildings on residential streets, are required to conform to established building lines, which may be back of the street lines, although the city does not acquire title to the intervening space. No attempt has

been made to standardize street widths and there is much variation in the proportion of the streets devoted to roadways and
sidewalks.

Harrisburg, Pa.

A City Planning Commission has been created under authority
of an act of the Legislature of 1913. While this commission
has no veto power, it is said that its recommendations are given
great weight in the City Council. No city officer has any jurisdiction over the commission.

This city has undertaken some comprehensive planning and
considerable has been accomplished. All property owners, before they can have plans for real estate development recorded,
must have such plans approved by the City Planning Commission.

No action has yet been taken toward the limitation of building heights and there is no authority to establish building lines in
addition to street lines, altho the securing of such authority
is contemplated. There are no standard street widths, but in
residential districts streets sixty feet wide have roadways of
twenty-five feet.

Hartford, Conn.

This was probably the first city to establish a city plan commission, this being done by a special act of legislature in 1907.
The powers of the commission are advisory only, with no veto
power, altho it is authorized to initiate city planning movements. The act creating the commission provides that it shall
consist of the Mayor, the President of the Board of Street Commissioners, the President of the Board of Park Commissioners,
the City Engineer, two members of the Board of Aldermen, and
two citizens, neither of whom shall hold any other office. No
member of the commission is to receive any compensation for
serving on the commission. All questions concerning the location of public buildings, parkways, streets or parks must be referred to this commission for its consideration and report before
final action is taken. The Common Council may also refer to
the commission the construction of any public work not expressly
within the province of other city authorities and may delegate to
the commission all powers deemed necessary to complete such
work in all details. The commission may cause maps or plans
to be made of the city or any portion thereof. The city, acting
thru the commission or otherwise, is given power to enter
upon and hold in fee real estate within the corporate limits for
the establishment of boulevards, parks, streets, sites for buildings, etc., and it may convey any real estate thus acquired and
not necessary for such improvement, with or without reservations
concerning the future use and occupancy of the property.

Following the establishment of the commission, a report was made on a comprehensive plan for the future development of the city, the recommendations of which are gradually being carried out.

The city has no control over the location of streets in private property or over the planning of territory outside, but contiguous to, the city limits.

The city has for many years established building lines, which in some cases are back of the street lines, but does not acquire title to the spaces between the two lines.

Houston, Texas

This city has no planning commission. The platting of private property is controlled by regulations which prohibit the laying out or subdivision into lots, blocks and streets or the selling of any property so laid out unless the plan shall have been approved by the City Engineer and the dedication of the streets accepted by the City Council. A penalty of not less than $25 nor more than $200 is imposed for failure to conform with this provision, and each week's failure to obtain the approval of the City Engineer constitutes a separate offense. The rules provide, among other things, that proposed streets must conform to those in abutting subdivisions, or, if the adjoining property is not subdivided, they must conform to the prolongation of other streets, unless topographic or other considerations make some other arrangement advisable.

This city does not establish building lines back of the street lines, nor has it any standard street widths, altho the greater part of the city was laid out with streets eighty feet in width, with two principal thorofares crossing the city, each one hundred feet in width, and one boulevard one hundred and twenty-six feet wide. In recent additions there is a tendency to reduce the street widths, but a minimum width of fifty feet is required.

Memphis, Tenn.

This city has not established a planning commission. The City Engineer is the only city officer who attempts to exercise any jurisdiction over city planning matters, and his authority is very limited. The City Engineer and the commissioners have nominal control over the platting of private subdivisions, but it is said that such control is largely nominal and can not be enforced.

The City Engineer states that he does not believe that any progress can be made in his city, or in any city in his state, until a new State Constitution is adopted. When this was written the question of adopting a new Constitution was under consideration and, if authorized, he believed it probable that city planning commissions would be provided for.

Milwaukee, Wis.

The powers of the city planning commission are vested in the Board of Public Land Commissioners, altho the state has by statute, authorized every city of the first, second and third classes to create a commission on city plan, to consist of seven members. Cities are also authorized to regulate and restrict the location of trades and industries and the location of buildings designed for specific uses, but such districts shall not be established by any city unless it shall have created a city plan commission.

The Board of Land Commissioners has been engaged primarily in the opening and extension of important streets in the outskirts of the city and has given attention to the widening of certain streets at once, in order to avoid future expense in the removal of buildings. A beginning has also been made in the creation of certain industrial zones and also in the preparation of a comprehensive plan for the future development of the city. A city planning engineer has been engaged for this purpose.

Minneapolis, Minn.

No city planning commission has been created. Much attention has been devoted to the subject by improvement societies and civic organizations, but these bodies appear to be entirely unofficial.

That much study has been given to planning for the future development of the city is indicated by the illustrations and descriptive matter relating to Minneapolis in the volume on City Planning Progress, published in 1917 by the American Institute of Architects.

The city exercises no control over the planning of territory contiguous to but outside the city limits. Work is now in progress on a zoning system, while there are ordinances limiting the heights of buildings.

The city has authority to fix building lines back of the street lines, but does not acquire title to the property between the two lines.

Montreal

No city planning commission has been created, nor is there any authority for such a commission. No comprehensive planning has been undertaken and the city has no control over the platting of private property.

There is a limitation as to the height of buildings, which fixes a flat limit of 130 feet and not more than ten stories.

The city has authority to establish building lines back of the street lines.

Newark, N. J.

There is a City Plan Commission, consisting of nine members appointed by the Mayor, created under authority of a law passed in 1913. Its powers are entirely advisory, it being authorized to consider and investigate and to make such recommendations as it may deem advisable.

The Commission has prepared a comprehensive plan for the future development of the city, but it has no way of controlling the development of property outside the present city limits.

In 1917, legislation was secured providing for the location of building districts and restrictions. The city has authority to establish building lines, but as this was acquired within the past year, such authority has not yet been exercised. It is said that its primary object is to permit the progressive widening of streets already built up.

New Orleans, La.

This city has no city planning commission, except that the City Council can exercise some control over the planning of new subdivisions, by reason of the fact that plans must be submitted to the Council for approval and these plans can be accepted or modified.

There is a restriction as to building heights, the city being divided into three districts. The restrictions run all the way from a flat limit of 45 feet to a height two and a half times the width of the widest street upon which the building abuts.

There is no standard width for streets, but in residential sections they are usually 50 feet wide, with roadways of 22 feet.

A characteristic feature of the streets of this city is the establishment of "neutral grounds" in the middle of streets, in which the street railway tracks are located.

New York

This city has not created a planning commission, but a great deal of work has been done thru special committees and civic associations, and a number of comprehensive plans have been prepared, but they have never been finally adopted.

Perhaps the most notable accomplishment of New York was the adoption of a comprehensive zoning plan in 1916, under which the entire city is divided into districts, for each of which are specified the height to which buildings may be erected, the use to which property may be put—whether residential, business or industrial—and the proportion of the land which may be covered by buildings. The districts laid out in connection with these three separate restrictions are not identical and, in fact, bear little relation to each other. While it was anticipated that there would be much objection to the adoption of a zoning plan, it has met with almost universal approval. The development of the plan for each of the five boros of the city is under the control of the President of the boro, there being in each boro a topographical bureau. These plans must be submitted to and approved by the Board of Estimate and Apportionment before they become effective. This Board thus has a veto power, but has little, if any, power of initiative.

The city has lately been given the right to establish building lines back of the street lines, tho this right has thus far been exercised in only a few instances.

Control over the subdivision of private property has been secured by the enactment of a law prohibiting the acceptance, for filing, of any plan for subdivision unless such plan shall first have been approved by the Board of Estimate and Apportionment, but the city is unable to exercise any control over the plotting of land outside but contiguous to city limits.

Norfolk, Va.

The City Council has created a City Plan Commission, composed of some of its own members and representatives from several of the business organizations of the city. It has advisory powers only; it can suggest plans, but has no power to carry them out. No city official is given jurisdiction in city planning matters.

About twenty-five years ago the city undertook the preparation of a comprehensive scheme for future development, and a state law required all suburban property to conform with this plan, but before the plan was actually completed, parties who did not approve the law succeeded in having it repealed, and nothing came of the comprehensive plan. The city can exercise no actual control over the development of territory outside its limits but contiguous thereto, although the City Council recently adopted a resolution in which it was pointed out that certain adjacent territory would probably be annexed to the city in the near future and requesting the owners of such property to lay out the same in conformity, as nearly as might be, with the general plan of the city of Norfolk, and to that end they were asked to confer with the City Engineer and obtain his approval of such plans. It does not appear that this invitation has been generally accepted.

The city has no authority to establish building lines in addition to street lines, although it is said that this power is very much desired.

Philadelphia, Pa.

This city has established a permanent Committee on Comprehensive Plan, attached to the Department of Public Works. It consists of seventeen members, seven of whom are city officers. It has only advisory powers and no power of veto, but it exercises a very powerful influence in connection with the initiation of city planning improvements and its suggestions carry much weight. The actual work of the development of the comprehensive plan is in the hands of the Board of Surveyors, composed of fifteen engineers. This Board has very unusual powers and its approval is necessary before any streets can be laid out by the city plan. A great deal of constructive work has been accomplished thru this Board, as much perhaps as in any city in this country. The notable things which have been done can not be enumerated, but have been described in detail in the annual reports of the Bureau of Surveys for the last twenty years.

The city has entire control over the subdivision of private property and legislation has been asked which will extend this control over a zone three miles beyond the city boundaries.

The city is now engaged in the formulation of regulations governing the height, use and area of buildings, a Zoning Commission having been established for this purpose in 1916.

The city has no authority to establish building lines in addition to street lines, but the Zoning Commission, above referred to, is considering the establishment of compulsory setbacks for certain districts.

Pittsburg, Pa.

This city has established a City Planning Commission, the functions of which are almost entirely advisory. It is, however, able to exercise control over the subdivision of private property within the city.

The Commission has undertaken the study of and made comprehensive plans for various new thorofares and street widenings, but no attempt has yet been made to carry out any of the plans, on account of financial conditions.

The city has not adopted any zoning system, but the advisability of doing so is under consideration.

Rochester, N. Y.

The City Charter has authorized the establishment of a City Planning Commission, but it has not yet been appointed. The commission shall be composed of four citizen members and the Corporation Counsel. Its powers are to be advisory only, with a suspensive power of veto. A Superintendent of City Planning is to be appointed by the City Engineer, which superintendent shall, with the approval of the Board, have the power to initiate improvements.

While the city has not undertaken the carrying out of any comprehensive plan, several reports have been made and some improvements have been carried out in line with the recommendations contained in these reports. The new City Charter will give to the municipality some control over the development of territory outside its boundaries but contiguous thereto, and it also authorizes the establishment of a zoning system.

The city has authority to establish building lines back of the street lines, but does not acquire property outside of the street lines.

San Antonio, Texas

This city has not established any planning commission, and answers every one of the questions in the negative.

Savannah, Ga.

This city has not established a planning commission, nor is there any legislative authority for doing so. There is some control over private subdivisions, as they must be acted upon by the City Council after recommendations by the City Engineer.

No comprehensive planning has been undertaken, but the city has one power which is rare—namely, that no street plan for the development of property within two miles of the corporate limits of the city can be recorded until it shall first have been submitted to and approved by the Mayor and Aldermen of the city.

St. Louis, Mo.

St. Louis has a City Plan Commission, consisting of nine members, appointed by the Board of Public Service, each member for a term of four years, these terms overlapping. There are also five ex-officio members, or fourteen in all.

The powers of the Commission are advisory only. The Board of Public Service is the authority thru which the Commission must carry out any of its plans. The Engineer of the Commission is the principal city planning official. A definite program has been laid out and much has already been accomplished. A number of special reports issued by the Commission will be found exceedingly interesting.

The city can refuse to accept plans which are not satisfactory, but it has not an effective control over private subdivisions, and none whatever over developments outside the city limits. A study for zoning regulations is now in progress.

While the charter authorizes the city to establish building lines, this power can not be used owing to adverse court decisions.

Syracuse, N. Y.

This city has a City Planning Commission, constituted under a state law passed in 1913 and a city ordinance adopted in 1915. There are nine members, three of whom are appointed each year by the Mayor. The statute is said to be obscure and confers little but advisory power, except that under certain conditions the city may not act except after report from the Commission. The City Engineer is the authority having control over city planning matters.

The Planning Commission has undertaken the preparation of a general plan for the future development of the city, but is seriously handicapped by the absence of a complete topographic survey of the city and its immediate surroundings.

The law under which the Commission was created appears to give it some control over the planning of property outside but contiguous to the city.

Plans are under way for the establishment of a zoning system somewhat similar to that adopted by New York.

Utica, N. Y.

This city has never established a commission. It can exercise certain control over the development of private property thru an ordinance which forbids the offering for sale of any property fronting on a street unless a plan for the street shall have been approved by the City Engineer. There is no such control over property outside the city limits but contiguous thereto, nor is there any authority to establish building lines outside the street lines.

The foregoing abstract of replies received will indicate that American cities are becoming alive to the necessity of more far-sighted plans.

Of the twenty-seven replies, five are from cities with a population of less than 100,000; ten from cities of between 100,000 and 250,000, and twelve from cities of over 250,000, and it will be seen that some of the relatively smaller cities are showing the keenest interest in this subject.

GARBAGE UTILIZATION

The U. S. Food Administration, Garbage Utilization Division, has issued a booklet on Garbage Utilization with particular reference to utilization by feeding, which will be sent on request to members of the Society.

THE CITY TRAFFIC

Notes by Louis L. Tribus, Consulting Engineer, Chairman of Committee on Traffic and Transportation

The whole world is in turmoil over traffic, upon railroads, highways, canals, lakes, rivers and seas. So many experts from civil life are in the field that plain engineers who have devoted their lives to the subject are hanging their heads in shame, as the shoe manufacturer, the broker and the lawyer tell how things should be done, and worse still, proceed to do them. In the past the engineer has been unable to get the money to do things thoroly, now millions are spent and wasted without a question. Criticism is easy, but speedy accomplishment is more difficult; yet speed is essential, so there exists some excuse even for the waste.

This country (and others) has lost all appreciation of the value of money. Let a project be big enough and millions without stint are provided by very comfortable bond issues, to be paid off in the anticipated most prosperous future. Interest payments, it is true, must be considered, but if private banking can not provide, the government is expected to come to the rescue. Of course all must have some relationship to the war, and patriotism will do the rest. There must be no discordant note, however, for that would tend to lessen patriotic support, for the one thing that broadly counts today is winning the war for humanity and true Christian democracy.

Viewing the financial situation for a moment; as far as the United States is concerned, the vast sums of money expended circulate in our own land, even much of the enormous expenditures of Britain and France also, so that the end of the war would not see our coffers depleted, even tho there be enormous bond issues to be gradually met by taxation of all the people. The days call for big things, with changes occurring so rapidly that society committees can do little but register facts and go slow on prophecy.

Not long ago 40 to 50 freight cars made a full train, now 80 to 100 of double capacity are often coupled up; 600-foot steamers were "whoppers," now 1,000-foot lengths are nearly reached and fully anticipated.

Trolley service for local passengers and some freight five years ago were pushing steam roads hard; now the motor bus and motor truck are giving both a rub.

Canals were being abandoned, but with larger barges and mechanical propulsion, activity is again awakening, as the greater carrying capacity in bulk freight and increased speed make for economical transportation.

In the air, the birds are being put to blush by the aeroplanes, tho as yet their traffic is chiefly human freight and death-dealing bombs; but mail transportation is being planned for early operation.

Under the surface the submarine carrier has demonstrated its feasibility and the subway mole its economic value.

What do these facts indicate? That the self-sufficient community is no more; that the self-contained state is impossible and that the self-satisfied nation is an entity of the past. Free trade, that propaganda of the last generation, is virtually to be forced upon the world by necessities and a realized brotherhood of man. The terrible world war has, in spite of its horrors, done more already for world enlightenment and unselfish cooperation and helpfulness than all the ages that have gone before; true socialism and Christian unity. Transportation and traffic make this possible; conveyances and their motive power; highways and their coverings.

A society of *Municipal* Improvement rather denotes a limited range of activity, hence its Traffic Committee should not go farther afield than to consider such functions as pertain to cities primarily, yet in the last analysis the city depends on the farmer; the farmer on the highway and railroad; the railroad on the financier; the financier on the government, the government on all the people; a veritable "House that Jack built," no complete segregation of interests possible.

The Lincoln and Dixie Highways and the Santa Fe Trail are but phases of the broadening sentiment; and the recent much-written-of government motor-truck train, an evidence of *development*. •

In our largest cities, three levels of transportation facilities are found; the subway for passengers and we may anticipate, shortly, also for local freight; the surface for all normal street movements, and the elevated again for passengers and perhaps express service. Serious thought has been given to the subject of two-story sidewalks in some of the more congested streets (for many years a hobby of the writer) as well as underground moving platforms for pedestrians. Recently a proposal has been put forward for a pair of elevated driveways on Sixth avenue, New York, for thru motor traffic and elevated sidewalks for the relief they would furnish. Such a service would largely ease the burden on several of the avenues, permitting speed impossible on the surface and aiding a very large long-distance movement north and south.

Subways and elevated roads have been built by specialists, but the surface has been fair game for all sorts of engineers and every kind of a politician, with much disaster, though some commendable successes.

Usually the determination of character of pavements has been finally in the hands of elected officials, as well as ordinances controlling their use. A proposed ordinance that might designate the width of motor or other trucks; the weight per wheel or per inch of tread; the length of body or the total load, is referred to some inactive committee and quietly given trench-gas. Why? Because some friends, manufacturers or truckmen might be restrained in their business. Speed control is all right, for other aldermanic constituents may be endangered as to life and limb by the wild driving of the so-considered privileged classes. Regulated traffic, even half way, makes for convenience, safety and ultimate economy, but we may hope for further intelligent regulations.

Formerly, pavements themselves had large influence on traffic, much more than at present, due to change of motive power and traction conditions. Pavements have two prime features; foundations to support the loads and wearing coats over which to move them. When horses were the sole motive power, grades added their limitations, but today they can be largely ignored, i. e. within reasonable limits. Nonslippery smoothness is desired for the surface, but there must be initial resistance to abrasion, even tho the rubber tire lessens that form of wear.

Motor trucks with padded wheels pound pavements to pieces, first cracking their foundations, those with smooth tires crush by dead weight, and the motive thrust of all drive wheels tends to push the component parts of the pavement out of position, with some forward wave movement due to weight. A few years since, loads exceeding three tons were a rarity; today those of six and more are common; then, speeds of six miles per hour for the heavy loads were the normal limit; now twelve miles or more is unfortunately too nearly the rule. What has been the result? Nothing less than the breaking down of virtually every pavement that was not laid on a substantial foundation, and possessed a wearing surface equal to or better than some bituminous form.

Much has been said lately about "military" roads; there is no difference in the last analysis between such and ordinary highways, other than that the proportion of heavy loads transported, such as ordnance and munitions, may be larger than of ordinary heavy motoring; with the ordnance, greater compression per inch of tire may be the rule, consequently the stoutest foundations are required. Unlike old time ideas, this will make essential the construction of the most substantial pavements on the inter-city highways and those leading from great manufacturing plants on the outskirts, with rather less necessity perchance within the cities' central districts; for separation and segregation of heavy industries is becoming the rule and large storage of heavy raw materials in the cities is tending to decrease. Further routing of thru traffic to avoid the congested cities, with adequate sorting terminals, will also help not only rail freight, but more rapid service for distributing bulk necessities and manufacturing materials. As to country roads the earth turnpike must go; nothing short of concrete, with or without a wearing coat, will stand the service called for.

Surface street cars are being hard pushed by the jitney and the motor bus. These offer so much greater flexibility of service that popularity is with them.

Traffic regulation under police management is one of the generally adopted boons of the times; practically essential to the lives of pedestrians, who have to cross the path of the fast moving vehicles, often carelessly or brutally driven.

The increased width of motor trucks is a traffic element that has not received much attention, tho it has already changed the effective width of streets that accommodated four lines of travel so that but three can operate, and has reduced three lines to two. Were it not for the greater average speed, street capacity per hour would be greatly lessened; probably, however, speed has a little more than made up for the curtailment. This is a phase of conflict between community rights and official duty and private advantage. Should the user of very wide motor trucks, in regular service, be permitted thus to occupy, thru such widths, so large a proportion of the thorofare that others can not be easily accommodated? Some answer yes, business is paramount, and if streets are not wide enough for modern traffic, then widen them or cut others. Others answer no; custom has established a normal maximum of about seven feet for vehicles to which the public has become accustomed and to which street development has been generally adjusted; therefore if a larger use be desired, let the special interest pay the price, not necessarily by being barred from travel, but thru stiff license fees, which in the aggregate would somewhat adjust matters by providing city revenue and lessening ordinary taxation. Of course occasional use of the streets for some interfering traffic may be permitted, even to house moving, but special fees should be exacted. Roads are standardized the world over, therefore let the vehicles conform to them; extra lengths may be permitted, for that factor does not interfere with general travel.

Scarcely a direct feature of traffic, yet incidental to it, is the greater speed of loading and unloading thru the use of the vehicle's own power, consequently producing much less interference thru stationary occupancy of street space. This makes for greater aggregate carrying capacity per day, increasing the advantages of motors over horse-drawn vehicles.

A committee's comment or report would not pass without at least a reference to a traffic census. Its value was formerly vital in determining the class of a pavement; today, of greater importance for pointing to the need of additional streets or widenings or regulation of traffic, or even the zoning of industries. A study of the class of traffic might well decide the limitation of hours for certain vehicles and the prescription of certain routes for them to take. Restrictions are sometimes a general blessing and even of advantage to the interest curbed. An occasional traffic census is exceedingly desirable, together with official measuring and weighing of typical vehicles, but its application must lie in intelligent hands to bring out its best values.

New York City has made very extensive studies of traffic conditions and development of industries, resulting in a prospective large regulation of occupancy and prospective use of districts, with practical control of transportation as an incidental feature. Many other points were considered in the building-limitation and zoning law, but for this review we need only note the traffic as automatically affected thereby.

The ultimate object of all regulation is to conserve and enhance the value of property thru greater comfort, convenience and economy of municipal activities.

The Civic Center idea and the City Beautiful were but the first crude ideas in the big problems that make for municipal betterment. Street traffic, material and human, is a dominant factor and becomes the crux of City Planning. It extends afield to the neighboring community and even the more distant ones also. Boston bears some relationship to San Francisco and we may soon say to Calcutta and Valparaiso, for the uttermost ends of the earth are affected by inter-traffic facilities.

But these war days are compelling; traffic must be accommodated; pavements must stand the strain; roads must be wide enough; maintenance must be perfect; control must be prompt and efficient. No time now for experimenting; money must be spent and that wisely; the engineer must meet the demand, for traffic must have the right of way without let or hindrance; food, fuel, manufactures, necessities of life first. Then when the war days are over the great readjustments will make our cities and the world at large vastly better to live in. Then the men and women of accomplishment may well be glad and the Honor Roll flags of peace will take their turn in flying and those of war take their place in proud history.

REPORT OF THE COMMITTEE ON PAVING

W. A. Howell, Newark, N. J., Chairman

The year 1917 was a most unsatisfactory year for the prosecution of paving work in most cities in this country and Canada, and 1918 does not promise to be any better, in fact the indications are that conditions will be worse. With the prevailing shortage of labor, high prices of materials, government embargo on cars and paving materials, paving work not absolutely necessary is not being considered at all in most cities of the country. The paving history of 1917 was the record of paving construction delayed and hampered by government embargo on cars needed for the shipment of materials at granite quarries, concrete stone quarries, gravel banks, paving brick plants, and at other points where paving materials were manufactured. It was easier to get an empty car placed on a siding for almost any kind of household or factory supplies, than it was to have a car placed on a siding at a granite quarry, to be loaded with a shipment of paving blocks or curb. The taking over of the railroads by the United States Government has made the paving situation still more difficult.

The Government bending all of its mighty energies towards the successful flotation of Liberty Bonds, does not look with favor upon the issuance at this time by either, State, County, or City, of paving bonds. An official in charge of financial matters whether national, state, or municipal, generally fails to comprehend the necessity of keeping the main highways, especially the roads that might be considered as military roads, in first class condition, as to maintenance. In the opinion of the writer, money expended for the construction or reconstruction of military roads, is just as well spent, as money used for the construction of cantonments. A first class military road might decide the fate of a nation, by helping indirectly to win a great battle.

The recent passage by a number of the more important states of remedial legislation, will put an end for all time to the use of steel-tired motor vehicles on the public highways. In the state of the writer (New Jersey) and more particularly in the City of Newark, the damage caused by the use of these steel-tired motor trailers to the city during the last five years, has amounted to many thousands of dollars.

The Chairman of this Committee has communicated with a number of City Engineers and other officials in charge of paving work, and perhaps it will be interesting for the Society at large to note what is engaging the attention of these men in various parts of the country.

St. Louis, Mo. (Mr. Horner)—writes: "The present cost of paving has resulted in a decision by the Board of Public Service to proceed with construction only under one of two conditions,

First, in the case of main traffic ways where the paving is considered essential to the city at large;

Second, in the case of residence streets now ready for letting, where a majority of the property owners ask that the job be let at once."

Minneapolis, Minn. (Mr. Cappelen)—"We have not changed our methods worth mentioning, but we have been greatly handicapped in receiving material due to the embargo of cars by the United States Government, so it is very doubtful if we can finish the program as outlined."

Buffalo, N. Y. (Mr. Norton thru Mr. Babcock) advises us that "the high cost of labor and material is beginning to show in the postponement of some new paving. As it requires about four months to go thru our charter proceedings for paving, most of the work now being performed was bid for last year, or early this year, and the amount performed so far has not been greatly affected by cost, but later on the cost may very likely influence." (This was written during the early fall of 1917.)

Cincinnati, Ohio (F. S. Krug)—"Our principal work this year (1917) consisted of paving, with recut granite blocks, old worn-out granite roadways, approximately 20,000 yards of this type of pavement having been laid during the current year (1917). The work in short consists in recutting and redressing the existing blocks, so as to form one or more blocks of smaller size. The newly cut blocks vary in size as follows: in length, 5 to 8 inches; in width, $3\frac{1}{2}$ to 5 inches; in depth, $4\frac{3}{4}$ to $5\frac{1}{4}$ inches. Concrete mixed in proportion of 1:3:6 and averaging about 2 inches in depth is applied to the existing concrete bed. On the newly formed paving base is then spread a layer of clean sand $1\frac{1}{4}$ inches in depth, on which the recut blocks are laid. After the blocks are laid the joints are filled about half full with clean dry pebbles, only in sufficient quantity to prevent the blocks rocking when being rolled. Following the rolling, a pitch filler at a temperature of 300° F. is applied after the pebbles have been scratched out of the joints to a depth of $2\frac{1}{2}$ inches below the top of the blocks. Additional pebbles are then swept into the remaining joint, which is again poured with paving pitch. The entire surface of the paving is then given a flush coat of paving pitch by means of a squeegee in a manner to completely fill all of the joints, leaving a light bituminous coat on the top of the blocks. A $\frac{1}{4}$-inch covering of clean dry pebbles is then evenly applied to the flush coated surface and rolled into same with a steam roller. The total yardage of all kinds of pavements laid during 1917 is 83,400 against 143,379 yards laid during 1916.

Philadelphia, Pa. (W. P. Taylor)—It has been the policy of the city so far to continue its street improvements without regard to war conditions, so that approximately the same expenditures are being made this year (1917) as in preceding years. The high cost of labor and materials has almost doubled the cost of most classes of work and this, of course, has in a measure cut down the yardage of pavements laid, altho, as stated, the money expended is practically the same. The city program about four years ago included the resurfacing of all the old macadam roads with bituminous materials, and the suburban roads were put in such good condition in 1914 that the problem since that time has been one merely of maintenance. The bituminous concrete roads are repaired by patching, while the macadam roads in the suburban districts are given an annual surface treatment with bituminous materials. In general the methods of work in this city follow those of preceding years, changes being principally those of detail. One change that has been instituted in the granite block and brick pavements is the substitution of a dry sand-cement cushion for the sand cushion that was used heretofore.

Toronto, Canada (R. C. Harris, Commissioner of Works)— "The war conditions, under which we have been living for the past three years, have exercised a very powerful influence upon work of this nature (paving), which has been cut to a very small amount during 1917. Up to the present time (October 5, 1917) we have laid approximately 15,100 sq. yds. of asphalt, 9,134 sq. yds. of reinforced concrete and 567 yds. of plain concrete. At the present time two or three jobs are under way, the most notable one being a granite block pavement, which is being laid upon a mortar cushion, placed upon the green concrete, the grout being applied as soon as the surface of the pavement has been trued off properly. The result of this is, of course, practically a monolithic structure. Great difficulty has been experienced this year (1917) with respect to labor and material, men being scarce and those available not being up to the standard of former years. The difficulty with material is not so much in the production as in transportation.

Rochester, N. Y. (Arthur Poole, City Engineer)—"The following is a brief summary of the work finished, and expected to be completed, during the current year (1917): 174,440 sq. yds. asphalt pavement; 10,850 sq. yds. asphalt block pavement; 12,450 sq. yds. asphalt resurfacing; 3,360 sq. yds. brick pavement; 1,530 sq. yds. Medina block stone pavement. Our asphalt resurfacing has been on old Medina stone entirely. We have not done any resurfacing on old macadam pavements during 1917, but have some under consideration. The high cost of materials and the shortage of labor have affected the work, also labor troubles in the early part of the summer of 1917 kept us back considerably. We have not done nearly as much paving work this year (1917) as in former years."

City of Chicago (Julius G. Gabelman, Chief Street Engineer)— We have changed the construction of brick pavements by eliminating the sand cushion and substituting therefor a mortar cushion composed of one part portland cement to four parts sand. Pitch filler for brick pavements has also been eliminated, and asphalt filler or cement grout filler put in place thereof. We appear to be getting our best results from an asphalt filler. The high cost of labor and materials has not affected the amount of paving in this city. We are also figuring on laying a hard sandstone block pavement on streets where the grade is over 3 per cent. This would include bridge and subway approaches and streets on hillsides.

Boro of Brooklyn (H. H. Schmidt, Chief Engineer)— During the first three quarters of the year 1917 the following contracts were completed.

This year (1917) concrete base laid............................125,000 square yards
Granite block paving laid with cement grout joints........ 50,000 " "
Wood block pavement laid .... 2,000 " "
Sheet asphalt and binder laid.................................... 80,000 " "
Bituminous macadam laid (asphalt)............................ 25,000 " "
Topeka pavement laid .... 2,000 " "
Artificial stone sidewalks laid................................... 50,000 " "

Springfield, Mass. (F. H. Clark, Superintendent of Streets and Engineering)—Owing to the high cost of labor and transportation difficulties, the work of the paving division of this city has been largely along lines of resurfacing old macadam roads with bituminous top, using both tar penetration and mixed asphalt. Only about 25,000 sq. yds. of permanent pavement have been constructed. Several miles of new bituminous macadam have been built. It would be safe to say that at the end of the season (1917) more yards of streets will have been surfaced than during any other year in the history of the city. Nothing has been done with wood block, brick or granite except to replace about 8,000 yards of wood and brick with new wood.

Pittsburg, Pa. (N. S. Sprague, Chief Engineer)—During the past season an unusually large amount of assessment work (new work) has been accomplished. The effect of the war in this city has brought with it much prosperity, owing to the industries which are peculiar to this city. There apparently has been no curtailment of original street improvements on account of the abnormal price of labor and materials. On the contrary, an unusually large number of petitions for street improvements from abutting property owners on unimproved streets have been received. There has been much difficulty, however, on the part of the contractors in securing sufficient labor to execute the work promptly, which has resulted in forcing them, wherever conditions would permit, to the use of machinery. Nearly all contracts were delayed beyond the stipulated time of completion (during 1917), owing to the congestion on the railroads, resulting in serious delay in the delivery of materials, and in some cases it has been impossible to get materials called for by the specifications and the department has been confronted with the problem of accepting material different from the specifications, or have the improvement greatly delayed. If these conditions continue, it is very likely that the specifications for street paving will be modified and changed so as to meet the conditions as they now exist.

Boston, Mass. (Joshua Atwood, Engineer in Charge, Highway Division), October 4, 1917—"In common with all other municipalities we have been affected by the high cost of labor and materials, and still more so by freight embargoes and lack of labor. There are more jobs than men, and the result is that labor is independent. We are continuing to lay sheet asphalt, bitulithic and also granite block with cement grout joints, on existing macadam foundation, where the traffic is not too heavy, and the results are quite satisfactory. We are now laying a large area of granite block paving with the so-called "split block." The old blocks that were in the roadway are taken up, culled and then split in the middle and trimmed, thereby getting two good blocks which, when laid and grouted, make an excellent pavement with quite a saving in cost. We are paving many of our principal business streets with special cut granite blocks on concrete base with grout joints and also using wood blocks and asphalt. The following is the approximate amount of paving done this year (1917):

	Yardage
Resurfacing present asphalt pavements	156,397
Paving and repairing asphalt on concrete foundation	170,775
Paving asphalt on present concrete foundation	17,155
Paving 2-in. asphalt block on concrete foundation	5,293
Paving and repairing grade granite	96,265
Paving with special 4-in. granite blocks	3,400
Paving granite on sand	1,110
	450,395

Cleveland, Ohio (Robert Hoffmann, Chief Engineer)—We have built a number of pavements this year (1917) of monolithic form of brick construction. As far as observed, this type of pavement promises to be satisfactory. The cost of labor and materials in connection with paving work have been higher by 15 to 50 per cent. than under normal conditions in the last year (1916). These higher prices did not affect directly the amount of paving done in this city during the year 1917, as a rather extensive program was provided for, and financed in such a manner that the work could proceed even though prices were somewhat higher. Labor conditions and delivery of material have had some effect upon the amount of work completed, but on the whole, the progress of the paving work proved quite satisfactory during the year 1917.

Detroit, Mich. (George H. Fenkell, Commissioner), October 29, 1917—"At the end of the present season (1917) we will have newly paved 40 miles of streets, and resurfaced and repaved about 15 miles. Of this new work 80 per cent. is asphaltic concrete, the balance being distributed for equal miles of sheet asphalt, creosoted block and brick. We have also laid about 20 miles of one-course pavement in alleys this year (1917). The high cost of labor has not resulted in a lessened demand for paving, but we have had the progress of our work considerably retarded from our inability to secure materials. Concerning the attention paid to resurfacing of old Telford or macadam roads with bitulithic, warrenite, asphaltic concrete, or any other bituminous covering, will state that on our Grand Boulevard, which is practically in the center of the city (14 miles long of single and double driveways, 30 to 60 feet wide), the macadam base has been resurfaced with sheet asphalt, which is in perfect condition. The work of resurfacing the boulevard was begun in 1914 and completed in 1917. We have laid some brick pavements upon a bituminous cushion with a sand filler. All other brick, granite and stone pavements are laid on a cushion composed of four parts sand and one part cement. Grout is used as a filler. During the past two years we have laid about four miles of creosoted block upon a bituminous cushion, using a fine dry sand as a filler. This has given very good service. About 12,000 sq. yds. of creosoted block treated with distillate oil will be laid this year (1917).

LANDSCAPE GARDENING

The American Society of Landscape Architects is co-operating with Houghton Mifflin Company in the editing and publishing of a series of authoritative books on landscape gardening, the first of which was a reproduction of Repton's "The Art of Landscape Gardening," the record of English advancement in that art a hundred years ago. The second volume is a reprinting of Prince von Pueckler-Muskau's "Hints on Landscape Gardening" which bears the same relation to the history of the art in Germany, tho the prince seems to have been more catholic and to have accepted the good wherever he found it. His book was fully illustrated and most of the illustrations have been reproduced. After some chapters devoted to the general principles to be followed and of his experience out of which he had developed them, the author gives a most interesting and valuable description of their application to his own large estate at Muskau, in the form of foot and carriage journeys about the park, with plans of the area before and after the developments had been made and views of the various detailed results obtained. Even allowing for the modern collections of experience, the book is quite as valuable for the student as it was when first published, nearly a century ago.

The Society is made up of the leaders in the profession and is doing its present and future members as well as the public an inestimable service in promoting the publication of this series.

REPORT OF THE COMMITTEE ON FIRE PROTECTION

Alcide Chaussé, Montreal, Que., Chairman

As in former years, I have noted for the object of this annual report the activities relative to Fire Protection and Prevention and the "resumé" of these notes is as follows:

The National Fire Protection Association, assembled in Washington for its twenty-first annual meeting, in May, 1917, called attention to the new and unusual hazards to life and property created thruout America by the world war, which demand the utmost vigilance and initiative not only from those in authority, but from the private citizen as well. Every individual should consider himself a fire warden of the nation at this critical time and should equip himself to serve his country by safeguarding to the extent of his intelligence and ability every form of natural and created resource. The elimination of waste, at all times the duty of good citizenship, is at this moment our profoundest public and private responsibility.

In its warfare against the needless sacrifice of human lives and property by fire the Association advocated the following measures:

1. The adoption by municipalities of the Standard Building Code of the National Board of Fire Underwriters to the end that fire-resistive building construction may be encouraged, the use of inflammable roof coverings prohibited, adequate exit facilities from buildings assured, and interiors so designed and fire-stopped as to make easy the extinguishment of fires therein.

2. The adoption by all states of minimum building requirements for the protection of state and county hospitals, asylums and similar institutions outside city limits and of small communities in which the establishment and enforcement of a building code is impracticable.

3. The enactment by each state of the fire marshal law advocated by the Fire Marshals' Association of North America to the end that official investigation may be made of the causes of all fires, preventable fires may be eliminated by public education, and the crime of arson stamped out.

4. The adoption of the Association's suggested ordinance providing for the systematic inspection of all buildings by city fire marshals or local firemen, to insure the vigorous enforcement of rules for cleanliness, good housekeeping, and the maintenance of safe and unobstructed exits, fire-fighting apparatus and other protective devices.

5. The enactment of ordinances similar to that of Cleveland, Ohio, fixing the cost of extinguishing preventable fires upon

citizens disregarding fire prevention orders, and a more general legal recognition of the common law principle of personal liability for damage resulting from fires due to carelessness or neglect.

6. The wider general use of the automatic sprinkler as a fire-extinguishing agent and life saver and the more general adoption of the fire division-wall as an important live-saving exit-facility.

7. A careful study of the technical surveys of cities made by the engineers of the Committee on Fire Prevention of the National Board of Fire Underwriters covering the items of water supplies, their adequacy and reliability, fire department efficiency, fire alarm systems and conflagration hazards, and of the possibility of cooperation among neighboring cities thru mutual aid and the standardization of hose couplings.

8. The adoption of the Association's suggested laws and ordinances for state and municipal regulation of the transportation, storage and use of inflammable liquids and explosives.

9. The universal adoption and use of the safety match and legislation prohibiting smoking in all parts of factories, industrial and mercantile buildings except in such fireproof rooms as may be especially approved for the purpose by fire departments.

10. The education of children and the public generally in careful habits regarding the use of fire.

11. The coordination of all these activities, thru a central administrative officer or body of the state or city having primary jurisdiction, for the purpose of promoting uniformity of action and efficient cooperation.

In the furtherance of these objects the Association appealed for the cooperation of all citizens. It asked them to help in the dissemination of its valuable literature and in the use of the standards of fire protection so carefully worked out by its committees to the end that the lives and substance of our people shall not continue to be dissipated by a reckless and easily preventable waste.

Between fifteen and twenty building officials of American municipalities, charged with responsibility for the safety of at least 15,000,000 people thru structural safeguards, and half a dozen or so of material men, representatives of associations formed of material and equipment companies, underwriters' engineers, etc., participated in the third annual session of the Building Officials' Conference, held at Washington, Friday, May 11, following the adjournment of the annual meeting of the National Fire Protection Association. The conference, recognizing the fact that it is still, in a measure, in the formative stage, continued in office its chairman, secretary and executive committee, who have labored unceasingly to put it on a firm foundation. Rudolph P. Miller, president of the Board of Standards and Appeals, New York City, was reelected chairman, and Sydney J. Williams, chief inspector of the Wisconsin Industrial Commission, Madison, secretary-treasurer.

There was very little in this session of the Conference, compared with the first and second sessions, touching on fire hazards and fire prevention. Chairman Miller, outlining the scope and work of the New Board of Standards and Appeals, showed the application of its activities to the fire hazard, and Mr. Moore, of the Boro of Queens, describing the zoning system, pointed out and emphasized its effect on fire-hazardous occupancies.

Mr. Davidson gave an illustrated talk on accident protection, particularly with reference to scaffolding; Mr. Moore and Mr. Davidson discussed sidewalk bridges for building construction, and Secretary Williams outlined the scope and form of building department organization, as gathered from a survey of upward of 100 American cities. This included many interesting tabulations, ranging from the number of permits per inspector to the percentage of fees received to the cost of the department. It will be published in the proceedings of the Conference.

A motion of Captain Mason for the creation of a number of standing committees to consider structural standards and practices, permissible use of specific materials and modifications of building requirements to be allowed for the installation of fire-control equipment, particularly automatic sprinklers, was referred to the executive committee with power.

The Kansas Bureau has adopted the following recommendations for improvements:

Stairways, elevators, hatchways, chutes and dumb waiters, when not in standard fireproof or semi-fireproof constructed shafts, should be cut off at each floor-opening by traps as herein specified, viz.:

(a) Traps to be made of $\frac{7}{8}$-in. kiln-dried matched pine or other non-resinous wood free from unsound knots and sap; to be securely nailed to battens with No. 13 gage flat-head, full-barbed wire nails, 2 inches long, driven in flush and clinched so as to leave a smooth surface on both sides. Battens to be $\frac{7}{8}$-in. thick, not less than 6 inches wide, and not more than 3 feet on centers. Traps to be covered on under side with tin sheets 14 x 20 in., not less than 107 lbs. to the box of 112 sheets, all joints single locked; covering to lap top side of trap not less than 4 inches and nail heads not to be exposed except where covering laps on top side. Traps to lap openings at least 3 inches. Hinges to be substantial wrought iron of "T" or strap type, with non-corrosive pins, securely bolted to trap and if possible bolted to floor. Never use nails for hinge fastenings.

(b) Traps to be made similar to (a) in all respects except

that trap is to be made of two thicknesses of ⅞-in. with boards laid at right angles, or single thickness of 1½-in. matched pine or other non-resinous wood.

(c) Traps to be made of two thicknesses of ⅞-in., otherwise same as (b) except that trap is to be without battens and entirely covered with tin, as per requirements for standard fire doors. All traps to close automatically by fusible link or electric attachments; details covering location of links and thermostats may be obtained upon application and to be subject to the approval of this office. All traps on one shaft to be operated by the fusing of any one link or thermostat; all wires, chains and pulleys to be protected if necessary against mechanical injury by substantial guard strips, or from being rendered inoperative by piling stock or other material against same. All weights to be boxed in if outside of shaft and so arranged that one side of boxing can easily be removed for accessibility. Traps to be provided with automatic flaps for covering all cable, guide and counterweight openings when same are closed; a spring must be put on the back of all flaps for closing same when the traps are released.

Note—In buildings of ordinary joisted construction, stairway enclosure of plaster or matched flooring of same thickness as floor, with door of same construction and self-closing with metal rope and weight or suitable spring attachment, may be accepted for stairway cutoffs. Door to be provided with a suitable snap-catch to hold same rigidly closed. Windows or transoms, if any, to be stationary and of approved wired glass.

A suggestion is made by the Ohio State Fire Marshal that during the observance of the spring clean-up and paint-up campaign, citizens should also be urged to examine and correct any defects in chimneys, furnaces and other heating apparatus. If citizens wait until fall, it is likely that cold weather will arrive before the inspection is made. The Ohio official is lending the full support of his department to clean-up campaigns in Cincinnati, Cleveland and other Ohio cities.

The Kansas State Fire Prevention Association has adopted the plan of pledging each member to make at the least a certain number of inspections during the year. The average number pledged by members is three. As there are sixty-six members in this association, there should be no difficulty in obtaining the number of men necessary to make the inspection in Kansas, especially since the assistance of inspectors from the fire-marshal office is always available. State Fire Marshal Hussey sends deputies to assist in actual making of inspections and also in conducting public meetings. As an example of the good will which is aroused by visits of the association, Frank Britton, the secretary, reported that in one day he had received five letters from a town where an inspection was recently held, announcing that corrections requested had been made and asking for additional suggestions for improvement.

The approved method of removing the danger of the old shingle roof, especially on structures which are not of sufficient value to warrant an entirely new roof covering, is the placing of tin over the shingles. Fire marshals are ordering old shingle roofs, especially where they are along the railroad or in other exposed positions, covered with incombustible material. The form in the Indiana state fire marshal's office ordering this change reads, "See that roof covering is of metal or of other incombustible material." In most instances the property-owner covers the roof with metal. In many cases where economic consideration would prevent the placing of a new roof with fire-resistive qualities, the tin-covered roof may be successfully recommended.

A fire-prevention code, containing requirements governing building construction and hazards of occupancies, was passed by the 1916 session of the Louisiana legislature. This code is to be enforced by the state fire marshal. As the statute setting forth the code stated that the cities and towns might define the portion of the city to which the code would apply, there was some doubt regarding the general application of the law. The attorney-general of the state has now ruled that the act is to apply thruout the state and in all locations until restrictions as to limits are made by the various towns and cities. Fire-marshal Campbell and his men have recently inspected the cities of Baton Rouge and Monroe and have made substantial progress in obtaining enforcement of the fire-prevention code in those cities.

Regular inspections of special-hazard occupancies are made wherever possible by the Chicago Fire Prevention Bureau. Thus the inspectors expect to reach every garage in the city twice each year, dry-cleaning establishments twice each year, and to examine all sprinkler equipments three times each year. Motion-picture theaters and opera houses are inspected every night. There are 598 of these theaters in Chicago. One-half of them are inspected each night by the regular force of the bureau and one-half by firemen from the engine houses. A report on every theater is turned into the chief inspector every morning and orders for correction of ordinance violations are given immediate attention. This system is so arranged that it is practically impossible for failure to examine any theater on a given night to escape the check-up of the chief inspector. These daily inspection reports of theaters are not filed except in cases where orders must be issued. Every theater must have a licensed theater guard and those with stages must have a stage fireman. It does not seem possible that a fire panic in a Chicago theater could be charged to the negligence of the Fire Prevention Bureau.

This same systematic method extends to the enforcement of all orders issued by the bureau. Orders expiring on a given date are placed in a file, which is taken out on the day after expiration of the time limit and an order-copy is given to the proper inspector for reinspection. When a citizen receives an order from the Chicago Fire Prevention Bureau he knows that on the day after the order expires an inspector will be there to find out whether or not the order has been obeyed. He knows further that if it has not been obeyed immediate steps will be taken to see that the order is enforced.

Minnesota is the second state in the Union to enact into law stringent rules and regulations governing the construction and · use of motion-picture theaters, placing enforcement powers in the hands of the state fire marshal. Michigan was the pioneer in this movement. Other states, among which are Connecticut and Massachusetts, have mild regulations governing motion-picture theaters, enforcement being in the hands of the state police.

The Minnesota statute deals completely with the hazards of the motion-picture theaters and grants ample powers for enforcement to the state fire marshal. These theaters can operate only after obtaining a license each year from the state fire marshal. Before granting this license, the state fire marshal must approve the construction and fittings of the theater. An annual license fee of $5 will be paid by each motion-picture theater owner to the fire-marshal department to be used by it in promoting any of its work. A severe penalty is provided for operation without a license and the fire marshal in enforcing orders may also cut off the electric current supplying the theater.

The statute includes complete specification for booth construction and electrical equipments, provides that the state fire marshal may examine operators as to their fitness and that no operator shall be less than 18 years of age, prohibits the exposure of inflammable films except while being transferred from the two magazines, and sets forth complete regulations governing exits, aisles and seats. Schools and churches are exempted from the requirements of the act where motion-pictures are to be used for a charitable, benevolent or educational purpose and are not used regularly, but only on special occasions, and in these cases only when a representative of the local fire department is present.

The powers of the Minnesota state fire marshal are further extended by a new act granting the authority to condemn buildings in dilapidated condition where so situated as to endanger life or limbs. The fire-marshal law proposed by the Fire Marshals' Association of North America provides that buildings may be condemned only when "so situated as to endanger other property." No matter how dangerous a building may be for its occupants, the state fire marshals, where this law is on the statute books as in Indiana, can not condemn the building unless it is so situated as to endanger other property in the event of fire. The amended Minnesota law also adds to the authority of the fire marshal for obtaining correction of many other defects.

The following resolutions have been adopted by the Fire Marshal in Chief of the Fire Department of Texas:

"Experience has taught us that carelessness and ignorance are responsible for the origin of the majority of fires in cities, and that a large per cent. of such fires can be prevented. We hereby resolve to enforce to the letter all fire prevention laws, ordinances and regulations, and remedy conditions in our city by making frequent inspections of the business and manufacturing districts, including the residence district, whenever and wherever possible, and insist upon the removal of all rubbish and inflammable material from the premises. We resolve further to take every precaution for the prevention of fires, protection of property and the safety of the public, realizing that the responsibility rests upon our shoulders as fire marshal and chief of the fire department.

"The average yearly fire loss in this country, to say nothing of the wages lost by the people thrown out of employment, the rents loss and the profits gone, is around $225,000,000. The fire loss in the United States and Canada every year is greater than of all the other countries of the world combined. This surely is an enormous tax on the people of this country, and I have come to the conclusion that, to a considerable extent, I am responsible for this loss. Therefore, I hereby resolve that, in the future, I will not issue a fire insurance policy to a person unknown to me without first making an investigation as to his character and reputation. I will personally ascertain that the property upon which I issue a policy is not over-insured, as I realize that many fires are set because of over-insurance in an attempt to sell out at a price above the value of the property, and, in this manner, defraud the insurance company, when, as a matter of fact, in the end the honest policyholder and the general public pays the loss and not the insurance company. Further, I resolve to cancel or reduce the amount of any policy when informed by the fire marshal, the chief of the fire department, or any other person in authority that the amount of the policy is greater than the value of the property.

"For many years in Texas we have failed to convict in arson cases on circumstantial evidence, even when we were thoroly convinced beyond a reasonable doubt that the defendants were guilty. We have allowed our verdicts to be influenced by sympathy for the prisoners or their families, and we have taken the position, after listening to the arguments of the attorneys for the defendants, that the insurance companies—usually foreign corporations—have accepted the premiums and should pay the loss, not realizing that insurance companies are merely self-constituted agents of the people for the purpose of collecting the fire tax and distributing it among those who lose, and that the tax collected is based upon the amount of property involved; that we ourselves and other honest policyholders pay out of our own pockets every dollar paid to people who burn their property for the insurance. We, therefore, resolve that, in the future, we will do our duty as the law requires, that the firebug may be given his just deserts."

That builders of defective and dangerous chimneys should be liable to criminal prosecution if fire occurs as a result of their negligence is the contention of many fire prevention workers. The principle upon which this contention is based was endorsed by Benjamin Franklin about 1735.

Dangerous burning of chimney-soot resulted in the payment of a fine by property owners of Philadelphia in early colonial days. Chimney sweeps were employed to clean out soot and take care of flues. As owners could not conveniently inspect to see that a thoro cleaning was made by the sweep, the latter was no doubt often tempted to shirk his task. In discussing this matter, Franklin said, "I have known foul chimneys to burn most furiously a few days after they are clean, making large fires. Everybody among us is allowed to sweep chimneys that please to undertake the business; and, if a chimney fires thru the fault of the sweeper, the owner pays the fine and the sweeper goes free. The thing is not right. Those who undertake the sweeping of chimneys and employ servants for the purpose ought to be licensed by the mayor; and if any chimney fires and flames out fifteen days after sweeping the fine should be paid by the sweeper, for it is his fault."

Fires occurring in chimneys are due primarily to accumulations of soot. Accumulations of soot are due to imperfect combustion of fuel and to neglect to clean the chimney at proper intervals. Wood and bituminous or soft coal under the best conditions produce more soot than anthracite or hard coal.

When a change is made from the use of anthracite to the use of soft coal conditions will usually be bad, unless the necessary alterations have been made under expert supervision by a competent workman. Bituminous coal requires more draft to insure good combustion than does anthracite, and a furnace designed for the burning of anthracite is pretty certain to cause a considerable unnecessary wastage in the form of soot when bituminous coal is burned in it.

Quick, hot fires, such as are often built to take off the chill of a cool evening in the fall, are particularly likely to cause soot in the chimney to take fire. The burning of accumulations of waste, paper, etc., in stoves, furnaces or fireplaces in the spring or fall is also a dangerous practice in this respect.

1. It is essential that furnaces should be properly designed and installed with reference to the kind of fuel to be used.

2. Much can be done by intelligent firing. Comparatively small charges of coal put on at frequent intervals and spread upon a portion of the fire bed only will produce better combustion than is possible with large charges at infrequent intervals. The object of not covering the whole fire bed with coal is to permit the gases from the freshly fired coal to be quickly ignited. As soon as fresh coal has been "coked" it should be spread out over the entire bed, when it will burn as a bright fire without further smoke. A continually and freely smoking chimney is a sure sign of imperfect combustion.

3. Stoves and furnaces should be periodically examined to see that they are in proper repair.

4. Stoves or furnaces should never be used for the burning of garbage.

The best method, of course, is a thoro cleaning by an expert chimney sweep. Where the services of such a man are not available, the common method of lowering a brick wrapped in carpet by a rope from the top of the chimney and swinging it around inside will be found effective. A method sometimes followed, but involving more risk to the amateur, is to empty a pail of small coals down the chimney. Cleaning with a piece of fir tree at the end of a rope, with a weight to carry it down, is also satisfactory.

The burning of zinc scraps over a hot fire is reported to have been attended with good results in some cases where the chimney was thoroly filled with the fumes, which deposited their heavy white zinc oxide powder on the soot, thus causing it to fall. To determine the amount of zinc required it is, however, necessary to take into account the size and construction of the chimney. Where the chimney is wide at the base, with the sides sloping gradually inward, this method will probably give better results than under other conditions.

Attempts to remove soot by chemical means are not recommended, as fumes sufficiently powerful to act on the soot might injure the mortar, and thus the remedy might prove worse than the disease.

Stovepipes and flues should be carefully examined from time to time to see that they are in good repair and should be thoroly cleaned out at least once a year. Special attention is necessary to the conditions of those portions of a stovepipe which may be within ventilated thimbles used for the protection of partitions, etc., thru which the pipe happens to pass. Deterioration of the pipe and thimble due to rust, which would be detected in exposed pipe, often escapes notice within the thimble and is only discovered when a soot fire occurs and causes sparks to drop into the partition.

Fires in chimneys can sometimes be extinguished with hand chemical extinguishers from below. Bicarbonate of soda thrown upon the fire will unquestionably retard the blaze, though it is extremely unsafe to rely upon this method for total extinguishment. In every case it is safer to call the fire department at once, while making every effort to extinguish the fire before the firemen arrive. Such fires sometimes become very serious, and no chances should be taken. A large proportion even of the less serious fires can only be extinguished with chemical extinguishers turned in from the top after all drafts have been closed.

In British Columbia the British practice has been adopted of treating chimney fires as legal offenses punishable on conviction by fine. This method of dealing with the problem would seem to be best suited to provinces or countries in which chimney-sweeping is a recognized trade (as England and other European countries) with qualified workmen in every town.

The situation in most American cities would probably be most satisfactorily met by the enactment of an ordinance along the lines of the by-law at present in force in the city of Montreal, Canada. This ordinance is as follows:

"Each chimney used in the city in connection with a coal or wood burning stove, grate or range, or heating apparatus, shall be swept twice, each year, if the Superintendent of Buildings deems it necessary, at such times as may be fixed by the said Superintendent of Buildings, by sweeps appointed by the Board of Commissioners. The said sweeps shall be under the control of the Superintendent of Buildings; they shall obey his commands and use the appliances and implements approved by him.

"(a) The Superintendent of Buildings shall divide the city into as many sweeping districts as he may deem necessary and shall have such division of said districts approved by the Board of Commissioners. There shall be for each district one sweep, and the said sweep and his employes shall be licensed.

"(b) Before sweeping the chimney of any building whatsoever, the said sweeps shall previously give to the occupant of such building at least two days' notice in writing. Such notice, which shall also contain the name of the sweep, his address, the number of his telephone and the number of the district, shall be as per following form:

No.........................

Office of the Building Inspector,
City Hall.

Montreal,........................19....

You are hereby notified that the sweeps will, after two (2) days from this date, proceed to sweep the chimneys of the following buildings ....

in accordance with the provisions of By-law No. 260 of the City of Montreal.

You are therefore requested to give them the necessary assistance.

Superintendent of Buildings.

(Name of the licensed sweep.)

Sweep District No...

No. ....Street

Telephone.............................

"(c.) The Board of Commissioners may also have the chimney sweeping done by civic employes in one or more districts or may have such work performed by contract. The persons entrusted with such work in virtue of this paragraph shall comply with the provisions of this by-law.

"(d) Every sweep license shall consist of a certificate issued and signed by the Superintendent of Buildings. Such certificate shall indicate the name, address and age of the licensee and the name of the district for which he is appointed. Such license may be revoked and annulled at any time by the Board of Commissioners on a report from the Superintendent of Buildings and shall be issued only for one year from May to May. In the event of a license being issued after the 1st of May, the same shall be valid only up to the 1st of May following.

"(e) The following fees shall be paid by the occupant of any house or building for the sweeping of chimneys: For each flue in a house, there shall be paid for each story 5 cents.

"(f) If the house is heated by the proprietor, the said proprietor shall pay for the sweeping.

"(g) When any sweep is especially called upon outside of his ordinary rounds to sweep any chimney, the charge in that case shall be 50 cents for each flue.

"(h) Such fees shall be payable immediately by the occupant of the house or building wherein the chimneys have been swept or by the proprietor in the case of paragraph (f). .

"(i) Any person who shall refuse or neglect to pay such fees, or shall prevent any sweep from entering any house or building, or shall in any way obstruct or molest him in the discharge of his duties, shall be liable to the penalty hereinafter provided.

"(j) It shall be the duty of the owners of any building or house to provide suitable means of communication so that the sweeps may have access to the roofs and to the tops of the chimneys.

"(k) By 'chimney-sweeping' is meant the cleaning of the inner sides of the chimneys or flues. The sweeps shall not be held to remove the soot or other rubbish resulting from sweep-ings; the soot and other materials and rubbish shall be removed by the occupants as soon as the sweeping is completed.

"(1) Every sweep shall keep a book in which the sweepings done by him shall be entered daily, and the said book may be examined at any time by the Superintendent of Buildings. If the sweeping of chimneys is done by contract, the contractor shall keep a similar book for each district assigned to him."

The penalty is a fine not exceeding $40 and costs or two months in jail.

The Standard Specifications for the Construction of Steam Boilers and Other Pressure Vessels and for Their Care in Service

The Committee on Fire Protection of the American Society of Municipal Improvements having examined the "Standard Speci-fications for the construction of Steam Boilers and other Pres-sure Vessels and for their Care in Service," as formulated by the American Uniform Boiler Law Society, Erie, Pa., beg to submit same for adoption by the American Society of Munici-pay Improvements.

The specifications or "rules" are published by the American Uniform Boiler Law Society in a pamphlet of 148 pages, 32 pages of which are occupied by a very full index, and can be obtained by any one interested from the secretary at Erie, Pa.

SHADE TREES

The embellishment of city streets with shade trees is developing a science at the same time that the art of landscape gardening is being applied to it. The extremely artificial nature of the planting and growth of trees in narrow street lawns makes the science largely a new one, and one which is essential to comfortable and sanitary existence in cities as well as desirable from the con-sideration of beauty. Mr. Solotaroff's book on "Shade Trees in Towns and Cities" is the first one devoted to this subject exclu-sively and is the most complete in its scientific study of the prob-lems of tree planting, care, and maintenance, and gives consider-able attention also to the artistic point of view. It is published by John Wiley and Sons.

WHO PAYS FOR RESURFACING PAVEMENTS

An investigation by the Clearing House of Information was made at the request of a member and gives some valuable information regarding the methods of securing the resurfacing of worn pavements and meeting the cost of the same. Three general questions were asked: First, as to method of meeting the cost of the original pavement. Second, as to payment by the city of cost of repairs and maintenance. Third, as to method of securing resurfacing or reconstruction of pavement and of raising the funds to pay for the same.

Many cities make careful distinctions between maintenance, repairs, resurfacing and reconstruction, and secure the funds for these different kinds of work from different sources. It is believed that these distinctions, where made, are shown in the following tabular statements of the answers to the questions asked in the questionnaire sent to members. .

The responses are quite widely distributed, coming from about 70 cities in 33 states and Canadian provinces.

The meanings of the letters and numbers are given in the foot notes at the end of the tables. They are in three groups.

Capital letters stand for the principal word in the answer to the question.

Small letters refer to the boards or officials involved in the operations.

Numbers refer to notes giving special methods which must be explained, the table not being large enough to contain them.

In the first table, A, are given the answers to the questions regarding the method of meeting the cost of the original pavement.

Column 1 gives the answers to the question, Do the funds come from assessment on the property benefited. It will be noted that in the great majority of cities this is the method. The proportions assessed on the property and raised in other ways are given in a few instances. Special methods of distributing the cost are explained in the foot notes.

Column 2 states whether the cost of original construction is met from general city funds. It will be noted that in many cities the city pays the cost of paving intersections, being considered a property owner to this extent. The proportion definitely fixed for the city to pay is shown in other instances. In Ohio, cities pay for the intersections and two per cent. of the remainder also. In Tennessee the city pays for the grading of the street, for the intersections, and for one-third of the remainder. Other special provisions are explained in the footnotes.

Column 3 states kinds of bonds issued, if any, and what area ultimately pays the bonds. Thus C A denotes that city bonds are issued to pay the cost and these bonds are paid from assessments made on the property benefited; D T that bonds of the paving district are issued which are paid from taxes levied on the district; P A that bonds on the property itself are issued, which are paid from assessments; etc.

The fourth column shows, together with the other columns and the foot notes, how the funds are raised in case there are two or more sources for them.

City bonds (C) are issued by the city and are a charge against the city. They may be paid by general taxes or by assessments on the property improved as stated in each case. District bonds (D) may be issued on the responsibility of the improvement district and paid from proceeds of assessments or taxes on the property in the district; or they may be issued by the city and paid by assessments on the property benefited, not being a lien on the general funds but on the property assessed. Abutting property bonds (P) are issued for the amounts of the deferred payments on each piece of property assessed and are a lien on such property alone. Tax or assessment bills (B) are liens on the property assessed, issued for the amounts of the assessment and sold or given to the contractors in payment for their work.

A.   How Cost of Original Pavement is Met

City	1	2	3	
Alabama				
Birmingham ....y	—	CA(1)	—	
Arkansas				
Pine Bluff ....y	—	DT(2)	—	
California				
Pasadena ....y	I(3)	PA(4)	—	
San Francisco ....y	—	—	—	
Colorado				
Denver ....y	—		—	
Connecticut				
Hartford .... ⅔	⅓		(5)	
Florida				
West Palm Beach ....y	—	—	—	
Georgia				
Savannah ....y	y	—	(6)	
Illinois (49)				
Evanston ....y	—	PA(4)	—	
Moline ....y	—	PA(4)	—	
Oak Park ....y(7)	—	DA	—	
Waukegan ....y	—	—	—	

City		2	3	
INDIANA				
Indianapolis	y	I(8)	PA(4)	y
Richmond	4-5	2-5	PA(4)	(5)
South Bend	y	I(3)	PA(4)	y
IOWA				
Sioux City	y	—	—	—
KANSAS				
McPherson	y(7)	I	DA(26)	y
Pittsburg	y	I	DA	y
Wichita	y	I	PA	y
KENTUCKY				
Louisville	y	—	—	—
Owensboro	y	I	DA	y
LOUISIANA				
New Orleans	—	y	—	—
MARYLAND				
Baltimore	—	y	CT	
MASSACHUSETTS				
Boston	y	—	—	—
Brookline	—	y	C(9)	—
Fitchburg	—	y	CT	—
Springfield	½(10)	y	—	—
MICHIGAN				
Ann Arbor	1-5	I 4-5 (3)	y	(5)
MINNESOTA				
Minneapolis	y	I(11)	—	y
MISSOURI				
Kansas City	y	(12)	BP	—
St. Louis	y	(13)	BP	—
NEW JERSEY				
Atlantic City	y	y	CTA	(14)
East Orange	y	—	—	—
Essex County	—	—	CT	—
Roosevelt	—	y	—	—
NEW YORK				
Albany	y	—	CA	—
Buffalo	y	—.	—	—
Elmira	2-5	3-5	CT(15)	(5)
New York	y	—	—	—
Oswego	y	I(16)	—	y
Rochester	y	(17)	—	—
Syracuse	y	—	—	—
Utica	⅓	⅔	TCA	(24)

City		2	3	4
OHIO				
Cleveland ....y(19)		I 2%	CTA(20)	(18)
Columbus ....y		I 2%	CTA(20)	(18)
Lakewood ....y		I 2%	CTA(20)	(18)
OREGON				
Portland .... —		y	BCA	(25)
PENNSYLVANIA				
Bradford ....y		—	—	—
Butler ....y		—	—	—
Erie ....y		I	CA(1)	(5)
Farrell .... ⅔		⅓	—	(5)
Harrisburg ....y		I	—	(5)
Oil City ....y		I	CA(1)	(5)
Pittsburg ....y		—	—	—
Wilkes-Barre ....y		—	—	—
RHODE ISLAND				
Pawtucket .... —		y	—	—
SOUTH CAROLINA				
Columbia .... ½		½	—	(5)
TENNESSEE				
Greenville .... ⅔		GI ⅓	CTA	(21)
TEXAS				
San Antonio .... ⅔		I ⅓	CT(3)	(5)
VIRGINIA				
Danville .... —		y	(15)	—
WASHINGTON				
Everett ....y		—	—	—
WISCONSIN				
Beloit ....y		I	CT(3)	(22)
Madison ....y		—	CA(1)	—
Milwaukee ....y		I	—	(22)
CANADA				
Victoria, B. C............y		—	CA(1)	—
Ottawa, Ont. ....y		—	—	—
Toronto, Ont. ....y		—	CA(1)	—
Montreal, Que. ....y		I(23)	—	(5)

B. How Cost of Maintenance Is Met

The following cities pay all cost of repairs and maintenance of pavements after construction guaranties expire:

ALABAMA, Birmingham; ARKANSAS, Pine Bluff; CALIFORNIA, Pasadena, San Francisco; COLORADO, Denver; CONNECTICUT, Hartford; FLORIDA, West Palm Beach; GEORGIA, Savannah; ILLINOIS, Moline, Oak Park, Waukegan; INDIANA, Indianapolis, Richmond, South Bend; IOWA, Sioux City; KANSAS, Mc-

Pherson, Pittsburg, Wichita; KENTUCKY, Louisville, Owensboro; LOUISIANA, New Orleans; MARYLAND, Baltimore; MASSACHUSETTS, Boston, Brookline, Fitchburg (from street maintenance tax as long as it can be done economically), Springfield; MICHIGAN, Ann Arbor; MINNESOTA, Minneapolis; MISSOURI, St. Louis; NEW JERSEY, Atlantic City, East Orange, Essex County, Roosevelt; NEW YORK, Albany, Buffalo, Elmira, New York, Oswego, Rochester, Syracuse, Utica; OHIO, Cleveland, Columbus, Lakewood; PENNSYLVANIA, Bradford, Butler, Erie, Farrell, Harrisburg, Oil City, Pittsburg, Wilkes-Barre; RHODE ISLAND, Pawtucket; SOUTH CAROLINA, Columbia; TENNESSEE, Greeneville; TEXAS, San Antonio; VIRGINIA, Danville; WISCONSIN, Beloit, Madison, Milwaukee; CANADA, Victoria, B. C., for 10 years, Ottawa, Ont., by 5-year repair contracts, Toronto, Ont., Montreal, Que.

Evanston, Ill., pays from 50 to 67 per cent. of the cost of repairs to pavements, the city's portion being paid from a street and bridge tax and general funds.

In Kansas City, Mo., the cost of all repairs is proportioned uniformly against all of the property fronting on the street, contract for the repair and maintenance of which has been let. A tax bill is issued not oftener than once a year for the amount assessed on each piece of property, which is payable within thirty days and bears 7 per cent. interest if it becomes delinquent.

Everett, Wash., thus far has taken care of small repairs not caused by cuts, which are paid for by party responsible. Has as yet no system of maintenance.

In Table C the first column shows by the small letter, explained in the second group of footnotes, what authority determines when the street shall be resurfaced or reconstructed.

The second column shows whether the procedure followed in resurfacing is the same as that given in Table A or not.

The third column shows whether the procedure followed in reconstruction is the same as that given in Table A or not.

The fourth column shows who pays for resurfacing or reconstruction and method of meeting cost if different from that shown in Table A.

C. How Cost of Repaving Is Met

	2	3	4
ALABAMA			
Birmingham c	y	y	p
ARKANSAS			
Pine Bluff............... p	y	y	p

		2	3	4
CALIFORNIA				
Pasadena	cc	y	y	(28)
San Francisco	c	n	—	c
COLORADO				
Denver	m	n	n	
CONNECTICUT				
Hartford	sc	n	n	
FLORIDA				
West Palm Beach	co	y	y	P
GEORGIA				
Savannah	co	(29)	y	(29)
ILLINOIS				
Evanston	c	(30)	y	(30)
Moline	b	y	y	cp
Oak Park	b	y	y	(7)
Waukegan	b	y	y	p
INDIANA				
Indianapolis	b	y	y	(4)
Richmond	c	(31)	y	p
South Bend	b	y	y	p
IOWA				
Sioux City	co	y	y	p
KANSAS				
McPherson	—	y	y	
Pittsburg	p	y	y	(32) (28)
Wichita	p	y	y	(33)
KENTUCKY				
Louisville	b	n	n	c
Owensboro	co	y	y	p
LOUISIANA				
New Orleans	co	n	n	(34)
MARYLAND				
Baltimore	،	y	y	
MASSACHUSETTS				
Boston	—	—	—	c
Brookline	ss	n	y	(35)c
Fitchburg	co	y	y	c
Springfield	ss	y	y	c
MICHIGAN				
Ann Arbor	co	—	—	
MINNESOTA				
Minneapolis	co	y	y	p
MISSOURI				
Kansas City	e	y	y	p
St. Louis	b	(36)	y	(36)

		2	3	4
NEW JERSEY				
Atlantic City	cc	y	y	c
East Orange	co	n	y	(37)
Essex County	e	—	n	C
Roosevelt	e	y	y	c
NEW YORK				
Albany	co	(38)	(38)	c
Buffalo	cp	y	y	(39)
Elmira	b	y	y	(40)
New York	bp	n	y	c
Oswego	cp	y	y	(41)
Rochester	co	y	y	(42)
Syracuse	co	—	—	(43)
Utica	—	y	y	(24)
OHIO				
Cleveland	co	·y	y	(44)
Columbus	co	y	y	(45)
Lakewood	c	y	y	(46)
PENNSYLVANIA				
Bradford	co	—	—	
Butler	co	—	—	
Erie	cp	—	—	
Farrell	c	—	—	ᴜ
Harrisburg	—	—	—	c
Oil City	co	n	n	c
Pittsburg	b	n	n	c
Wilkes-Barre	co	—	—	c
RHODE ISLAND				
Pawtucket	co	y	y	
SOUTH CAROLINA				
Columbia	co	none yet repaved		
TENNESSEE				
Greenville	—	y	y	(21)
TEXAS				
San Antonio	ss	y	y	(47)
VIRGINIA				
Danville	co	y	y	(15)
WASHINGTON				
Everett	—	y	y	n
WISCONSIN				
Beloit	co	y	y	(22)
Madison	b	y	y	n
Milwaukee	cp	y	y	(48)

		2	3	4
CANADA				
Victoria, B. C.	e	y	y	n
Ottawa, Ont.	cp	y	y	—
Toronto, Ont.	e	y	y	n
Montreal, Que.	—	y	y	y

A—Funds raised by assessments on property.
B—Tax or assessment bills issued as direct liens on property.
C—City or county bonds issued to pay cost.
D—Bonds on paving district issued to pay cost.
G—Grading (different procedure from paving).
I—Street intersections separated from street abutting on private property in procedure.
P—Assessment made on abutting property.
T—General municipal taxes are source of funds.

b—Board of Local or Public Works or Improvements, or like body; official titles are various.
bp—Boro President.
c—City.
cc—City Commission.
co—City Council.
cp—Commissioner of Public Works.
e—Engineer of Highways.
m—Manager of Improvements and Parks.
n—No.
p—Property owners.
sc—Board of Street Commissioners.
ss—Superintendent of Streets.
y—Yes.

(1) City bonds are paid from proceeds of assessments on the property benefited.

(2) Bonds issued by improvement districts are paid by taxes on the districts.

(3) Cost of street intersections is paid from city funds.

(4) Bonds issued against the property benefited are paid by assessments upon the property.

(5) Portions indicated are paid by assessment on property benefited and from general funds or paving bond issues.

(6) Part of cost of pavement is paid by assessment on property abutting, and part from general city funds. In the special case of the street improved under the ordinances sent as samples, one-third the total cost was paid from the city treasury and two-thirds was paid by a single assessment on the abutting property, the city being considered a property owner to the extent of the width of intersecting streets and lanes.

(7) The property benefited includes property one-half block each way from the street paved. Bonds are issued and paid by tax on the improved district so defined.

(8) Cost of paving street intersections is paid in cash by the city if possible. If necessary, cost of intersections may be assessed on valuation of all lands and lots in the city, which is made a special assessment district for the purpose. This assessment is made annually, large enough to pay the cost of all work done during the year.

(9) Cost of street paving is usually paid from the general funds, but is occasionally paid from proceeds of paving bond issues.

(10) Assessment of one-half of cost on property benefited is made if the street is a new one. Nearly all street construction is done by municipal labor, only three small contracts have been let in five years.

(11) City pays also the assessments which would be made on property exempt from assessment.

(12) Tax bills payable in four annual instalments are given contractors for work, for each piece of property assessed. Improvements are paid for practically always by assessment on property benefited. Very rarely the improvement of traffic ways is paid for from general funds.

(13) Tax bills are given contractor, which are liens on the particular pieces of property covered by them. It is proposed in case of certain boulevards to assess on the property benefited the cost of an ordinary street, the excess of cost to be paid from general funds of the city.

(14) Ordinances provide that a just and equitable assessment of benefits shall be made on the property benefited and that any excess of cost shall be paid from city funds. Paving bonds are issued and are paid from proceeds of assessments and general taxes.

(15) City's share is sometimes raised by issuing bonds, which are paid from proceeds of city taxes.

(16) Property benefited is assessed bid price for pavement, curb, etc., in front of it plus for inspection, contingencies, etc., 5 per cent. on long block, 10 per cent. on short block or 15 per cent. if there is a single-track car line. This practically seems to leave the city to pay a part or all of the cost of paving street and alley intersections.

(17) The city council has power to assess a part or all of the cost of paving a street against the city, but actually this is limited to assessing on the city 25 per cent. of cost of resurfacing **street if it is extensive, but not** if it is an entire reconstruction.

(18) The city pays the cost of paving street intersections and 2 per cent. of the remaining cost.

(19)   Special assessments are made (a) as a percentage of the tax value of the property assessed; (b) in proportion to the benefits which may result from the improvement; (c) by the foot frontage of the property bounding or abutting upon the improvement.   Street improvements are made by (b), which is usually assumed to be (c).

(20)   City's portion is paid from proceeds of bond issues, met from general city taxes.   City bonds or notes may be issued in anticipation of collection of assessments, interest to be included in the assessment.

(21)   Town pays for grading, draining, other preliminary work, one-third of paving, street and alley intersections, pavement abutting public buildings.   Abutting property pays two-thirds of cost of paving, one-third on each side of street.   City bonds paid from general taxes and serial 1-10 yr. bonds paid from proceeds of assessments on paving districts are sold to pay cost of improvement.

(22)   City pays for street intersections.   If cost of pavement is more than $3 a sq. yd. city pays the excess in Beloit and one-half the excess in Milwaukee.

(23)   Cost of paving street intersections is paid by the city, also the cost of any excess in width of street over 50 feet.

(24)   City pays one-third of cost of pavement and two-thirds is assessed on abutting property, which is paid in cash, or bonds of city are issued, which are paid from deferred payments of assessments with interest.

(25)   Tax bills are issued for each piece of property assessed and taken by the contractor.   If unpaid in thirty days they are collected as other delinquent taxes unless property owner elects to pay in instalments.   Tax bills are then replaced by city bonds, which are paid by the proceeds of the deferred payments of assessments.   City bonds draw 1 per cent. less interest than deferred payments of assessments, thus giving a fund for expenses.

(26)   The bonds issued in anticipation of collection of assessments are first offered to the state school fund commission and if it does not have funds to invest they are readily sold at 4½ per cent., non-taxable.

(27)   Paid from proceeds of wheel tax and auto licenses, as long as the fund is large enough, then streets on which repairs are too heavy are resurfaced by assessment.

(28)   City pays for resurfacing or reconstructing street intersections, property is assessed for remainder.

(29)   City council decides whether street should be resurfaced or reconstructed.   If reconstructed, the cost is met by assessment.   If resurfaced, city pays cost in some instances.   In case of ordinances filed with report, city was assessed one-third of cost, street railroad cost of paving track space, and property

owners two-thirds of cost of plain pavement. Procedure was same as for original construction after old pavement was condemned as unsanitary and worn out. City's share is paid from general city revenues.

(30) A pavement may be resurfaced by the city and the abutting property owners or by special assessment, in the latter case the procedure being the same as for reconstruction or for original construction by this method as outlined in Note 7 above.

(31) City pays cost of resurfacing. If street is reconstructed procedure is same as for new construction as under Table A.

(32) The district for paving or repaving a street extends to the center of the alley in rear of abutting property, or, if none, 300 feet back from street line.

(33) If property owners petition for resurfacing or reconstruction of street procedure is same as for new construction. If city resurfaces or reconstructs without petition, the city pays the bill out of general funds.

(34) City pays for resurfacing streets from general fund. Cost of reconstruction is divided between city and property owners, proportion not given.

(35) Procedure for reconstruction is same as for new construction and is paid for from general funds or bond issues raised by general taxation.

(36) City does a small amount of resurfacing by the general maintenance force, but most of resurfacing is done, the same as reconstruction, by same procedure as new construction.

(37) City pays for resurfacing, the need for which is determined by the road committee of the city council. Part of cost of reconstruction is paid by city and part by property owners, the necessity of reconstruction being decided by the city council. The city's share of the cost is met by improvement bonds which are paid by general tax.

(38) As city pays for resurfacing, no petition is required and the need for it is determined by the city council on advice of the Commissioner of Public Works and the City Engineer. Fifteen-year bonds are issued, which are paid from general taxes. Reconstruction is authorized by ordinance of the city council and paid for by city, same as resurfacing.

(39) The city pays one-third the cost of resurfacing and reconstruction and two-thirds is assessed on property.

(40) The city pays three-fifths the cost of resurfacing and reconstruction and two-fifths is assessed on property. The city's share is paid from the general funds or proceeds of paving bonds, met by tax on city.

(41) Procedure is same as for new construction except that usually about one-half the cost of reconstruction is paid by city

from funds of Department of Works. The city has issued no paving bonds for twenty years.

(42) For some years city council has assessed one-fourth of cost of resurfacing asphalt or brick on the city, and three-fourths on abutting property. Reconstruction is treated same as new construction.

(43) One-tenth of cost of resurfacing and reconstruction is paid from the budget of the year and nine-tenths from the proceeds of ten-year local improvement bonds, which are paid by taxes on entire city.

(44) The city council, on advice of the Commissioner of Engineering, decides when a street shall be resurfaced or reconstructed. The procedure and method of payment are the same as in the case of new construction except that the city usually pays 50 per cent. of the cost from bond issues met by general taxes.

(45) Same procedure as for new construction except that city pays 50 per cent. of cost plus cost of intersections from general taxes, the other 50 per cent. being assessed as benefits on the abutting property.

(46) The state law for repaving pays 50 per cent. by general tax and 50 per cent. by assessment on frontage, but the city charter provides that for any replacement made within twenty years after the original construction the city shall pay two-thirds from general taxes and assess one-third on the abutting property.

(47) Payment same as for new construction except in case of partial resurfacing.

(48) Fifty per cent. of all cost of resurfacing or reconstruction above $3 a sq. yd. is paid by the city from general funds and 50 per cent. by assessment on abutting property.

(49) Funds may be raised by general tax, frontage tax or by assessment of private and public benefits.

Analyses of the complicated local improvement laws of Illinois have been published by the National Paving Brick Manufacturers' Association, Cleveland, Ohio, and the Portland Cement Association, Chicago, which can probably be had for the asking. These laws provide that the cost of local improvements may be met either by general taxation, special taxation or special assessment, or by a combination of general taxation with either of the others. The general custom, however, is to make special assessment in which may be included an assessment of a part of the cost as public benefits upon the public generally. Serial bonds may be issued to cover deferred payments on assessments and are paid as these deferred payments come due. Repairs are usually made and paid for by the city. In resurfacing and reconstruction the same process is followed as in original construction.

A charter provision of Indianapolis, Ind., reads: "Improvement by resurfacing upon a foundation already in place shall be deemed an improvement within the meaning of this act."

The Kansas law concerning paving is couched in the following terms, which show that the procedure is the same for repaving as for the original work: "When the mayor and council shall deem it necessary to grade, pave, curb, gutter, or regrade, repave, recurb, or regutter, any street, alley, or avenue, or any part thereof, within the limits of the city, for which a special tax is to be levied as herein provided, said mayor and council shall by resolution cause the same to be done and such improvement necessary, and such resolution shall be published in the official paper of the city for five consecutive days if the same is a daily and for two consecutive weeks if the same is a weekly, and if a majority of the resident property owners of real property liable to taxation for such improvement shall not within twenty days thereafter file with the city clerk their protest in writing against said improvement, then the mayor and council shall have the power to cause such improvements to be made and contract therefor, and to levy taxes therefor as provided by law, and the construction may be done during or after the collection of the special assessments, as may be deemed proper by the mayor and council; also whenever a majority of the resident property owners of real property liable to taxation for the improvement petition the mayor and council to pave, grade, curb, gutter or otherwise improve any street, alley, avenue or any part thereof, the mayor and council shall cause said work to be done, shall contract therefor, and levy the taxes therefor as provided by law: Provided, That the cost of the paving, grading, curbing, guttering, and otherwise improving the areas and squares formed by the crossing of streets, as well as the cost of making said improvements in streets, alleys and avenues running along and through city property, shall be paid for by a general tax levied by the mayor and council upon all property of the city." Bonds issued are city bonds, but are paid from the proceeds of assessments on the property benefited.

Section 2833 of the Louisville charter provides that "When the improvement is the *original* construction of any street, road, lane, alley, or avenue, such improvement shall be made at the exclusive cost of the owners of lots in each fourth of a square to be equally apportioned by the Board of Public Works, according to the number of square feet owned by them respectively, and in such improvements the cost of curbing shall constitute a part of the cost of the construction of the streets or avenue, and not of the sidewalk. Each subdivision of the territory bounded on all sides by principal streets shall be deemed a square. When the territory contiguous to any public way is not defined into squares by principal streets, the ordinance providing for the improvement of such public ways shall state the depth, not exceeding five hundred feet, on both sides of said improvements to be assessed for the cost of making the same, including the cost of the improvement of the intersections, if any, of said public way, according to the number of square feet owned by the parties respectively within the depth, as set out in the ordinance." Repaving is paid for by the city out of general funds.

Kentucky cities of the third class make their resurfacing under the following statute provisions: "The improvement of any public way or sidewalk by original or re-construction or by resurfacing upon a foundation already in place, shall be deemed an improvement within the provisions of this act." Also, "The city may pay the cost of the improvement of intersections with other public ways, including one-half of the width of the street or alley being improved, opposite other streets or alleys which run into but do not cross the street or alley so being improved, and of that proportion of any street abutting upon property belonging to the city, or it may assess the cost thereof against the property abutting on the street or way or part thereof ordered improved." The county is treated the same as private property owners. The city may decide for ten-year period what proportion of the cost of street paving, excluding sidewalks, will be paid from general funds. The city council or board of commissioners decides what improvements shall be made or remade, with what materials and in what way. Assessments are made on property benefited and may be paid in ten equal annual instalments. The city may issue bonds to cover the deferred payments, which are paid by them tho they pledge the credit of the city as well as the security offered by these deferred payments. A sinking fund is provided to pay the city's portion of the cost if not paid in cash and any delinquencies in the deferred payments. The law governing cities of the second class is very nearly the same.

Kansas City, Mo., is exceptional in that, after the guaranty period on a new pavement has expired, a contract is let for repairing and maintaining the pavement and not oftener than once each year special tax bills are issued against the property assessed for the original pavement on the street or streets covered by the repair contract. The amount of these tax bills is determined by measuring the repairs made, and computing their cost under the terms of the contract and distributing the total cost over the frontage on the street covered by the repair contract. Since all the costs of the pavement are paid by the property, repair contracts can be extended to cover practical resurfacing or reconstruction if more economical or more equitable than reconstruction.

In St. Louis, Mo., the provisions regarding reconstruction are the same as for the original construction and the cost is assessed one-third on the frontage and two-thirds on the area of the lots abutting on the improvement. The city must pay for maintenance and repairs. At least one-fourth the cost of reconstruction of a street must be paid by the city if done within ten years after the original construction.

The charter of Rochester, N. Y., gives the common council "power to require the opening, laying out, paving, repaving, grading, regrading, repairing, sprinkling, cleaning, sodding, embellishment, alteration, widening and discontinuance of public streets, highways and places, and the cutting and sowing of grass and planting and care of trees therein," and it "may direct that the whole of the expense of a public improvement or work be assessed upon the property deemed benefited or, subject to the approval of the Board of Estimate and Apportionment, that the whole or part thereof be charged to the city at large and the remainder, if any, assessed upon the property deemed benefited."

The charter of Cleveland provides that "the council shall have the power by ordinance to provide for the construction, reconstruction, repair and maintenance by contract or directly by the employment of labor, of all things in the nature of local improvements, and to provide for the payment of any part of the cost of any such improvement by levying and collecting special assessments upon abutting, adjacent and contiguous or other specially benefited property. The amount assessed against the property specially benefited to pay for such local improvements shall not exceed the amount of benefits accruing to such property." Special assessments may be made on tax value, in proportion to benefits, or by front footage. The council decides what portion the city shall pay, which shall not be less than 2 per cent. of the total cost of the improvement. If an improvement is replaced within fifteen years of the date of a prior assessment for local improvement, the assessment shall not exceed 50 per cent. of the cost of the improvement. Estimates must be made of the life of all improvements made since the new charter and the above provision applies to replacements made within the period so fixed but not to those made after it has expired. The city may issue bonds in anticipation of collection of assessments.

The charter of Lakewood, Ohio, has the same provisions, also one limiting local assessments for improvements to one-third the actual value of the lot assessed within any period of five years; one Cleveland provision being modified to provide that assessments for replacements of existing streets made within twenty years of the date of the original construction shall not exceed one-third the cost of the replacement, and that the life of new streets shall be estimated and assessments made within that estimated time for replacements shall not exceed one-third the cost.

The local improvement act governing Toronto, Ont., expressly excepts from the list of local improvements "work of ordinary repair or maintenance." Assessments are made by front footage, including engineering, advertising and notices, interest on loans, cost of issue and sale and discount of bonds, compensation for lands and damages thereto. The city pays for street intersections and for surface drainage. Special modifications of the frontage rule are provided for. A part of the cost of an improvement can be assessed on the city. City bonds may be issued, to be paid from proceeds of deferred payments of assessments. The annual instalments shall not continue longer than the estimated life of the pavement, fixed in the ordinance authorizing it. Repairs must be paid for by the city. On complaint of party injured the courts may compel the city to make repairs.

Montreal, Que., assesses cost of paving on abutting property, the city paying the cost of intersections.

A brief study of these data shows considerable variation in the principles underlying the practices followed and still greater variations in the details of practice, and gives much force to the desire expressed by one member, a city attorney, that the Society appoint a committee to work on the project of aiding in the securing of uniformity in laws governing public improvements, of which this matter of repair and reconstruction of streets is a very small part.

The original reports from members from which the above data are taken are in some cases fuller than the tables indicate and are on file and can be studied by any one desiring to do so. In the file are also the following documents:

Savannah, Ga.; copies of published procedure on public improvements, including reports of committee on streets and lanes, reports of chief and assistant chief engineer, resolutions ordering paving or repaving, ordinances governing the construction, preparation of assessment rolls and collection of same and ordinances establishing the official statement and assessment roll.

Illinois; pamphlet giving Outlines of Procedure and forms for construction of local improvements by special assessment.

Owensboro, Ky.; act relative to control and improvement of public streets, alleys, sidewalks, roads, lanes, avenues, highways, and thorofares in cities of the third class. Court decision on validity of act. Street improvement resolutions. Street improvement ordinances. Specifications for street construction.

Kansas City, Mo.; contract and specifications for constructing brick or block pavement. Specifications for repairing and maintaining asphalt pavement. Ordinance providing for and authorizing the work of paving.

St. Louis, Mo.; provisions of charter governing public work.

Atlantic City, N. J.; ordinance providing for street improvement.

Cleveland, Ohio; charter of city and amendments thereto.

Lakewood, Ohio; charter of city and published ordinance governing the improvement of a street.

Toronto, Ont.; the local improvement act of Ontario, with the forms required by the statute.

Montreal, Que.; charter of the city and amendments thereto.

REPORT OF SPECIAL COMMITTEE ON REVISION OF CONSTITUTION

George W. Tillson, ·Brooklyn, N. Y., Chairman

At the Newark convention of the Society held in 1916 a committee of five, of which Geo. W. Tillson was named Chairman, was authorized, by resolution regularly adopted, for the purpose of revising the constitution of the Society. The Chairman was given the power to designate the remainder of the committee. He subsequently appointed Prof. A. H. Blanchard, Nelson P. Lewis, Morris R. Sherrerd, and A. Prescott Folwell as the additional members.

The committee was directed to present its report to the Secretary six weeks prior to the 1917 convention. As no convention was held in 1917, the committee took no action in that year. At a meeting of the Executive Committee held in New York in 1917 the Committee on the Revision agreed to prepare its report so that it might be printed in the April, 1918, Transactions of the Society.

The Committee therefore met in New York on February 12, 1918. The entire Committee as well as the President of the Society were present. The constitution as a whole was gone over and discussed in great detail, as were communications from different members regarding several points at issue.

After careful consideration of all the questions involved the attached constitution was unanimously adopted and is hereby transmitted for presentation to the Society.

Respectfully,

GEO. W. TILLSON, Chairman,
ARTHUR H. BLANCHARD,
NELSON P. LEWIS,
MORRIS R. SHERRERD,
A. PRESCOTT FOLWELL.

REVISION OF CONSTITUTION
AMERICAN SOCIETY OF MUNICIPAL IMPROVEMENTS

Submitted by Committee on Revision of Constitution: George W. Tillson, Chairman, A. Prescott Folwell, Nelson P. Lewis, Morris R. Sherrerd and Arthur H. Blanchard

ARTICLE I
NAME AND OBJECT

SECTION 1. This Society shall be known as "The American Society of Municipal Improvements." Its object shall be to disseminate information and experience upon, and to promote the best methods to be employed in the management of municipal departments, and in the construction of municipal works, by means of annual conventions, the reading and discussion of papers upon municipal improvements, and by social and friendly intercourse at such conventions; and to circulate among its members, by means of an annual publication, the information thus obtained.

ARTICLE II

MEMBERSHIP

SECTION 1. There shall be three classes of membership, viz.: Active Members, Associate Members and Affiliated Members.

SECTION 2. Any engineer, officer or director who shall have charge of or supervision over, or any person employed as a consulting engineer on any public, municipal, county, or state department work, or any mayor, councilman or other official of any municipality, county or state is eligible to Active membership in this Society. A municipality may be represented by as many active members as it may desire, the representatives of the City holding such memberships being subject to appointment each year by the municipality. Provided, however, that the names of all appointees shall be submitted to the Executive Committee for action previous to the convention.

SECTION 3. Any proper person, interested in municipal improvements or work as a contractor or contracting agent or who is a manufacturer of or dealer in municipal supplies, may become an Associate Member, and shall enjoy all the rights and privileges of Active membership, excepting that of holding office, voting or addressing the convention without its consent.

SECTION 4. Any one interested in the subject of municipal improvements, but not included in either of the above classes of members, may be admitted as an Affiliated Member. Such members shall enjoy all the rights and privileges of Associate membership.

SECTION 5. Any member who shall have ceased to perform duties that make him eligible for Active membership may, if he so elect, retain such membership, unless he shall have come under the restrictive requirements of Associate membership, when he shall retain membership as an Associate Member only. Decision as to the classification or change in classification of all members shall rest with the Executive Committee; but an appeal may be taken from such decision to the Society at any regular annual convention. A two-third vote of all members voting shall be necessary to overrule the Executive Committee.

SECTION 6. Every application for membership shall be in writing, stating the age and residence of the applicant, his official position and past experience in public work.

Every such application shall be considered by the Executive Committee within two months of its receipt by the Secretary. A two-third vote of the Committee shall be necessary for election, which shall take effect upon the payment of the dues to the end of the current year. In case of the rejection of any applicant by the Committee, he may appeal to the Society at the next annual convention, when a two-third vote of all the Active Members voting shall admit him to membership.

SECTION 7. Any member may withdraw from the Society upon payment of all dues to date, and by notifying the Secretary thereof in writing.

SECTION 8. Any member may be expelled from the Society at a regular convention of the same, upon the recommendation of the Executive Committee, adopted by a two-third vote of all the Active Members voting.

ARTICLE III

FEES AND DUES

SECTION 1. Each Active and each Affiliated Member shall pay five dollars per annum, and each Associate Member shall pay ten dollars per annum, all dues to be payable in advance, on or before the first day of the annual convention; except that if more than one representative of a given company be Members, one shall pay a fee of ten dollars, and the others five dollars each. A Member admitted after March 15 of any year shall pay, for the balance of that year, one-half the annual dues.

SECTION 2. Any Member who shall be in arrears for more than one year's dues may be considered as no longer a Member of this Society, and his name may be discontinued from the roll of the Society at the discretion of the Executive Committee.

ARTICLE IV

OFFICERS AND COMMITTEES

SECTION 1. The officers of this Society shall consist of a President, three Vice-Presidents, a Secretary, and a Treasurer, not more than two of whom shall be residents of the same state; and who, with the five latest living past Presidents who have retained their membership, shall act as an Executive Committee for and in behalf of the Society.

SECTION 2. There shall also be elected a Finance Committee consisting of three members of the Society.

SECTION 3. In case of any of the above positions, excepting Presidency, becoming vacant, or in case of their absence during the annual convention, the President shall fill such vacancy by appointment from the membership.

SECTION 4. There shall be appointed annually the following general and specification Committees:

General Committees

1. Street Paving, Sidewalks and Street Design.
2. Parks and Parkways.
3. City Planning.
4. Traffic and Transportation.
5. Street Lighting.
6. Street Cleaning, Refuse Disposal and Snow Removal.
7. Sewerage and Sanitation.
8. Water Works and Water Supply.
9. Municipal Legislation and Finance.
10. Fire Prevention.
11. Public Markets.
12. Convention Papers.
13. Convention Arrangements.

The Chairman of the last named Committee shall be a resident of the city in which the next following convention is to be held, provided there is a member of the Society residing in that city.

The Secretary of the Society shall be the Chairman of the Committee on Convention Papers.

Each General Committee shall consist of three members. No Committee shall incur any liabilities unless the same shall have been authorized by the Executive Committee.

Specification Committees

1. Sheet-Asphalt Pavements.
2. Bituminous Macadam, Bituminous Concrete and Asphalt Block Pavements.
3. Broken Stone and Gravel Roads with or without Bituminous Surface Treatments.
4. Brick Pavements.
5. Cement-Concrete Pavements.
6. Stone Block Pavements.
7. Wood Block Pavements.
8. Sidewalks and Curbs.
9. Sewers.

Each Specification Committee shall consist of five Active Members.

All Committees shall be appointed by the President unless otherwise specified in this Constitution.

ARTICLE V

ELECTION OF OFFICERS

SECTION 1. The officers of this Society shall be elected by ballot on the second day of each annual convention, a majority of the votes cast electing.

SECTION 2. The President shall not be eligible for immediate re-election, except by a unanimous vote.

SECTION 3. The officers elected shall assume office immediately after the close of the annual meeting at which they were elected.

SECTION 4. The ballot for any officer may be waived by unanimous consent.

ARTICLE VI

DUTIES OF OFFICERS AND COMMITTEES

SECTION 1. The President shall preside at the convention of the Society and at meetings of the Executive Committee, and shall perform such other duties as are incumbent upon the office. In the absence of the President, or upon his becoming ineligible, the Vice-Presidents in the order of seniority shall assume and perform the duties of the office.

SECTION 2. The Secretary shall keep accurate minutes of the proceedings of the Society and of the Executive Committee; shall conduct all correspondence; shall issue notices of any convention of the Society not less than four weeks prior to the date of such convention; shall collect and receipt for all fees and dues and pay them to the Treasurer, taking his receipt for the same; and keep accurate account between the Society and its members. He shall keep an accurate list of the members of the Society.

The Secretary shall receive a salary, the amount of which shall be determined by the Executive Committee. In addition, his expenses incurred in attending conventions of this Society shall be paid by the Society; and he is authorized to incur in the name of the Society, the expenses necessary to the conduct of his office, including an assistant during the convention.

SECTION 3. The Treasurer shall receive from the Secretary and safely keep all moneys belonging to the Society, giving his receipt therefor; shall pay all bills by vouchers countersigned by the President and Secretary; shall keep correct account of the funds of the Society, and submit to it at its annual convention a report of all receipts and disbursements during the preceding year. He shall give a bond in an amount required by the Executive Committee, the cost of which shall be paid by the Society.

SECTION 4. The Executive Committee shall manage all the affairs of the Society subject to the action and approval of the Society at its conventions. At its meetings, five members shall constitute a quorum, not less than three of whom shall be officers of the Society. All the business of the Executive Committee shall be decided by a majority vote. The Executive Committee shall meet at least once each year on the morning of the first day of the annual convention of the Society, and as much oftener as the President may determine.

SECTION 5. The Finance Committee shall meet on the morning of the first day, and previous to the annual convention of the Society, to examine and audit the Secretary's and Treasurer's accounts and annual statements, and report thereon to the Society.

SECTION 6. It shall be the duty of each of the General Committees, Nos. 1 to 11, inclusive, to prepare a report and submit the same at the annual convention. Also to obtain for presentation at the conventions papers on the subjects covered by said Committee, when requested so to do by the Committee on Convention Papers.

SECTION 7. It shall be the duty of each Specification Committee to keep in touch with the developments relating to its work, and report to the annual convention any recommended changes in adopted or any new specifications.

The Committees shall prepare their tentative reports and send the same to the Secretary six weeks previous to the opening of the convention. If, in the judgment of the Executive Committee, the financial condition of the Society will warrant the expense, the Secretary shall send to each member of the Society a printed copy of each report. If the expense of preprinting be not warranted, a typewritten copy shall be sent to each member who discussed the subject at the previous convention and also to any person requesting the same.

During the first two days of the convention each Committee shall hold a hearing, due notice of which as to time and place shall be given in the program, for a discussion of its report by all interested parties. After the hearing has been closed the Committee shall submit its final report to the convention at the time previously determined upon by the Committee on Convention Papers.

After discussion of the report upon the floor of the convention, a vote shall be had upon the submission of the proposed specifications, or amendment of existing specifications, to letter ballot or reference back to the Committee. If a letter ballot be ordered it shall, within thirty days after the close of the convention, be sent to all who were Active Members at the time the letter ballot was ordered. The votes shall be canvassed by the Executive Committee, or a Sub-Committee appointed by the Executive Committee, at a date not less than thirty or more than sixty days after the mailing of the ballots. If a majority of those entitled to vote favor the specifications or their amendment, they shall be adopted.

Any member wishing to make any changes in existing, or to suggest new specifications shall present the same to the appropriate Committee or to the annual convention, which after due consideration may refer the same to the appropriate Committee for report at the next convention or reject them entirely.

SECTION 8. The Committee on Convention Papers, of which the President shall be a member, shall prepare the program for the annual convention and shall have the power to edit, revise, reject, and control the publication of any paper submitted for presentation at said conventions.

SECTION 9. The Committee on Convention Arrangements shall have charge of the details of the convention next following the appointment of said Committee, subject to the provisions of this Constitution, and the instructions of the Executive Committee.

ARTICLE VII

CONVENTIONS

SECTION 1. The annual convention of the Society shall be held in such city as the majority of the members voting shall decide; selection of place of convention to be made after the officers shall have been elected. The date and duration of the convention shall be determined by the Executive Committee, which shall notify the members concerning the same not later than the first of June; but such date shall be in either September, October or November.

SECTION 2. At any annual convention of the Society twenty members shall constitute a quorum for the transaction of business.

SECTION 3. Any member, with the concurrence of the presiding officer, may admit friends to the convention of the Society; but such person or persons shall not without the consent of the meeting be permitted to take part in any discussion.

SECTION 4. All papers, drawings, etc., submitted to the convention of the Society shall be and remain the property of the Society.

ARTICLE VIII

ORDER OF BUSINESS

SECTION 1. At the annual convention of the Society the order of business at the first session shall be as follows:

1. The President's address.
2. Reports of the Secretary and Treasurer.
3. Report of the Executive Committee.

4. Report of the Finance Committee.
5. New Business.
6. Unfinished Business.

Election of officers and selection of the place of the convention shall take place during the second day.

SECTION 2. All questions shall be decided by vote, and all differences of opinion in regard to points of order shall be settled by parliamentary practice as set forth in Cushing's Manual.

ARTICLE IX

AMENDMENTS

SECTION 1. Proposed amendments to this Constitution must be reduced to writing and signed by not less than ten Active Members, and be submitted and acted upon as follows: Amendments must be submitted on the first day of the convention and shall be made an order of business for the third day of the convention, and, if approved, or amended in any manner consistent with the intent of the original amendment or amendments, by a majority vote, the amendment or amendments shall be sent out for letter ballot. An affirmative vote of two-thirds of all ballots cast shall be necessary for the adoption of any amendment.

This Constitution shall take effect upon its adoption.

MEMBERS IN THE WAR

The following is the list of members in the service of the United States and the Allies, as nearly up to date as possible to make it. Corrections and additions are requested from any one who knows the facts. Do not wait for the most interested person to send the information; he may be too busy to see this list. A few concerning whom the information is fragmentary are included, with special request for further data.

H. N. Ruttan, Brigadier-General (retired), Consulting Engineer, 802 Confederation Life Bldg., Winnipeg, Manitoba, Canada.

Frederic A. Snyder, Colonel, 103d Engineers; Division Engineer of 28th Division, Camp Mills, L. I., N. Y.

Walter W. Crosby, Lieutenant-Colonel, National Army, care of Chief of Chief of Engineers, War Department, Washington, D. C.

William D. Uhler, Lieutenant-Colonel, Quartermaster's Corps, N. A., Office of Quartermaster-General, U. S. A., Washington, D. C.

Henry M. Waite, Lieutenant-Colonel, Signal Corps, National Army, American Expeditionary Forces, France.

Webster L. Benham, Major, Quartermaster's Reserve Corps; Engineer Officer in Charge of Camp Utilities, Camp Funston, Ft. Riley, Kansas.

R. Keith Compton, Major, Engineers, U. S. R., in charge of buildings, docks, roads, sewage system, water supply, etc., Curtis Bay Ordnance Depot, South Baltimore, Md.

Lawrence E. Curfman, Major, U. S. R., 314th Engineers, Camp Funston, Kas.

Henry W. Durham, Major, 41st Engineers, N. A., American Expeditionary Forces, France.

John B. Hawley, Major, 503d Regiment of Engineers, Service Battalion, American Expeditionary Forces, France.

Lawrence E. Hess, Major, 309th Regiment of Engineers, Camp Taylor, Louisville, Ky.

Edgar A. Kingsley, Major, Engineers, U. S. R., U. S. A. P. O. 708, American Expeditionary Forces, France.

Ernest McCullough, Major, Engineers, U. S. R., Gas Service, Headquarters American Expeditionary Forces, France.

Eugene W. Stern, Major, Engineers, U. S. R., Superintendent of Roads, care of C. G. Base Sec. 2, U. S. A. P. O. 705, American Expeditionary Forces, France.

Gustave R. Tuska, Major, Engineers, U. S. R., 68 William St., New York City.

Joshua Atwood, Captain of Infantry, National Army, Headquarters of Northeastern Department, Boston, Mass.

Franklin R. Allen, Captain, U. S. R., 8th Company of Engineers, Camp Lee, Va.

Paul Hansen, Captain of Engineers (detached), General Headquarters, American Expeditionary Forces, France.

John F. Mangold, Captain, U. S. R., unassigned, Rapid City, S. D.

G. T. McClean, Captain, U. S. R., 29th Engineers, American Expeditionary Forces, France.

Dana Q. McComb, Captain, U. S. R., 3d Engineers, Ft. Mills, Corregidor, Philippine Islands.

Roger L. Morrison, Captain (honorably discharged), College Station, Tex.

J. F. Richardson, Captain, Ordnance Department, Camp Lee, Petersburg, Va.

Herbert Spencer, Captain, Engineers, U. S. R., Co. H, 23d Engineers, American Expeditionary Forces, France.

Bruce Aldrich, First Lieutenant, 115th Regiment of Infantry, Camp McClellan, Anniston, Ala.

Charles W. Linsley (rank Lieutenant, junior grade), Assistant Civil Engineer, U. S. N., R. F., care Public Works Office, Naval Operating Base, Hampton Roads, Va.

Lawrence V. Sheridan, Co. F, 306th Ammunition Train, Camp Jackson, Columbia, S. C.

Robert Stallings, Sergeant, Headquarters Co., 3d Anti-Aircraft Battalion, Ft. Morgan, Ala.

John E. Ballinger, in charge of sewers, drains and paving, Public Works Office, Naval Operating Base, Hampton Roads, Va.

W. L. Stevenson, Sanitary Engineer, Dept. of Health and Sanitation, U. S. Shipping Board, 140 N. Broad St., Philadelphia, Pa.

CONVENTIONS AND PAST PRESIDENTS OF THE SOCIETY.

First	1894	Buffalo	M. J. Murphy, St. Louis
Second	1895	Cincinnati	M. J. Murphy, St. Louis
Third	1896	Chicago	Geo. H. Benzenberg, Milwaukee
Fourth	1897	Nashville	August Hermann, Cincinnati
Fifth	1898	Washington	H. Van Duyne (deceased) Newark
Sixth	1899	Toronto	Nelson P. Lewis, New York
Seventh	1900	Milwaukee	A. D. Thompson, Peoria
Eighth	1901	Niagara Falls	Robert E. McMath, St. Louis
Ninth	1902	Rochester	E. A. Fisher, Rochester
Tenth	1903	Indianapolis	C. H. Rust, Victoria
Eleventh	1904	St. Louis	G. M. Ballard (deceased) Newark
Twelfth	1905	Montreal	A. Prescott Folwell, New York
Thirteenth	1906	Birmingham	Charles C. Brown, Bloomington
Fourteenth	1907	Detroit	Morris R. Sherrerd, New York
Fifteenth	1908	Atlantic City	Geo. W. Tillson, Brooklyn
Sixteenth	1909	Little Rock	James Owen, Newark
Seventeenth	1910	Erie	Julian Kendrick, Birmingham
Eighteenth	1911	Grand Rapids	Fred Giddings, Lake Charles
Nineteenth	1912	Dallas	E. A. Kingsley, San Antonio
Twentieth	1913	Wilmington	B. E. Briggs, Erie
Twenty-First	1914	Boston	Edward H. Christ, Grand Rapids
Twenty-Second	1915	Dayton	Wm. A. Howell, Newark
Twenty-Third	1916	Newark	A. F. Macallum, Ottawa
None	1917	Convention omitted on account of the war.	
Twenty-Fourth	1918	Buffalo	N. S. Sprague, Pittsburgh

NORMAN S. SPRAGUE
President

E. R. CONANT
First Vice-President

G. H. NORTON
Second Vice-President

R. K. COMPTON
Third Vice-President

CHARLES CARROLL BROWN
Secretary

F. J. CELLARIUS
Treasurer

OFFICERS OF THE SOCIETY FOR THE YEARS 1917-1918

President................................NORMAN S. SPRAGUE..Pittsburg, Pa.
First Vice-President........E. R. CONANT....................Savannah, Ga.
Second Vice-President....GEO. H. NORTON.............Buffalo, N. Y.
Third Vice-President......R. KEITH COMPTON......Baltimore, Md.
Secretary............................CHARLES C. BROWN......Bloomington, Ill.
Treasurer............................F. J. CELLARIUS..............Dayton, O.

FINANCE COMMITTEE

GEO. A. CARPENTER, Chairman..............................Pawtucket, R. I.
F. A. REIMER..Newark, N. J.
HAL MOSELEY..Dallas, Texas

EXECUTIVE COMMITTEE

The officers of the Society, together with the Past Presidents who have retained their continuous membership, constitute the Executive Committee. The Past Presidents are given on page 200.

STANDING COMMITTEES, 1917-18

STREET PAVING

W. A. HOWELL, Chairman..Newark, N. J.
H. C. ALLEN..Syracuse, N. Y.
J. H. WEATHERFORD..Memphis, Tenn.

SIDEWALKS AND STREET DESIGN

S. SAMMELMAN, Chairman..St. Louis, Mo.
H. A. VARNEY..Brookline, Mass.
J. E. BALLINGER..Jacksonville, Fla.

PARKS AND PARKWAYS

C. F. PUTNAM, Chairman..Roxbury, Mass.
G. A. PARKER..Hartford, Conn.
L. V. SHERIDAN..Cambridge, Mass.

CITY PLANNING

N. P. LEWIS, Chairman..New York, N. Y.
F. L. OLMSTED..Brookline, Mass.
H. BARTHOLOMEW..St. Louis, Mo.

TRAFFIC AND TRANSPORTATION

L. L. TRIBUS, Chairman..New York, N. Y.
H. S. MORSE..Detroit, Mich.
E. E. SANDS..Houston, Texas

STREET LIGHTING

T .W. WOOLEY, Chairman..Schenectady, N. Y.
C. W. KOINER..Pasadena, Cal.
J. H. WEATHERFORD..Memphis, Tenn.

STREET CLEANING AND REFUSE DISPOSAL

G. H. NORTON, Chairman..Buffalo, N. Y.
R. HERING...New York, N. Y.
R. C. HARRIS..Toronto, Ont.

SEWAGE AND SANITATION

F. A. DALLYN, Chairman..Toronto, Ont.
G. T. HAMMOND...Brooklyn, N. Y.
C. A. EMERSON..Harrisburg, Pa.

WATER WORKS AND WATER SUPPLY

F. W. CAPPELEN, Chairman......................................Minneapolis, Minn.
G. G. EARL...New Orleans, La.
G. W. FULLER..New York, N. Y.

MUNICIPAL LEGISLATION AND FINANCE

A. R. DENMAN, Chairman..Newark, N. J.
G. C. CUMMIN..Jackson, Mich.
EUGENE W. STERN..New York, N. Y.

FIRE PREVENTION

ALCIDE CHAUSSE, Chairman....................................Montreal, Que.
J. H. DINGLE..Charleston, S. C.
F. R. LANAGAN..Albany, N. Y.

STANDARD FORMS

A. PRESCOTT FOLWELL, Chairman..........................New York, N. Y.
E. S. RANKIN...Newark, N. J.
L. D. CUTCHEON..Grand Rapids, Mich.

Sub-Committees on Standard Forms

STREET CLEANING AND REFUSE DISPOSAL

B. F. MILLER, JR...Meadville, Pa.

SIDEWALKS AND CURBS

HENRY MAETZEL..Columbus, Ohio

SEWERS

GEORGE T. HAMMOND..Brooklyn, N. Y.

STREET PAVING AND REPAIR

C. D. POLLOCK..New York, N. Y.

STANDARD SPECIFICATIONS—GENERAL COMMITTEE

G. W. TILLSON, Chairman..Brooklyn, N. Y.
E. A. FISHER..Rochester, N. Y.
M. R. SHERRERD...Newark, N. J.

Sub-Committees on Standard Specifications

ASPHALT PAVING

F. P. SMITH, Chairman..New York, N. Y.
E. A. KINGSLEY...San Antonio, Tex.
H. H. CRAVER..Pittsburg, Pa.
*BRUCE ALDRICH..Baltimore, Md.
*WALTER H. TAYLOR, JR...Norfolk, Va.

Bituminous Paving

R. K. COMPTON, Chairman..................................Baltimore, Md.
A. W. DOW...New York, N. Y.
W. D. UHLER...Harrisburg, Pa.

Broken Stone and Gravel Roads

A. H. BLANCHARD, Chairman..............................New York, N. Y.
LINN WHITE...Chicago, Ill.
F. A. REIMER...Newark, N. J.
*T. H. BRANNAN...Columbus, Ohio
*WM. H. CONNELL..Philadelphia, Pa.
*W. W. CROSBY..Baltimore, Md.
*PREVOST HUBBARD...Washington, D. C.
*ANDREW LENDERINK ....Kalamazoo, Mich.
*R. A. MacGREGOR...New York, N. Y.

Brick Paving

E. H. CHRIST, Chairman...................................Grand Rapids, Mich.
S. C. CORSON...Norristown, Pa.
HENRY MAETZEL..Columbus, Ohio
*F. J. CELLARIUS...Dayton, Ohio
*GEORGE F. FISK..Buffalo, N. Y.
*ANDREW LENDERINK ....Kalamazoo, Mich.

Concrete Paving

A. W. DEAN, Chairman.....................................Winchester, Mass.
W. A. HANSELL...Atlanta, Ga.
F. O. EICHELBERGER.......................................Dayton, Ohio

Stone Block Paving

H. H. SCHMIDT, Chairman..................................Brooklyn, N. Y.
W. H. CONNELL...Philadelphia, Pa.
E. R. CONANT..Savannah, Ga.

Wood Block Paving

E. R. DUTTON, Chairman...................................Minneapolis, Minn.
F. KLEEBERG...New York, N. Y.
J. C. HALLOCK..Newark, N. J.

Sewers

E. J. FORT, Chairman....................................New York, N. Y.
W. W. HORNER...St. Louis, Mo.
T. C. HATTON..Milwaukee, Wis.

Convention Papers

C. C. BROWN, Chairman...................................Chicago, Ill.
A. P. FOLWELL...New York, N. Y.
G. A. CARPENTER.......................................Pawtucket, R. I.

Convention Arrangements

GEO. H. NORTON, Chairman...............................Buffalo, N. Y.
CHARLES C. BROWN, Secretary...........................Bloomington, Ill.

SPECIAL COMMITTEES

Standard Tests for Bituminous Materials

A. H. BLANCHARD, Chairman.............................New York, N. Y.
PREVOST HUBBARD.......................................Washington, D. C.

F. P. SMITH..New York, N. Y.
*LESTER KIRSCHBRAUN...Chicago, Ill.
*FELIX KLEEBERG...New York, N. Y.

Membership

E. R. CONANT, Chairman...Savannah, Ga.
JOSHUA ATWOOD..Boston, Mass.
R. K. COMPTON...Baltimore, Md.

Revision of Constitution

GEORGE W. TILLSON, Chairman...........................Brooklyn, N. Y.
ARTHUR H. BLANCHARD..New York City
NELSON P. LEWIS..New York City
MORRIS R. SHERRERD..Newark, N. J.
A. PRESCOTT FOLWELL...New York City

Convention Exhibits

C. E. P. BABCOCK, Chairman.....................................Buffalo, N. Y.
E. W. PIMM..Boston, Mass.
W. C. PERKINS..Conneaut, Ohio

---

*Appointed by Chairman.

ACTIVE

(Italics show member's address before he entered the service.)

Membership
Dates From

Ackerman, J. Walter, Chief Engineer and Superintendent of Water
Works, Auburn, N. Y..1905

Albright, Chester E., Chief of Bureau of Surveys, Municipal Dele-
gate from Philadelphia, Pa..1918

Aldrich, Bruce, *Chief Asphalt Inspector, Municipal Laboratory, 22
Harrison St., Baltimore, Md.* First Lieutenant, 115th Infantry,
Camp McClellan, Anniston, Ala..1917

Aldridge, William, Chief Computer and Estimator, City Engineering
Department, 333 McGee St., Winnipeg, Manitoba, Can.....................1912

Allen, F. R., *City Engineer, Pine Bluff, Ark.,* Captain, U. S. R., 8th
Company of Engineers, Camp Lee, Va..1911

Allen, Henry C., City Engineer, Syracuse, N. Y..1917

Allin, Thomas D., Commissioner of Public Works, City Hall, Pasa-
dena, Calif..1905

Ambler, John N., Consulting Engineer for Winston, Winston, N. C...1908

Anderson, Frederick J., City Engineer, City Hall, South Bend, Ind.....1915

Ash, Louis R., City Manager, Wichita, Kan...1911

Askwith, F. C., Deputy Engineer, 203 Powell Ave., Ottawa, Ontario,
Canada 1916

Atwood, Joshua, *Chief Engineer, Paving Service, Public Works Department, 501 City Hall Annex, Boston, Mass.,* Captain of Infantry, N. A. Northwestern Headquarters, Boston, Mass................1914

Babcock, C. E. P., Deputy City Engineer, Municipal Delegate from
Buffalo, N. Y..1914

Bæchlin, Ernest, Town Engineer, National Bank Building, Bloom-
field, N. J..1916

Baillairge, W. D., City Engineer, Quebec, Que., Canada........................1912

Baker, Henry E., Consulting Engineer, Watertown, N. Y., now Hang
Chow, Chekiang, China...1905

Ballinger, John E., *Engineer of Highways, Jacksonville, Florida.* In
charge of sewers, drains and paving, Public Works Office, Naval
Operating Base, Hampton Roads, Va...1913

Barbour, Frank A., Consulting Engineer, 1120 Tremont Building, Bos-
ton, Mass. 1914

Barlow, James E., City Manager, City Hall, Dayton, Ohio....................1910

Barlow, John R., Montreal, Que., Canada...1910

Barrett, C. H., Mayor, Gloucester, Mass...1917

Bartholomew, Harland, Engineer City Plan Commission, Municipal
Courts Building, St. Louis, Mo...1914

Bastis, Albert, Member City Council, Ways and Means, and Finance
Committees, Municipal Delegate from Minneapolis, Minn...............1917

Baylis, J. R., Bacteriologist, Montebello Filters, 3402 Harford Ave.,
Baltimore, Md..1911

Beggs, James L., Commissioner Streets and Public Improvement, 2049
N. Tremont St., Kansas City, Kan...1915

Belt, Edwin K., Assistant City Engineer, 525 Woodward Ave., Kala-
mazoo, Mich...1915

Benham, Webster L., *Consulting Engineer, 13th Floor Colcord Building, Oklahoma City, Okla,* Major, Q. M. C., U. S. R., Officer in
Charge of Camp Utilities, Camp Funston, Kan......................................1916

Benzenberg, George H., Member of Sewer Commission, 1310 Wells
Building, Milwaukee, Wis...1894

Berthe, L. T., City Engineer, President Berthe Engineering Co., Char-
leston, Mo...1917

Bingham, Clarence A., General Manager, 271 Winter Street, Nor-
wood, Mass...1915

Blanchard, Arthur H., Consulting Highway Engineer, Broadway and
117th St., New York City..1909
Boudinot, Allen R., City Engineer, Davenport, Iowa.......................1914
Bourleau, Edward, Superintendent of Streets, 28 Pendleton Avenue,
Chicopee, Mass...1917
Brandon, Walter W., Superintendent of Water Works, Anderson,
Indiana 1915
Brannan, Thomas H., Superintendent Asphalt Construction, City En-
gineer's Office, Columbus, Ohio..1913
Brehm, George C., City Hall, Marlboro, Mass................................1917
Brennan, W. C., Secretary City Corporation, Hamilton, Ont., Can.......1909
Briggs, B. E., Consulting Engineer, 207 Marine Bank Building, Erie,
Pennsylvania 1902
Brower, Irving C., Commissioner Public Works, 426 Hamilton St.,
Evanston, Ill..1915
Brown, Charles Carroll, Consulting Engineer, Bloomington, Ill., and
Indianapolis, Ind..1895
Brown, Matthew, City Engineer, 211 S. State St., Emporia, Kan.......1911
Brown, Thurber A., City Engineer, 416 E. Church St., Elmira, N. Y...1908
Brown, William M., Chief Engineer, Passaic Valley Sewerage Com-
mission, 820 Essex Building, Newark, N. J.................................1913
Buchanan, N. B., City Engineer and Secretary Tupelo Engineering
Company, Tupelo, Miss...1909
Bull, Irving C., Bull & Roberts, 100 Maiden Lane, New York City.......1912
Burkholder, Frank, Director of Public Service, Municipal Delegate
from Troy, Ohio..1918

Caldwell, Wallace L., District Manager Pittsburgh Testing Labora-
tory, 215 Clark Building, Birmingham, Ala..................................1913
Calkins, D. J. F., Acting City Engineer, Municipal Delegate from
Everett, Wash...——
Campbell, Edward F., Engineer for Pelham Manor and North Pel-
ham, 230 Huguenot St., New Rochelle, N. Y. 1916
Cannon, S. Q., City Engineer, Salt Lake City, Utah.......................1915
Cappelen, F. W., City Engineer, Municipal Delegate from Minneapolis,
Minnesota 1895
Carpenter, George A., City Engineer, Pawtucket, R. I....................1905
Carson, H. O., City Engineer, 218-219 Odd Fellows Building, Butler,
Pennsylvania 1917
Carter, Hugh R., State Highway Engineer, New State Capitol, Little
Rock, Ark...1909
Cellarius, Frederick J., Consulting Engineer, 1001 Commercial Build-
ing, Dayton, Ohio...1910
Chambers, John, Chief Engineer, Municipal Delegate from Louis-
ville, Ky...1918
Charles, Frederick R., Civil Engineer, Richmond, Ind....................1910
Chase, Guy H., Commissioner of Streets and Engineering, Fitch-
burg, Mass..1917
Chaussé, Alcide, City Architect and Superintendent of Buildings. P.
O. Box 304, Montreal, Que., Canada..1901
Chrisman, O. D., City Engineer, Court House, Springfield, Mo...........1917
Christ, Edward H., Civil and Consulting Engineer, Norris Building,
Grand Rapids, Mich..1908
Clark, Frederick H., Superintendent of Streets and Engineering, 328
Municipal Bldg., Springfield, Mass..1913
Codwise, Edward B., 298 Wall St., Kingston, N. Y.........................1906
Coile, C. E., Engineer for Green County Pike Commission and City
Engineer for Greenville, Tenn...1916
Colby, Elmer E., City Engineer, Chickasha, Okla...........................1909
Collins, Clarke P., Sanitary Engineer, City Hall, Johnstown, Pa...........1909

Collins, John L., Civil and Hydraulic Engineer, 30 Church St., New
York City 1910
Collins, Thomas E., City Engineer, City Hall, Elizabeth, N. J............1916
Compton, R. Keith, *Chairman and Consulting Engineer, Paving Com-
mission, 214 E. Lexington St., Baltimore, Md.*, Major, Engineers,
U. S. R., Curtis Bay Ordinance Depot, S. Baltimore, Md.................1915
Conant, Elbridge R., Chief Engineer, Savannah, Ga.............................1913
Condon, Pierce P., Superintendent of Streets, Watertown, Mass........1917
Cook, J. C., Chief Engineer, The J. B. McCrary Co., Municipal En-
gineers, 1408 Third National Bank Bldg., Atlanta, Ga...................1913
Cooksey, R. M., City Engineer, City Hall, Municipal Delegate from
Baltimore, Md. 1914
Cooper, C. M., City Engineer, Columbus, Kans..................................1913
Cornell, Douglass, City Hall, Buffalo, N. Y..1915
Corning, Dudley T., 334 City Hall, Philadelphia, Pa...........................1909
Corson, S. Cameron, Boro Engineer, City Hall, Norristown, Pa........1908
Coward, E. H., Civil Engineer, Miners Savings Bank Bldg., Pittston,
Pa. 1916
Cowden, M. B., City Engineer, Municipal Delegate from Harris-
burg, Pa. 1916
Cozzens, A. B., Secretary City Plan Commission, Firemen's Bldg.,
Newark, N. J..1917
Craig, George W., City Engineer, City Hall, Calgary, Alberta, Canada..1911
Craver, H. H., Chief Chemist, Pittsburg Testing Laboratory, Pitts-
burg, Pa. 1914
Crayton, G. A., Civil Engineer, with U. S. Office of Public Roads, 205
Broadway-Yamhill Bldg., Portland, Ore....................................1912
Crosby, Walter W., *Consulting Highway Engineer, 1431 Munsey
Bldg., Baltimore, Md.*, Lieutenant Colonel, 104th Regiment, En-
gineers, N. A., Camp McClellan, Anniston, Ala. Address, Care
Chief of Engineers, U. S. A., Washington, D. C.............................1909
Crowley, J. W., Commissioner Public Works, City Hall, Daven-
port, Ia. 1917
Cummin, Gaylord C., City Manager, Grand Rapids, Mich..................1915
Curfman, Lawrence E., *City Engineer, Pittsburg, Kans.*, Major, U. S.
R., 314th Engineers, Camp Funston, Kans.....................................1910
Currie, C. H., Consulting Engineer, Webster City, Ia........................1917
Cutcheon, L. D., Secretary and General Manager, Board of Public
Works, Grand Rapids, Mich..1906

Dallyn, Frederick Alfred, Provincial Sanitary Engineer, Province of
Ontario, 137 Jeffrey St., Toronto, Ont., Canada.............................1916
Dalton, E. L., 9-10 Murphy Bldg., Dallas, Texas................................1906
Darby, C. A., City Engineer, Sabetha, Kans.......................................1915
Datesman, George E., Director, Department of Public Works, City
Hall, Municipal Delegate from Philadelphia, Pa............................1916
Davis, Carleton E., Chief, Bureau of Water, Municipal Delegate from
Philadelphia, Pa. 1915
Davis, Charles O., Superintendent Street Sanitation, Milwaukee, Wis...1917
Davis, D. B., City Engineer, Richmond, Ind.......................................1918
Dean, Arthur W., Chief Engineer, Massachusetts Highway Commis-
sion, 34 Oxford St., Winchester, Mass..1914
De Lay, Theodore S., City Engineer, Creston, Ia...............................1910
Devlin, F. E., City Engineer and County Surveyor, County Court
House, Newton, Kans...1915
Devlin, Harry, Superintendent Buildings, Park Department, 2445 Val-
entine Ave., Bronx, New York City..1917
Dingle, James H., City Engineer, City Hall, Charleston, S. C............1908
Dorr, Edgar S., Chief Engineer, Sewer Service, 213 Savin-Hill Ave.,
Dorchester, Boston, Mass...
Doughty, Joshua, Jr., Town and County Engineer, Somerville, N. J....1918

Douthitt, M. J., City Engineer, City Hall, Waukegan, Ill................1911
Dow, A. W., Consulting Engineer, 131 E. 23rd St., New York City....1906
Drinkwater, Ernest, Town Engineer, 23 Lafayette Blvd., Montreal
    South. Res., 588 Desaulniers Blvd., St. Lambert, Que................1918
Driscoll, Michael, Superintendent Streets and Sewers, Town Hall,
    Brookline, Mass. 1914
Drowne, Henry B., 35 Kimberly Ave., Springfield, Mass................1912
Dubuc, Jules Henri, Engineer of Bridges and Subways, City Hall,
    Montreal, Que., Canada................1916
Duchastel, J. A., City Engineer, Outremont, Que., Canada................1917
Duck, Allen Douglas, City Engineer, Greenville, Texas................1913
Duff, Edward E., Jr., Boro Engineer, Municipal Bldg., Sewickley, Pa...1916
Dunlap, Fred C., Chief, Bureau of Highways, City Hall, Municipal
    Delegate from Philadelphia, Pa................1918
Durham, Henry Welles, *Consulting Engineer, 366 Fifth Ave., New
    York City,* Major, 41st Engineers, N. A., American Expeditionary
    Forces, France................1915
Durkin, Patrick, Superintendent of Public Works, 12 Mallory St.,
    Danbury, Conn. 1917
Dutton, E. R., Municipal Delegate from Minneapolis, Minn................1914

Earl, George G., General Superintendent, Sewerage and Water Board,
    New Orleans, La................1906
Eddy, Harrison P., Consulting Civil Engineer, 14 Beacon St., Bos-
    ton, Mass. 1914
Edgerly, R. J., City Engineer, Albany, Ga................1908
Eichelberger, F. O., City Engineer, 915 Cottage Grove Avenue, Day-
    ton, Ohio 1915
Ellingson, O. J. S., City Manager, 828 W. Houston St., Sherman, Tex...1918
Ellsworth, Frank V. P., Assistant City Engineer, San Antonio, Texas..1908
Emerson, C. A., Jr., Chief Engineer Pennsylvania State Department
    of Health, Harrisburg, Pa................1917
Erwin, M. C., Sewer Engineer, City Hall, San Antonio, Tex................1908
Estler, Charles E., Chairman Road Committee, Boonton, N. J...........1917
Evers, Henry A., Councilman, 263 Pontiac Ave., Cranston, R. I.........1917
Evinger, M. I., Consulting Engineer, 211 Securities Bldg., Des Moines,
    Ia. 1918

Finch, B. K., City Engineer, Wilkes-Barre, Pa................1908
Firth, Joseph, Superintendent Public Works, Winston-Salem, N. C.....1908
Fisher, E. A., Consulting Engineer, City of Rochester, Rochester,
    N. Y. 1896
Fisher, E. A., City Engineer, Lakewood, Ohio................1917
Fisk, George F., Assistant Engineer in Charge of Pavement Construc-
    tion, Bureau of Engineering, Department of Public Works, 7
    Municipal Bldg., Buffalo, N. Y................1916
Fletcher, Austin B., State Highway Engineer, Forum Bldg., Sacra-
    mento, Calif. 1912
Flood, Walter H., Consulting Chemical Engineer, 3725 Langley Ave.,
    Chicago, Ill. 1916
Folwell, A. Prescott, Editor Municipal Journal, 243 W. 39th St., New
    York City 1901
Freitas, George H., City Engineer, Modesto, Calif................1913
Fugate, Harry C., City Engineer, West Palm Beach, Fla........ 1916
Fuller, George W., Consulting Engineer, 170 Broadway, New York
    City 1906
Fulton, D. F., City Engineer, 37 City Hall, Yonkers, N. Y................1914
Funk, Elmo A., City Engineer, City Hall, Anderson, Ind................1915

Gainey, W. H., City Engineer, Valdosta, Ga................1906
Gault, Matthew, Superintendent of Sewers, City Hall, Worcester,
    Mass. 1917

Gaynor, Keyes C., 405 Frances Bldg., Sioux City, Ia................................1911
Giddings, Fred, Consulting Engineer, 1104 Kirkman St., Lake Charles,
    La. 1896
Giles, John A., Commissioner of Public Works, City Hall, Bing-
    hamton, N. Y..1911
Gillen, Charles P., Municipal Delegate from Newark, N. J................1914
Gillespie, Richard H., Chief Engineer Sewers and Highways, 286 E.
    201st St., Bronx, New York City...1912
Gleason, Joseph A., Deputy Commissioner of Public Property in
    Charge of Public Works, Municipal Delegate from New Orleans..1918
Goff, Edward E., City Engineer, 17 Exchange St., Cranston, R. I........1917
Goldstein, Harry I., Highway Inspector, Bureau of Highways, 4200
    Woodland Ave., Philadelphia, Pa...1916
Gorham, E. L., City Engineer, Lake Charles, La................................1914
Gottschalk, L. F., Engineer for City and County, Columbus, Neb........
Gray, E. R., Acting City Engineer, City Hall, Hamilton, Ont., Canada..1916

Hackney, John W., Atlantic City, N. J..1908
Hadert, John A., Commissioner of Public Works, City Hall, New
    Rochelle, N. Y. 1918
Hall, Wm. H., City Engineer, New Britain, Conn..............................1917
Hallock, James C., Deputy Chief Engineer, City Hall, Newark, N. J.....1908
Halsey, Edmund R., 41 Delaware Ave., S. Orange, N. J......................1908
Hamley, S. J., District Manager, Pittsburgh Testing Laboratory, 242
    Rockefeller Bldg., Cleveland, O..1917
Hammond, George T., Engineer of Design, Bureau of Sewers, 1013-
    1014 Mechanics Bank Bldg., Brooklyn, New York....................1908
Hamnett, W. S., Manager Pittsburg Testing Laboratory, 305 Prae-
    torian Bldg., Dallas, Tex...1912
Hansell, William A., Jr., Superintendent Public Works, Fulton County,
    501 County Court House, Atlanta, Ga......................................1916
Hansen, Paul, *Chief Sanitary Engineer, State Board of Health,
    Springfield, Ill.,* Captain of Engineers, U. S. R. (detached), Gen-
    eral Headquarters, American Expeditionary Forces, France.........1913
Hardee, W. J., City Engineer, and Chief Engineer Public Belt R. R.,
    Municipal Delegate from New Orleans, La................................1914
Harris, Harry F., County Engineer, Mercer County, N. J., Trenton,
    N. J. 1910
Harris, R. C., Superintendent of Public Works, Municipal Delegate
    from Toronto, Ont., Canada...1914
Harrison, Edwin M., Director Department of Streets and Public Im-
    provements, 31 N. Mountain Ave., Montclair, N. J...................1917
Hatton, T. Chalkley, Sewer Commissioner, Milwaukee, Wis..............1903
Hawley, John B., *Hoxie Bldg., Fort Worth, Tex.,* Major, U. S. R.,
    503d Regiment of Engineers, Service Battalion, American Expedi-
    tionary Forces, France..1912
Hawley, John B., City Engineer, 614 Main St., Boonton, N. J............1917
Heebink, G. E., City Engineer, Goodwin Block, Beloit, Wis..............1914
Heilman, Herbert W., Assistant Essex County Engineer, Newark,
    N. J. 1917
Helland, Hans, City Engineer, 1109 McCullough Ave., San Antonio,
    Tex. 1917
Henderson, Charles Elliott, City Engineer, St. Augustine, Fla...........1916
Hennen, Robert David, Engineer for County Commissioners, Mor-
    gantown, W. Va..1913
Henry, P. W., 120 Broadway, New York City................................1906
Hering, Rudolph, Consulting Engineer, 170 Broadway, New York
    City 1910
Herrmann, August, Wiggins Block, Cincinnati, O............................1894
Hill, Curtis, City Engineer, Municipal Delegate from Kansas City, Mo...1914
Hill, Nicholas S., Jr., 100 William St., New York City......................1911

Hills, George B., Engineer Manager, Isham Randolph & Co., Consulting Engineers, 1310 Heard Bank Bldg., Jacksonville, Fla........1913

Hillyer, William R., Deputy Commissioner of Water Supply, Gas and Electricity for Boro of Richmond, Port Richmond, New York City 1908

Hittell, John B., Civil Engineer, 5917 Winthrop Ave., Chicago, Ill........1908

Hodgdon, J. B., City Engineer, Joplin, Mo....................................1915

Hodges, Gilbert, Main St. Station, Franklin, N. H.........................1913

Hoffman, Robert, Chief Engineer Department of Public Service, Cleveland, O. 1908

Hoopes, Edgar M., Jr., Chief Engineer, Municipal Delegate from Wilmington, Del. 1915

Hoover, Clarence B., Chemist in Charge, Division of Sewage Disposal, City Hall, Columbus, O..1917

Horner, W. W., Engineer of Design, Sewers and Paving, 325 City Hall, St. Louis, Mo...1915

Horton, Irving S., Engineer, Fisher & O'Rourke, 937 Washington St., Reading, Pa. 1916

Howard, J. W., Consulting Engineer, Roads and Pavements, 1 Broadway, New York City...1901

Howe, Will B., City Engineer, Concord, N. H...............................1895

Howell, Carl L., Municipal Delegate from Buffalo, N. Y....................1914

Howell, Robert P., Town Engineer, Phillipsburg, N. J.......................1908

Howell, William A., Engineer of Streets and Highways, City Hall, Municipal Delegate from Newark, N. J....................................1907

Hubbard, Prevost, Chemical Engineer, Chief, Division of Road Material, Tests and Research, U. S. Office of Public Roads and Rural Engineering, Willard Bldg., Washington, D. C.........................1913

Hudson, Leo, Consulting Hydraulic and Sanitary Engineer, 3265 Piedmont Ave., Dortmont, Pittsburg, Pa..1912

Hughes, Hector James, Prof. Civil Engineering, Harvard University and Massachusetts Institute of Technology, 1-337 M. I. T., Cambridge, Mass. 1914

Hull, Horace H., City Engineer, Municipal Delegate from Memphis, Tenn.

Hunter, Lionel McL., Roadway Engineer, City Engineer's Office, 20 Willard Ave., Ottawa, Ont., Canada...1916

Huston, R. C., Consulting Engineer, 1010 Falls Bldg., Memphis, Tenn...1915

Hutchinson, A. E., Albuquerque, N. M...1915

Iredell, George S., Civil Engineer, Austin, Tex...............................1908

Jennings, F. W., Village Engineer, Bexley, O., 509 Hartman Bldg., Columbus, O. 1915

Johnson, George A., Consulting Engineer, 150 Nassau St., New York City 1917

Jones, Richard A., Superintendent of Streets, 27 Banks St., Waltham, Mass. 1917

Judson, William Pierson, Consulting Engineer, President Broadalbin Electric Light and Power Co., Broadalbin, Fulton County, N. Y.....1902

Kappele, A. P., Secretary Works Department, City Hall, Hamilton, Ont., Canada 1917

Kemper, Joseph, City Engineer, Municipal Delegate from Utica, N. Y...1917

Kendrick, Julian, City Engineer, Birmingham, Ala..........................1898

Kennedy, W. E., Superintendent Streets and Sewers, 154 Benedict St., Waterbury, Conn. 1917

Kershaw, G. Bertram, Consulting Engineer, 9 Victoria St., Westminster, London, S. W., England..

Keyes, John M., Chairman Board of Road Commissioners, Chairman Board of Health, Concord, Mass..1914

Kindrick, A. H., City Engineer, McAlester, Okla..1914
Kingsley, Edgar A., *Consulting Engineer Roads and Pavements, 110 W. Dewey Place, San Antonio, Texas,* Major of Engineers, U. S. R., U. S. Army P. O., 708, American Expeditionary Forces, France 1908
Kirkpatrick, Walter G., Municipal and Hydraulic Engineer, 703-704 Farley Bldg., Birmingham, Ala..1912
Kirschbraun, Lester, Consulting Engineer, 160 N. Fifth Ave., Chicago, Ill. 1909
Kistler, Dr. J. M., Alderman, Waterworks Committee, Municipal Delegate from Minneapolis, Minn..1916
Kleeberg, Felix, Chemist, Dept. of Public Works, Manhattan Boro, Municipal Building, New York City..1915
Klyce, B. H., 505 4th & 1st National Bank Bldg., Nashville, Tenn........1913
Knapp, N. A., Superintendent Highways, 38 Washington Ave., Greenwich, Conn. 1917
Kneale, Robert D., Consulting Engineer to City, County and State Highway Commissioner, Georgia School of Technology, Atlanta, Ga. 1917
Koiner, C. W., General Manager and Electrical Engineer, Municipal Lighting Works, Municipal Delegate from Pasadena, Cal............1913
Kraus, Jaros, Architect, Park Department, Flushing, N. Y................1917

Laberge, F. C., Consulting Engineer, 30 James St., Montreal, Que., Canada 1915
Lafaye, Edward E., Commissioner of Public Property, Municipal Delegate from New Orleans, La..1917
Lawrence, E. A., City Engineer, Westerville, Ohio, 509 Hartman Bldg., Columbus, Ohio 1915
Lea, Lucian D., City Engineer, Lead, S. D..1912
Lee, B. M., City Engineer, Asheville, N. C..1908
Lee, W. Loring, City Engineer, Sumter, S. C......................................1916
Legare, T. Keith, City Engineer, Columbia, S. C................................1916
Lenderink, Andrew, City Engineer, Kalamazoo, Mich......................1912
Levinson, Henry, City Engineer, Little Rock, Ark............................1909
Lewis, Nelson P., Chief Engineer, Board of Estimate and Apportionment, Municipal Bldg., New York City..1895
Linsley, Charles W., *Commissioner of Works, 52 E. Utica St., Oswego, N. Y.,* Assistant Civil Engineer, U. S. N., R. F. (Lieutenant, Junior Grade), Public Works Office, Naval Operating Base, Hampton Roads, Va..1915
Little, John C., Chief Engineer, The Roland Park Co., Roland Park, Baltimore, Md. 1910
Lovewell, Maurice N., Assistant Engineer, South Park Commissioners, 57th St. and Cottage Grove Ave., Chicago........................1912
Luster, W. H., Elizabeth, N. J..1905

Macallum, Andrew F., Commissioner of Public Works, Ottawa, Ont., Canada 1909
MacDonald, George E., Chairman Overseers of the Poor, Gloucester, Mass. 1917
MacDonald, James H., Road and Pavement Expert, New Haven, Conn. 1914
MacGregor, R. A., Assistant Engineer, Bureau of Highways, Manhattan Boro, Municipal Bldg., New York City............................1915
Mackie, George D., City Engineer Commissioner, City Hall, Moose Jaw, Sask., Canada..1916
Maetzel, Henry, City Engineer, Columbus, Ohio................................1908
Magruder, J. O., City Engineer, Danville, Va....................................1911
Mahnken, Alfred J., Consulting Engineer, 52 Hudson Place, Weehawken, N. J..1917

Mangold, John F., Rapid City, S. D., Captain U. S. R. (unassigned)....1913
Marchant, Kilby I., Superintendent Streets, 947 Washington St., Glou-
cester, Mass. 1917
McArthur, Franklin, City Engineer, Guelph, Ont., Canada....................1916
McCabe, John C., Chief Inspector and Engineer, Department of Safety
Engineering, 410 City Hall, Detroit, Mich..1912
McCandless, Robert, Clerk, Street Department, 33 Chauncey Ave.,
New Rochelle, New York..1917
McCarthy, John, City Engineer, Wymore, Neb.......................................1915
McCarthy, John J., Acting Purchasing Agent, Department Parks, 1149
75th St., Brooklyn, N. Y..1917
McCarthy, P. A., Consulting Engineer and City Engineer, Lufkin,
Texas 1917
McClean, G. T., *City Engineer, Astoria, Ore.* Captain U. S. R., 29th
Engineers, American Expeditionary Forces, France..........................1914
McClelland, Richard J., City Engineer, Kingston, Ont., Canada..........1917
McComb, Dana Q., *Testing Engineer, Pittsburg Testing Laboratory,
Miami, Florida.* Captain, U. S. R., 3d Engineers, Ft. Mills, Cor-
regidor, Philippine Islands..1917
McCoubry, Thomas, President Board of Aldermen, 51 Lemuel Ave.,
Chicopee, Mass. 1917
McCrary, S. K., City Engineer, 1011 Laramie St., Atchison, Kans........1909
McCullough, Ernest, Major of Engineers, U. S. R., Gas Service,
Headquarters, American Expeditionary Forces, France......................
McKellip, F. W., City Engineer, Faribault, Minn.
McMahon, Patrick F., Highway Commissioner, Brockton, Mass........1917
McMath, Robert E., 512 Bombard Ave., Webster Grove, Mo................1894
McNeal, John, Consulting Engineer and Contractor, Northampton
National Bank Bldg., Easton, Pa..1911
Meade, R. E., City Engineer, Florence, Ala..1906
Meigs, Joseph V., Chemist, City of Boston, Massachusetts Institute
of Technology, Cambridge, Massachusetts..1917
Mercier, Paul E., Chief Engineer and City Surveyor, City Hall, Mon-
treal, Que., Canada..1915
Meriwether, B. B., Care Birmingham Realty Co., Birmingham, Ala.....1908
Metz, L. V., Contractor, Erie, Pa..1910
Miller, B. F., Jr., City Engineer, 902 Grove St., Meadville, Pa.............1910
Miller, Daniel J., Boro Engineer, Bangor, Pa...1916
Miner, Franklin M., Assistant Engineer, Street Laying Out Depart-
ment, 404 City Hall Annex, Boston, Mass..1913
Moore, John W., Consulting Engineer, 3342 N. Illinois St., Indian-
apolis, Ind. 1915
Moorehouse, William B., Justice Peace, Member Town Board, Tarry-
town, New York..1917
Morales, Luis, Chief Engineer Bureau Water Supply, Linea entre 6 y
8, Vedado, Havana, Cuba..1917
Morgan, L. T., City Engineer and Superintendent of Water Works,
Box 43, Live Oak, Fla..1916
Morgan, R. D, City Engineer, Temple, Tex...1915
Morrison, Roger L., Professor of Highway Engineering, A. & M.
College, College Station, Tex. Captain U. S. R. (honorably dis-
charged) 1914
Morse, Howard Scott, Detroit Bureau of Governmental Research,
100 Griswold St., Detroit, Mich..1915
Moseley, Hal, City Engineer, Dallas, Tex..1915
Mullen, Charles A., Director Paving Department, Milton Hersey Co.,
Montreal, Que., Canada..1911
Murphy, M. D., Street and Sewer Director, Belvedere Apartments,
Wilmington, Del. 1912
Murray, Charles W., City Engineer, Miami, Fla....................................1918
Myers, William G., City Engineer, Harrisonburg, Va.............................1916

Near, W. P., City Engineer, St. Catherine, Ont., Canada..................1915
Nicholson, Maury, Assistant City Engineer, City Hall, Birmingham, Ala. 1908
Nicholson, Victor, Engineering Chemist, City of Chicago, 1533 S. Ashland Ave., Chicago, Ill..................1914
Noble, O. E., City Engineer, Manhattan, Kans..................1908
Norton, George H., City Engineer, 7 Municipal Bldg., Municipal Delegate from Buffalo, N. Y..................1914

Ogden, Henry N., Professor of Sanitary Engineering, Cornell University, Ithaca, N. Y..................1909
Ogier, James W., Assistant Engineer, City Engineer's Office, Baltimore, Md. 1914
Olmsted, Frederick L., Landscape Architect, Brookline, Mass..................1909
Osgood, Manley, City Engineer, President, Washtenaw Engineering Co., Ann Arbor, Mich..................1914
Owen, James, 196 Market St., Newark. N. J..................1904

Parent, Arthur, Superintendent City Lighting Department, Montreal, Que., Canada 1905
Parker, E. E., City Engineer, Madison, Wis..................1917
Parker, George A., Superintendent of Parks, Hartford, Conn..................1902
Parlin, Raymond W., Deputy Commissioner, Main Office, Department of Street Cleaning, Municipal Bldg., New York City..................1916
Parmelee, Louis R., City Engineer, Helena, Ark..................1913
Parobek, Anastasius, City Chemist, Trenton, N. J..................1914
Payton, Lyle, City Engineer, Moline, Ill..................1912
Peck, Leon F., Superintendent of Streets, Municipal Bldg., Hartford, Conn. 1913
Phul, William von, 2998 Pacific Ave., San Francisco, Cal..................1911
Pickersgill, H. M., Superintendent Public Works, Elmira, N. Y..................1917
Pierce, Herbert W., Commissioner Public Works, 26 City Hall, Rochester, N. Y..................1914
Pierson, Frank W., Street Commissioner, Municipal Delegate from Wilmington, Del. 1915
Plunkette, J. L., City Engineer, Rome, N. Y..................1917
Pollard, Seabury Gould, Consulting Water Supply Engineer, 3422 Burch Ave., Cincinnati, O..................1915
Pollock, Clarence D., Consulting Engineer (Pollock and Taber), Park Row Bldg., New York City..................1902
Poole, C. Arthur, City Engineer, Rochester, N. Y..................1918
Potter, Alexander, Consulting Civil Engineer, 50 Church St., New York City 1913
Preston, J. M., Dallas, Tex..................1908
Primeau, A. K., City Engineer, Muskegon Heights, Mich..................1916
Provost, A. J., Jr., 39-41 West 38th St. (Lederle and Provost), New York City 1904
Prow, John C., City and County Engineer, Salem, Ind..................1909
Putnam, Charles E., Engineer, Boston Park and Recreation Department, 105 Hutchings St., Roxbury, Mass..................1916

Ramsey, J. E., Municipal Delegate from Salisbury, N. C..................1915
Rankin, E. S., Engineer of Sewers and Drainage, Municipal Delegate from Newark, N. J..................1903
Redfern, Ira T., Village Engineer, South Orange, N. J..................1916
Reimer, Frederic A., County Engineer, Essex County, Newark, N. J. Major 104th Engineers, Camp McClellan, Ala. (resigned)..................1909
Reppert, Charles M., Division Engineer, Bureau of Construction, Department of Public Works, 5912 Douglas Ave., Pittsburg, Pa..................1908
Reynolds, A. M., Chief Engineer, Essex County Park Commission, 60 Clifton Ave., Newark, N. J..................1908
Rice, John M., Secretary Morris Knowles, Inc., Pittsburg, Pa..................1918

Richards, H. S., Assistant Superintendent, South Park Commission, 6930 Constance Ave., Chicago, Ill............1909

Ridgway, Robert, Public Service Commission, 49 Lafayette St., New York City 1908

Roberts, H. N., Jr., City Engineer and Superintendent of Water Department, 204 S. Main St., Longview, Tex............1915

Rogers, Niart, City Engineer, Asbury Park, N. J............1909

Root, Joseph E., Assistant Engineer, Division of Sewerage, 3436 Lyleburn Pl., Cincinnati, O............1915

Rowland, H. A., City Engineer, McPherson, Kans............1917

Rudolph, Charles A., Street and Sewer Director, 411 Delaware Ave., Municipal Delegate from Wilmington, Del............1912

Russell, G. Raymond, City Engineer, 1624 Stimson Ave., Rosedale, Kansas 1915

Rust, Charles H., City Engineer, Victoria, B. C., Canada............1898

Ruttan, H. N., Brigadier General (retired), Consulting Engineer, 801-802 Confederation Life Bldg., Winnipeg, Man., Canada............1904

Sammelman, Sylverius, in charge Street Design Division, Department of the President, 5951 Julian Ave., St. Louis, Mo............1915

Sands, Edward E., City Engineer, City Hall, Houston, Tex............1914

Sargent, Geo. H., City Engineer, LaGrange, Ga............1918

Sargent, Welland F., Commissioner of Public Works, Municipal Bldg., Oak Park, Ill............1910

Sarver, William Edward, City Engineer, Canton, O............1915

Sawyer, Walter H., Hydraulic Engineer, 11 Lisbon St., Lewiston, Me.

Scattergood, E. F., Electrical Engineer, Department of Public Service, 1415 Berkshire St., R. F. D. 8, No. 331 A, Los Angeles, Cal.....1913

Schmidt, H. H., Chief Engineer, Bureau of Highways, Room 502, 50 Court St., Brooklyn, N. Y............1915

Schmieder, Charles, Assistant Architect, Department Parks, 401 W. 50th St., New York City............1917

Shaner, H. L., City Engineer, Municipal Delegate from Lynchburg, Va. 1908

Shea, James B., Deputy Commissioner of Park and Recreation Commission of Boston, P. O. Box 108, Jamaica Plain, Mass............1916

Sheaf, Fred W., President of Boro Council, Rutherford, N. J............1917

Shelton, William H., City Engineer, 617 Central Ave., Dunkirk, N. Y...1916

Sherrerd, Morris R., Chief Engineer, Department of Public Works, Municipal Delegate from Newark, N. J............1896

Shockley, P. S., City Engineer and County Surveyor, News Bldg., Salisbury, Md. 1911

Simmons, Fred G., Commissioner Public Works, Milwaukee, Wis............1917

Simons, F. F., Boro Engineer of Roosevelt, N. J., Carteret, N. J............1917

Slattery, John L., Secretary-Treasurer St. John's Municipal Council, Municipal Delegate from St. Johns, Newfoundland............1901

Sloman, Arthur L., City Manager, Albion, Mich............1917

Smith, A. P., Councilman, Boonton, N. J............1917

Smith, Fred E., Surveyor Highways, Rockport, Mass............1917

Smith, Francis P., Consulting Engineer, 131-133 East 23rd St., New York City 1908

Smith, J. J., Grand Forks, N. D............1913

Smoot, L. D., Chief Engineer, Jacksonville, Fla............1913

Snow, Hubert A., Chairman Highway Commission, 25 Rockland St., Brockton, Mass. 1917

Snyder, Frederick Antes, *Chief Engineer, Town of Mount Royal, 230 St. James St., Montreal, Que., Canada.* Colonel, 103d Engineers, Division Engineer of 28th Division, Camp Mills, L. I., N. Y............1914

Sohier, William D., Chairman, Massachusetts Highway Commission, 15 Ashburton Place, Boston, Mass............1914

Sparks, George W., President Street and Sewer Board, Municipal Delegate from Wilmington, Del............1912

Sprague, Norman S., Chief Engineer, Bureau of Engineering, D. P. W., 421 City-County Bldg., Municipal Delegate from Pittsburg, Pa. 1908
Stallings, Robert, *Morrilton, Ark.* Sergeant, Headquarters Co., 3d Anti-Aircraft Battalion, Fort Morgan, Ala....................................1912
Starks, W. Fred, County Superintendent Highways, Glen Cove, N. Y...1917
Steed, Robert E., City Clerk, P. O. Box 919, Municipal Delegate from Norfolk, Va. 1911
Stern, Eugene W., *Chief Engineer Highways of Manhattan, New York City.* Major of Engineers, U. S. R., Superintendent of Roads, Care of C. G. Base, Sec. 2, U. S. A. P. O. 705, American Expeditionary Forces, France...1916
Stevenson, John D., Assistant Engineer, Bureau of Engineering, 1231 Monterey St., Pittsburg, Pa...1912
Stevenson, W. L., *Assistant Engineer, Sewage Disposal, City Hall, Philadelphia, Pa.* Sanitary Engineer, Department of Health and Sanitation, U. S. Shipping Board, 140 N. Broad St., Philadelphia, Pa.; Res. 57 E. Penn St., Germantown, Philadelphia, Pa..................1918
Strachan, Joseph, 352 Putnam Ave., Brooklyn, N. Y............................1905
Struthers, David L., City Engineer, Wilmington, N. C..........................1915
Sullivan, James H., Division Engineer, Public Works Department, City Hall, Boston, Mass..1913
Sumner, Charles R., City Engineer, Hermosa Beach, Calif...................1916
Swan, Jr., Abram, Engineer Streets, Municipal Bldg., Trenton, N. J...1917
Sweetman, Emmett F., City Engineer, Urbana, Ohio............................1915
Sylvester, Elbert W., City Engineer and Superintendent Public Works, Poughkeepsie, N. Y...1913

Talbot, A. N., Professor of Municipal and Sanitary Engineering, University of Illinois, Urbana, Ill...1903
Talbott, H. M., City Engineer, Owensboro, Ky..1914
Taplin, Arthur E., Consulting Engineer, Box 423, High Point, N. C.....1917
Taylor, W. H., Jr., City Engineer, Municipal Delegate from Norfolk, Va. 1917
Thayer, Joel A., Superintendent Streets, 386 Tremont St., Taunton, Mass. 1917
Thier, J. Ernest, Supervisor Roads, Montvale, N. J...............................1917
Thomas, J. Fred, Boro Engineer, City Bldg., Farrell, Pa......................1912
Thompson, S. C., Principal Assistant Engineer, Bureau of Highways, Boro of Bronx, New York City...1904
Thum, William, 123 Columbia St., Pasadena, Calif.........................1912
Tillson, George W., Consulting Engineer to Boro President, Boro Hall, Brooklyn, N. Y., 313 S. Catherine Ave., LaGrange, Ill........1896
Tribus, L. L., 15 Park Row, New York City...1908
Truss, J. D., Commissioner Public Improvements, City Hall, Birmingham, Ala. 1917
Turner, J. W., City Engineer, Lakeland, Fla...1917
Tuska, Gustave R., Consulting Engineer, 68 William St., New York City, Major of Engineers, U. S. R..1915

Uhler, Wm. D., *Chief Engineer, State Highway Department, Harrisburg, Pa.* Lieutenant-Colonel, Q. M. C., N. A., Office of Quartermaster General, U. S. A., Washington, D. C............................1914
Ulrich, Edmund B., City Engineer, Reading, Pa....................................1914
Upington, Sam F., Clerk Street Department, 182 Main St., New Rochelle, N. Y...1917

Vandewater, J. A., 7 Municipal Bldg., Municipal Delegate from Buffalo, N. Y..1914
Van Trump, Isaac, Consulting Asphalt Engineer, 2337 S. Paulina St., Chicago, Ill. 1911
Van Zuben, Frank J., City Engineer, Fort Worth, Tex........................1912
Varney, Henry A., Town Engineer, 15 Town Hall, Brookline, Mass...1916

Vars, Alexander, Town Engineer of Westfield, N. J., 814 Webster Pl.,
Plainfield, N. J..1916
Vosler, Ray, 1044 Mercer St., Youngstown, Ohio...............................1913

Waite, H. M., *City Manager, Dayton, Ohio.* Lieutenant-Colonel, Sig-
nal Corps, American Expeditionary Forces, France..........................1912
Ward, Kenneth B., Chief Engineer, Durham, N. C...........................1918
Warman, H. S., Superintendent Weights and Measures, Boonton,
N. J. 1913
Wasser, Thomas J., County Engineer, Court House, Jersey City,
N. J. 1913
Waterman, F. V., Town Engineer, East Providence, R. I...................1917
Watson, Robert M., Boro Engineer, Rutherford, N. J.......................1908
Weaver, H. J., City Engineer, Municipal Delegate from Elkhart, Ind...1918
Weber, B. B., City Engineer, City Bldg., Oil City, Pa......................1917
Weirbach, Charles D., City Engineer, 702 N. 6th St., Allentown, Pa....1916
Weller, W. Earl, City Engineer, 16 Davis St., Binghamton, N. Y......1916
Wentworth, Russell A., Acting City Engineer, Batavia, N. Y.............1918
Weston, Robert Spurr, Consulting Sanitary Engineer, 14 Beacon St.,
Boston, Mass. 1914
Wheeler, Holland, City Engineer, Lawrence, Kans...........................1905
White, Henry H., City Engineer, Muskogee, Okla............................1917
White, Linn, Chief Engineer, South Park Commissioners, Chicago,
Ill. 1908
Willigerod, William D., City Engineer, City Hall, East Orange, N. J...1913
Wilson, James, County Commissioner and State Highway Commis-
sioner, Court House, Wilmington, Del..1913
Wingfield, Nisbet, City Engineer and Commissioner Public Works,
Augusta, Ga. 1906
Wise, B. A., City Engineer, Bradford, Pa...1916
Wise, Colin R., City Engineer, 301 Gregory Ave., Passaic, N. J........1915
Withrow, Edgar P., Engineer in charge of Municipal Testing Labora-
tory, St. Louis, Mo...
Wolfinger, Wellington R., Assistant Engineer State Highway De-
partment, Allentown Trust Bldg., Allentown, Pa..........................
Woodworth, C. A., County Engineer, Ida Grove, Ia.........................1916
Wooley, W. Thomas, Schnectady, N. Y...1915
Wulff, Edward J., Consulting and Constructing Engineer, National
Bank Bldg., Tarrytown, N. Y..1917

Young, Alexander R., 3636 Virginia Ave., Kansas City, Mo..............1911

AFFILIATED

Adam, Carl F., Room 407, 130 S. Broadway, Los Angeles, Calif..........1914
Ballinger, Walter F., Ballinger and Perrot, Architects and Engineers,
17th and Arch Sts., Philadelphia, Pa..
Campbell, John, Superintendent Special Service Department, The
Edison Electric Illuminating Company, 39 Boylston St., Boston,
Mass. 1913
French, R. DeL., Arthur Surveyor & Co., 279 Beaver Hall Hill. Lec-
turer in Civil Engineering, McGill University, Montreal, Que.,
Canada 1915
Gould, J. W. DuB., 30 Church St., New York City...........................1913
Kopf, C. J., Boonton, N. J..1917
Lloyd, Alfred O., Secretary Chamber of Commerce, Chester, S. C......1916
Lothrop, G. W., Woonsocket, R. I..1913
Masury, Alfred F., Chief Engineer, International Motor Company,
64th St. and West End Ave., New York City.................................1917
Routh, James W., Chief Engineer, Rochester Bureau of Municipal
Research, 25 E. Main St., Rochester, N. Y....................................1916

Sawin, George A., Electrical Engineer, Public Service Electric Company, 759 Broad St., Newark, N. J...1914

Shakman, James G., Consulting Engineer, with Walter H. Flood, 5013 Grand Blvd., Chicago, Ill...1916

Sheridan, L. V., *Landscape Architect, 409 S. Clay St., Frankfort, Ind.*, Co. F, 306th Ammunition Train, Camp Jackson, Columbia, S. C. 1915

Teesdale, Clyde H., in Charge of Wood Preservation, Forest Products Laboratory, Madison, Wis...1914

Von Schrenk, Hermann, Consulting Engineer, Tower Grove and Flad Aves., St. Louis, Mo...1914

Webster, Edwin R., Consulting Municipal Engineer, Webster Bldg., Chicago, Ill. 1916

Municipal Members

BALTIMORE, MD.
R. M. Cooksey

BINGHAMTON, N. Y.
John A. Giles

BOSTON, MASS.
Joshua Atwood
E. S. Dorr
F. M. Miner
J. H. Sullivan

BRIDGEPORT, CONN.

BUFFALO, N. Y.
C. E. P. Babcock
G. F. Fisk
C. L. Howell
J. A. Vandewater

COLUMBUS, O.
Thos. H. Brannan
Henry Maetzel

DANVILLE, VA.
J. O. Magruder

ELIZABETH, N. J.
Thos. E. Collins

ELKHART, IND.
H. J. Weaver

EVANSTON, ILL.
Irving C. Brower

EVERETT, WASH.
D. J. F. Calkins

FARIBAULT, MINN.
F. W. McKellip

HARRISBURG, PA.
M. B. Cowden

KANSAS CITY, MO.
Curtis Hill

LOUISVILLE, KY.
John Chambers

LYNCHBURG, VA.
H. L. Shaner

MEMPHIS, TENN.
H. H. Hull

MINNEAPOLIS, MINN.
Albert Bastis
F. W. Cappelen
C. R. Dutton
J. M. Kistler

MONTREAL, QUE.
LIGHTING DEPT.
A. Parent

NEWARK, N. J.
C. P. Gillen
J. C. Hallock
W. A. Howell
E. S. Rankin
M. R. Sherrerd

NEW ORLEANS, LA.
J. A. Gleason
W. J. Hardee
E. E. Lafaye

NORFOLK, VA.
R. E. Steed
W. H. Taylor, Jr.

OMAHA, NEB.
Credit $15.

ONTARIO, PROVINCE OF
F. A. Dallyn

PASADENA, CALIF.
LIGHTING DEPT.
C W. Koiner

PASCO, WASH.
Credit, $15.00

PAWTUCKET, R. I.
Geo. A. Carpenter

PHILADELPHIA, PA.
C. E. Albright
G. E. Datesman
C. E. Davis
F. C. Dunlap

POUGHKEEPSIE, N. Y.
E. W. Sylvester

READING, PA.
E. B. Ulrich

RUTHERFORD, N. J.
   Fred W. Sheaf
ST. JOHNS, N. F.
   J. L. Slattery
SALISBURY, N. C.
   J. E. Ramsey
SHERMAN, TEX.
   O. J. S. Ellingson
TORONTO, ONT.
   R. C. Harris

TROY, O.
   Frank Burkholder
UTICA, N. Y.
   Jos. Kemper
WILKES-BARRE, PA.
   B. K. Finch
WILMINGTON, DEL.
   Edgar M. Hoopes
   F. W. Pierson
   C. A. Rudolph
   G. W. Sparks

ASSOCIATE

AMERICAN CAR SPRINKLER COMPANY, Worcester, Mass.........1917
   E. D. Perry, Assistant General Superintendent, Box 414, Worcester, Mass

AMERICAN CITY, THE, 93 Nassau St., New York City.................1913
   Harold S. Buttenheim, Editor, 93 Nassau St., New York City.

AMERICAN TAR CO., THE, 201 Devonshire St., Boston, Mass.........1914
   Charles P. Price, Manager, 201 Devonshire St., Boston, Mass.

ASPHALT AND SUPPLY COMPANY, Ltd., 103-7 Board of Trade
   Bldg., Montreal, Que., Canada..1917
   W. Alfred Morris, Engineer, Montreal, Que., Canada.

ATLAS COMPANY, THE, Lincoln, N. J.................................1915
   W. W. Dixon, Lincoln, N. J.

ATLAS PORTLAND CEMENT COMPANY, THE, 30 Broad St.,
   New York City...1914
   Wilbur T. Challar, Manager Road Department, 30 Broad St., New
   York City.

BAKER, JOHN, JR., 17 Battery Place, New York City.....................1911
   John Baker, Jr., 540 Otis Bldg., 10 S. LaSalle St., Chicago, Ill.
   J. J. Gartland, Jr., Manager Richmond Office, 1126 Mutual Assurance Society's Bldg., Richmond, Va.
   William Howe, Manager of Middle West Division, Otis Bldg.,
   Chicago, Ill.
   Dennis A. Kennedy, Manager New England Division, 701 Tremont Bldg., Boston, Mass.
   Wm. H. Kershaw, Manager Eastern Division, 17 Battery Place,
   New York City.
   T. H. Reed, Manager Southern Division, 1802 American Trust
   and Savings Bldg., Birmingham, Ala.
   James T. Ware, Manager Western Division, 212 Dwight Bldg.,
   Kansas City, Mo.
Baker, John, Jr., Rep., John Baker, Jr., 10 S. LaSalle St., Chicago, Ill.
Baker, W. D., Rep., Warner-Quinlan Asphalt Co., 79 Wall St., New
   York City.

BARBER ASPHALT PAVING COMPANY, THE, Land Title
   Bldg., Philadelphia, Pa..1913
   Charles W. Bayliss, Philadelphia, Pa.
   C. N. Forrest, New York Testing Laboratory, Maurer, N. J.
   J. S. Miller, Maurer, N. J.
   D. T. Pierce, Philadelphia, Pa.
   Clifford Richardson, 233 Broadway, New York City.
Barbour, J. G., Secretary, Metropolitan Paving Brick Co., Canton, O.

BARRETT CO., THE, 17 Battery Place, New York City.......................1906
    S. R. Church, 17 Battery Place, New York City.
    John A. Hull, Mgr. Warren Chem. & Mfg. Div., 17 Battery Place,
    New York.
    Philip P. Sharples, 17 Battery Place, New York City.
    B. M. Smith, Otis Bldg., Chicago, Ill.
Bartram, G. C., Rep. Lock Joint Pipe Co., East Orange, N. J.
Bayliss, Charles W., Rep., Barber Asphalt Paving Co., Land Title
    Bldg., Philadelphia, Pa.
Blackburn, W. T., Consulting Engineer, Dunn Wire-Cut-Lug Brick
    Co., Paris, Ill.
BLACKMER & POST PIPE CO., Boatmens Bank Bldg., St. Louis,
    Mo. 1912
    C. H. Miller, St. Louis, Mo.
Blair, Will P., Secretary, National Paving Brick Manufacturers Asso-
    ciation, 828-834 Brotherhood of Locomotive Engineers Bldg.,
    Cleveland, O.
BOOTH BROTHERS & HURRICANE ISLE GRANITE COM-
    PANY, 208 Broadway, New York City..1917
    Charles Mitchell, Treasurer, New York City.
Bramley, M. F., Rep., Cleveland Trinidad Paving Co., 886 The Arcade,
    Cleveland, O.
Budge, Guy G., Rep., Warren Bros. Co., Grand Forks, N. D.
Buttenheim, Harold S., Editor, The American City, 93 Nassau St.,
    New York City.

Challar, Wilbur T., Manager Road Department, Atlas Portland Ce-
    ment Co., 30 Broad St., New York City.
Cherrington, Frank W., Chief Engineer, Jennison-Wright Co., 2833
    Scottwood Ave., Toledo, O.
Church, S. R., Rep., The Barrett Co., 17 Battery Place, New York
    City.
CLAY PRODUCTS ASSOCIATION, 913 Chamber of Commerce,
    Chicago, Ill.
    G. H. Tefft, Secretary and General Manager, 913 Chamber of
    Commerce, Chicago, Ill.
CLEVELAND TRINIDAD PAVING COMPANY, 886 The Arcade,
    Cleveland, O. 1915
    M. F. Bramley, President, 886 The Arcade, Cleveland, O.
Collins, George R., Secretary and Treasurer, Harris Granite Quarries
    Co., Salisbury, N. C.
Cutter, Frank G., Assistant to the President, Warren Bros. Co., 1424
    Otis Bldg., Chicago, Ill.

Dixon, W. W., Rep., The Atlas Company, Lincoln, N. J.
D'Olier, William L., Chief Engineer, The Sanitation Corporation,
    1533 Girard Ave., Philadelphia, Pa.; Rep., Gillespie Manufactur-
    ing Corporation, Jersey City, N. J.
Draney, J. R., Sales Manager, U. S. Asphalt Refining Co., 90 West
    St., New York City.
Dunn, Frank B., President, Dunn Wire-Cut Lug Brick Co., Con-
    neaut, O.
DUNN WIRE-CUT LUG BRICK CO., Conneaut, O...............................1911
    W. T. Blackburn, Consulting Engineer, Paris, Ill.
    Frank B. Dunn, President, Conneaut, O.
    W. C. Perkins, Chief Engineer, Conneaut, O.
    F. T. Townsend, Assistant Engineer, 789 Main St., Conneaut, O.
    J. C. Travilla, Consulting Engineer, Mercantile National Bank
    Bldg., St. Louis, Mo.

DUSTOLINE FOR ROADS COMPANY, Summit, N. J.................1917
    Edwin R. Lamson, President, Summit, N. J.
Duty, Spencer M., President, Medal Paving Brick Co., Swetland
    Bldg., Cleveland, Ohio.

Farey, F. O., Rep., Robert W. Hunt & Co., Ltd., McGill Bldg., McGill
    St., Montreal, Que.
Farr, Leslie B., President, Harlem Contracting Co., 2 Rector St.,
    New York City.
Fay, Frank T., Road Oil Department, Sales Agent, Standard Oil Co.
    of New York, 50 Congress St., Boston, Mass.
FERRY & SONS, JAMES, INC., Atlantic City, N. J.................1917
    James V. Ferry, Treasurer, Atlantic City, N. J.
Ferry, James V., Treasurer, James Ferry & Sons, Inc., Atlantic
    City, N. J.
Fisher, Henry, Manager Standard Oil Co. of New York, 26 Broad-
    way, New York City.
Fletcher, Herbert E., President Hildreth Granite Co., West Chelms-
    ford, Mass.
Forrest, C. N., Rep., Barber Asphalt Paving Co., New York Testing
    Laboratory, Maurer, N. J.
Fulweiler, W. H., Chemist, The United Gas Improvement Co. Labora-
    tory, 1706 Broad St., Philadelphia, Pa.

Gartland, J. J., Jr., Manager Richmond Office, John Baker, Jr., 1126
    Mutual Assurance Society's Bldg., Richmond, Va.
GILLESPIE MANUFACTURING CORPORATION, Jersey City,
    N. J. 1914
    William L. D'Olier, Rep., 1533 Girard Ave., Philadelphia, Pa.;
    Chief Engineer, Sanitation Corporation, 50 Church St., New
    York.
Gillum, H. J., Rep., Pierce Oil Corporation, 628 Stock Exchange Bldg.,
    Chicago, Ill.
Granger, B. F., Sales Manager, Lock Joint Pipe Co., Jackson, Mich.
Gray, E. D., Rep., Imperial Oil Co., Ltd., Toronto, Ont., Canada.
GRANITE PAVING BLOCK MANUFACTURERS ASSOCIA-
    TION OF THE U. S., 31 State St., Boston, Mass.................1915
    Walter L. Weeden, Secretary, 31 State St., Boston, Mass.
Greenough, Maurice B., Engineer, National Paving Brick Manufac-
    turers' Association, 830 B. L. E. Bldg., Cleveland, O.................1915

HARLEM CONTRACTING CO., 2 Rector St., New York City........1908
    Leslie B. Farr, President, 2 Rector St., New York City.
HARRIS GRANITE QUARRIES CO., Salisbury, N. C.................1915
    George R. Collins, Secretary-Treasurer, Salisbury, N. C.
Head, James M., Attorney-at-Law, Rep., Warren Brothers Co., Bos-
    ton, Mass.
Helm, J. S., Rep., Standard Oil Company of Louisiana, New Orleans,
    La.
Hess, Lawrence E., *Rep., Republic Creosoting Co., Indianapolis, Ind.*
    Captain, 309th Engineers, Camp Taylor, Louisville, Ky.
HILDRETH GRANITE CO., 31 State St., Boston, Mass.................1914
    H. V. Hildreth, General Manager, 31 State St., Boston, Mass.
    Herbert E. Fletcher, President, West Chelmsford, Mass.
Hildreth, H. V., General Manager, Hildreth Granite Co., 31 State
    St., Boston, Mass.
Hirsch, Allan M., Treasurer, Lock Joint Pipe Co., Montclair, N. J.
Hogue, W. A., Rep., Warren Bros. Co., Charleston, W. Va.
Horn, J. Merrick, Rep., Warren Bros. Co., Ford Bldg., Wilmington,
    Del.

Howe, William, Rep. John Baker, Jr., Manager Middle West Division, Otis Bldg., Chicago, Ill.

Hull, John A., Rep., Warren Chemical and Manufacturing Division of The Barrett Company, 17 Battery Place, New York City.

HUNT, ROBERT W. & CO., 2200 Insurance Exchange Bldg., Chicago, Ill. 1913
H. H. Morgan, Manager Physical Testing Laboratories, 2200 Insurance Exchange Bldg., Chicago, Ill.
F. O. Farey, McGill Bldg., Montreal, Que., Canada.

IMPERIAL OIL COMPANY, Ltd., Toronto, Ont., Canada....................1917
E. D. Gray, Toronto, Ont. Canada.

Ingram, G. M., Vice-President, Warren Bros. Co., 606 Independent Life Bldg., Nashville, Tenn.

Jennison, H. G., President, Jennison-Wright Co., 313-315 Huron St., Toledo, O.

JENNISON-WRIGHT CO., 313-315 Huron St., Toledo, O..................1914
H. G. Jennison, President, 313-315 Huron St., Toledo, O.
Frank W. Cherrington, Chief Engineer, 2833 Scottwood Ave., Toledo, O.

Johnson, Alfred H., President, Texas Bitulithic Co., Praetorian Bldg., Dallas, Tex.

Kaull, Pardon S., Rep., Warren Bros. Co., Railway Exchange Bldg., St. Louis, Mo.

Kennedy, Dennis A., Manager New England Division, John Baker, Jr., 713-716 Tremont Bldg., Boston, Mass.

Kershaw, William H., Manager Eastern Division, John Baker, Jr., 17 Battery Place, New York City.

Kinney, William M., Inspecting Engineer, Universal Portland Cement Co., 208 S. LaSalle St., Chicago, Ill.

Lamson, Edwin R., President Dustoline for Roads Co., Summit, N. J.

LAMSON, GEORGE W., Railway Exchange Bldg., Chicago, Ill.......1911

Larkin, A. E., Rep., Republic Creosoting Co., 828 Plymouth Bldg., Minneapolis, Minn.

LEOPOLD, J. & CO., 233 Broadway, New York City..............................1915
J. L. Leopold, 233 Broadway, New York City.

Leopold, J. L., Rep., J. Leopold & Co., 233 Broadway, New York City.

Lewis, F. J., President, F. J. Lewis Manufacturing Co., 2500 S. Robey St., Chicago, Ill.

LEWIS MANUFACTURING CO., F. J., 2500 S. Robey St., Chicago, Ill. 1913
F. J. Lewis, President, 2500 S. Robey St., Chicago, Ill.

Lippincott, J. H., Rep., Warren Bros. Co., 742 Parker St., Newark, N. J.

LOCK JOINT PIPE CO., 165 Broadway, New York City..................1908
G. C. Bartram, East Orange, N. J.
B. F. Granger, Sales Manager, Jackson, Mich.
Allan M. Hirsch, Treasurer, Montclair, N. J.

Lydecker, Kenneth, Rep., Standard Oil Co. of New Jersey, Room 900, 26 Broadway, New York City.

Manning, F. L., Sales Manager, Peebles Paving Brick Co., Portsmouth, O.

McGRATH, GEORGE B., General Manager, The Southern Purchasing Co., 1025 James Bldg., Chattanooga, Tenn................................1909

McNEIL, DONALD, COMPANY, Jenkins Arcade Bldg., Pittsburg, Pa. 1915
Donald McNeil, Jenkins Arcade Bldg., Pittsburg, Pa.
McNeil, Donald, Rep., Donald McNeil Co., Jenkins Arcade Bldg., Pittsburgh, Pa.
MEDAL PAVING BRICK COMPANY, Swetland Bldg., Cleveland, Ohio 1911
Spencer M. Duty, President, Swetland Bldg., Cleveland, O.
METROPOLITAN PAVING BRICK COMPANY, THE, Canton, Ohio 1911
J. G. Barbour, Secretary, Canton, O.
Miller, C. H., Rep., Blackmer & Post Pipe Co., Boatmens Bank Bldg., St. Louis, Mo.
Miller, J. S., Rep., Barber Asphalt Paving Co., Maurer, N. J.
Mitchell, Charles, Treasurer, Booth Bros. & Hurricane Isle Granite Co., 208 Broadway, New York City.
Morgan, H. H., Manager Physical Testing Laboratories, Robert W. Hunt & Co., 2200 Insurance Exchange, Chicago, Ill.
Morris, W. Alfred, Engineer, Asphalt and Supply Co., Board of Trade Bldg., Montreal, Quebec, Canada.

NATIONAL PAVING BRICK MANUFACTURERS ASSOCIA-TION, 828-834 Brotherhood of Locomotive Engineers' Bldg., Cleveland, O. 1907
Will P. Blair, Secretary, 828-834 Brotherhood of Locomotive Engineers' Bldg., Cleveland, O.
Maurice B. Greenough, Engineer, 830 B. L. E. Bldg., Cleveland, O.

PACIFIC FLUSH TANK COMPANY, 4241 Ravenswood Ave., Chicago, Ill. 1915
E. L. Walcott, 4241 Ravenswood Ave., Chicago, Ill.
Park, Ernest S., Vice-President, Rodd Co., 1402 Commonwealth Bldg., Bldg., Pittsburg, Pa.
PARMLEY, WALTER C., Everett Bldg., Union Square, New York
PEEBLES PAVING BRICK COMPANY, Portsmouth, O..............1912
F. L. Manning, Sales Manager, Portsmouth, O.
Perkins, G. Howard, Superintendent of Refineries, Warren Bros. Co., Boston, Mass.
Perkins, W. C., Chief Engineer, Dunn Wire-Cut-Lug Brick Co., Conneaut, O.
Perry, E. D., Assistant General Superintendent, American Car Sprinkler Co., Box 414, Worcester, Mass.
Pierce, D. T., Executive Assistant, Rep., Barber Asphalt Paving Co., Land Title Bldg., Philadelphia, Pa.
PIERCE OIL CORPORATION, 420 Olive St., St. Louis, Mo............1914
H. J. Gillum, 628 Stock Exchange Bldg., Chicago, Ill.
PIONEER ASPHALT CO., Lawrenceville, Ill............1915
H. B. Pullar, President, Lawrenceville, Ill.
PITTSBURG FILTER MANUFACTURING COMPANY, Farmers' Bank Bldg., Pittsburg, Pa............1905
Price, Charles P., Manager, The American Tar Co., 201 Devonshire St., P. O. Box 2705, Boston, Mass.
Pullar, H. B., President, Pioneer Asphalt Co., Lawrenceville, Ill.......1916

Reed, Alexander, Rep., United States Wood Preserving Co., 165 Broadway, New York City 1908
Reed, T. H., Manager Southern Division, John Baker, Jr., 1802 American Trust and Savings Bank Bldg., Birmingham, Ala.
Reilly, P. C., President, Republic Creosoting Co., Merchants Bank Bldg., Indianapolis, Ind.

REINFORCED CONCRETE PIPE CO., CHICAGO, ILL...................1916
William O. Tracy, Chicago Club, Chicago, Ill.
REPUBLIC CREOSOTING COMPANY, Merchants Bank Bldg.,
Indianapolis, Ind. 1907
P. C. Reilly, President, Merchants Bank Bldg., Indianapolis, Ind.
A. E. Larkin, 828 Plymouth Bldg., Minneapolis, Minn.
Rice, John L., Rep., Sewer Pipe Manufacturers' Association, Akron,
Ohio.
Richardson, Clifford, Rep., Barber Asphalt Paving Co., 233 Broad-
way, New York City.
Richardson, Jeffers F., *Sales Manager, Buffalo Steam Roller Co., Box
990, Buffalo, N. Y.* Captain Ordnance Corps, Camp Lee, Peters-
burg, Va.
Robinson, E. M., Rep., Warren Bros. Co., 606 Independent Life Bldg.,
Nashville, Tenn.
ROCKPORT GRANITE COMPANY, Rockport, Mass.......................1915
C. Harry Rogers, Rockport, Mass.
RODD COMPANY, THE, 1402 Commonwealth Bldg., Pittsburg, Pa...1916
Ernest S. Park, Vice-President, 1402 Commonwealth Bldg., Pitts-
burg, Pa.
Rogers, C. Harry, Rep., Rockport Granite Co., Rockport, Mass.

SAINT MARYS SEWER PIPE COMPANY, St. Marys, Pa..........1910
Sanitation Corporation. See Gillespie Manufacturing Corporation.
Schutte, August E., Consulting Chemist, Warren Bros. Co., 142
Berkeley St., Boston, Mass.
SEWER PIPE MANUFACTURERS' ASSOCIATION, Akron, O...1917
John L. Rice, Rep., Akron, O.
Sharples, Philip P., Rep., The Barrett Co., 17 Battery Place, New
York City.
Sibley, John W., Secretary-Treasurer, Southern Paving Brick Manu-
facturers' Association, Brown-Marx Bldg., Birmingham, Ala
Smith, B. M., Rep., The Barrett Co., Otis Bldg., Chicago, Ill.
SOUTHERN PAVING BRICK MANUFACTURERS' ASSOCIA-
TION, Brown-Marx Bldg., Birmingham, Ala.................................1915
John W. Sibley, Secretary-Treasurer, Brown-Marx Bldg., Bir-
mingham, Ala.
Spencer, Herbert, *Engineer, Standard Oil Co. of New Jersey, 26
Broadway, New York City.* Captain U. S. R., Co. H, 23d En-
gineers, American Expeditionary Forces, France.
STANDARD ASPHALT AND REFINING COMPANY, 208 S.
LaSalle St., Chicago, Ill...1908
STANDARD OIL COMPANY OF LOUISIANA, New Orleans, La...1915
J. S. Helm, New Orleans, La.
STANDARD OIL COMPANY OF NEW JERSEY, Room 900, 26
Broadway, New York City...1913
Kenneth Lydecker, Room 900, 26 Broadway, New York City.
STANDARD OIL COMPANY OF NEW YORK, Room 1300, 26
Broadway, New York City.......:...1913
Frank T. Fay, Sales Agent, Road Oil Dept., 50 Congress St.,
Boston, Mass.
Henry Fisher, Manager, 26 Broadway, New York City.
STEVENS, GEORGE M., Salesman, 6 Beacon St., Boston, Mass.........1914

Tefft, G. H., Secretary and General Manager, Clay Products Association, 913 Chamber of Commerce Bldg., Chicago, Ill.
Tenny, George O., President, Atlantic Bitulithic Co., Virginia Railway and Power Bldg., Richmond, Va.

TEXAS BITULITHIC COMPANY, Praetorian Bldg., Dallas, Tex...1908
    Alfred H. Johnson, President, Praetorian Bldg., Dallas, Tex.
Thurston, George W., Secretary, The Western Paving Brick Manu-
    facturers' Association, 416 Dwight Bldg., Kansas City, Mo.
Townsend, F. T., Assistant Engineer, Dunn Wire-Cut Lug Brick Co.,
    789 Main St., Conneaut, O.
Tracy, William O., Reinforced Concrete Pipe Co., Chicago Club,
    Chicago, Ill.
Travilla, J. C., Consulting Engineer, Dunn Wire-Cut Lug Brick Co.,
    Mercantile National Bank Bldg., St. Louis, Mo.
Turner, R. W., Vice-President, Warren Bros. Co., 50 Church St.,
    New York City.

UNITED GAS IMPROVEMENT COMPANY, THE, 1706 N.
    Broad St., Philadelphia, Pa.......................................1913
    W. H. Fulweiler, Chemist, 1706 N. Broad St., Philadelphia, Pa.
UNITED STATES ASPHALT REFINING COMPANY, THE, 90
    West St., New York City.......................................1913
    J. R. Draney, Sales Manager, 90 West St., New York City.
    J. R. Valk, 1811 Harris Trust Bldg., Chicago, Ill.
UNITED STATES WOOD PRESERVING COMPANY, THE, 165
    Broadway, New York City.......................................1901
    Alexander Reed, 165 Broadway, New York City.
UNIVERSAL PORTLAND CEMENT COMPANY, 208 S. LaSalle
    St., Chicago, Ill.......................................1913
    William M. Kinney, Inspecting Engineer, 208 S. LaSalle St., Chi-
    cago, Ill.

Valk, James R., Rep., U. S. Asphalt Renfining Co., 1402 Harris Trust
    Bldg., Chicago, Ill.
Van Winkle, W. H., Jr., Rep., Water Works Equipment Co., 50
    Church St., New York City.

Walcott, E. L., Rep., Pacific Flush Tank Co., 4241 Ravenswood Ave.,
    Chicago, Ill.
Ware, James T., Manager Western Division John Baker, Jr., 212
    Dwight Bldg., Kansas City, Mo.
WARNER-QUINLAN ASPHALT COMPANY, 79 Wall St., New
    York City 1913
    W. D. Baker, 79 Wall St., New York City.
WARREN BROTHERS COMPANY, 142 Berkeley St., Boston,
    Mass. 1905
    Guy G. Budge, Grand Forks, N. D.
    Frank G. Cutter, 1424 Otis Bldg., Chicago, Ill.
    James M. Head, Attorney, 142 Berkeley St., Boston, Mass.
    W. A. Hogue, Charleston, W. Va.
    J. Merrick Horn, Ford Bldg., Wilmington, Del.
    G. M. Ingram, Nashville, Tenn.
    Pardon S. Kaull, Railway Exchange Bldg., St. Louis, Mo.
    J. H. Lippincott, Newark, N. J.
    G. Howard Perkins, Superintendent of Refineries, 142 Berkeley
    St., Boston, Mass.
    E. M. Robinson, Nashville, Tenn.
    August E. Schutte, Consulting Chemist, 142 Berkeley St., Boston,
    Mass.
    George O. Tenny, Richmond, Va.
    R. W. Turner, 50 Church St., New York City.
    George C. Warren, President, 142 Berkeley St., Boston, Mass.
    Ralph L. Warren, 142 Berkeley St., Boston, Mass.
    J. M. Woodruff, Box 1158, Richmond, Va.

Warren, George C., President, Warren Bros. Co., 142 Berkeley St., Boston, Mass.

Warren, Ralph L., Rep., Warren Bros. Co., 142 Berkeley St., Boston, Mass.

WATER WORKS EQUIPMENT COMPANY, 50 Church St., New York City 1917
W. H. Van Winkle, Jr., Rep., New York City.

Weeden, Walter L., Secretary, Rep., Granite Paving Block Manufacturers' Association of the United States, 31 State St., Boston, Mass.

WESTERN PAVING BRICK MANUFACTURERS' ASSOCIATION, 416 Dwight Bldg., Kansas City, Mo.....................................1912
George W. Thurston, Secretary, 416 Dwight Bldg., Kansas City, Mo.

Woodruff, J. M., Rep., Warren Bros. Co., Box 1158, Richmond, Va.

CHANGES IN MEMBERSHIP

Counts of members listed in 1916 Proceedings and above show the following:

	Active	Affiliated	Associate	Total
In 1916	465	21	134	620
In 1918	421	16	102	539
Loss	44	5	32	81

If each member will bring one new member to the Convention this fall we will make up this loss several times over. It is the result of no Convention last year, especially in municipal delegates. The following show the changes in personnel not already reported in the 1916 Proceedings.

NEW MEMBERS

ACTIVE

Chester E. Albright..Philadelphia, Pa. (mun. del.)
Bruce Aldrich...Baltimore, Md.
L. T. Berthe..Charleston, Mo.
Frank Burkholder..Troy, O. (mun. del.)
D. J. F. Calkins...Everett, Wash. (mun. del.)
O. D. Chrisman..Springfield, Mo.
D. B. Davis..Richmond, Ind.
Joshua Doughty, Jr...Somerville, N. J.
Ernest Drinkwater..St. Lambert, Que.
F. C. Dunlap...Philadelphia, Pa. (mun. del.)
O. J. S. Ellingson..Sherman, Tex. (mun. del.)
M. I. Evinger..Des Moines, Iowa
J. A. Gleason...New Orleans, La. (mun. del.)
L. F. Gottschalk..Columbus, Neb.
J. A. Hadert...New Rochelle, N. Y.
W. H. Hall...New Britain, Conn.
C. B. Hoover...Columbus, O.
H. H. Hull...Memphis, Tenn. (mun. del.)
G. B. Kershaw..London, England
A. J. Mahnken..Weehawken, N. J.
F. W. McKellip..Faribault, Minn. (mun. del.)
Hans Mumm, Jr...Everett, Wash. (mun. del.)
C. W. Murray..Miami, Fla.

The Sign of Good Wood Block Pavements

THERE is but one way to get perfect wood block pavements, and that is to see that the blocks are impregnated with the proper oil.

We originated the wood block paving industry in America. More than one-third of all the wood block pavements in this country are protected by our products. And, as a result of our twenty years of success in this business, we make the flat statement that by far the best oil for treating wood paving blocks is **Reilly's Improved** (Permanent) **Creosote Oil.**

Its superiority is due to the fact that it contains far more permanent body than any other oil. It cannot bleed—it cannot evaporate—it cannot dissolve out of the wood. Water is permanently sealed out of the wood, hence the blocks will not swell or disintegrate.

Reilly's Improved (Permanent) **Creosote Oil** costs contractors slightly more than inferior or adulterated products. The only sure way of securing this oil is to **write it into your contract.**

Invented—Patented—Manufactured and Sold Exclusively by

Republic Creosoting Company
Indianapolis, Indiana

Plants: Indianapolis Minneapolis Seattle Mobile

S. D. Newton	Knoxville, Tenn.
C. A. Poole	Rochester, N. Y.
J. M. Rice	Pittsburg, Pa.
G. H. Sargent	LaGrange, Ga.
W. H. Sawyer	Lewiston, Me.
W. L. Stevenson	Philadelphia, Pa. (mun. del.)
A. E. Taplin	High Point, N. C.
J. W. Turner	Lakeland, Fla.
K. B. Ward	Durham, N. C.
H. J. Weaver	Elkhart, Ind. (mun. del.)
R. A. Wentworth	Batavia, N. Y.
E. P. Withrow	St. Louis, Mo.
W. R. Wolfinger	Allentown, Pa.

AFFILIATED

W. F. Ballinger	Philadelphia, Pa.

New Representatives of Associate Members

G. C. Bartram	East Orange, N. J.
F. O. Farey	Montreal, Que.
M. B. Greenough	Cleveland, O.
Wm. Howe	Chicago, Ill.
D. T. Pierce	Philadelphia, Pa.
G. H. Tefft	Chicago, Ill.
J. C. Travilla	St. Louis, Mo.
W. L. Weeden	Boston, Mass.

MEMBERS REINSTATED

ACTIVE

E. R. Halsey	S. Orange, N. J.
E. McCullough	Chicago, Ill.

MEMBERS TRANSFERRED

H. L. Collier, Atlanta, Ga.	Associate to Active
M. B. Greenough, Cleveland, O.	Affiliated to Associate

RESIGNED

ACTIVE

L. P. Aloe	St. Louis, Mo.
C. S. Ashley	New Bedford, Mass.
Geo. Berry	Brooklyn, N. Y.
C. H. Davis	S. Yarmouth, Mass.
John A. Dean, Jr.	Owensboro, Ky.
H. S. Dennison	Framingham, Mass.
A. L. Fellows	Denver, Colo.
J. T. Fetherston	New York City
A. E. Foreman	Victoria, B. C.
E. J. Fort	Brooklyn, N. Y.
J. M. Goodell	Upper Montclair, N. J.

J. J. Goodfellow	San Angelo, Tex.
Wallace Greenalch	Albany, N. Y.
A. Hohenstein	St. Paul, Minn.
Richard Lamb	New York City
F. R. Lanagan	Albany, N. Y.
E. A. May	Patchogue, L. I.
E. D. Rich	Lansing, Mich.
A. J. Taylor	Wilmington, Del.
M. C. Welborn	Austin, Tex.
G. C. Whipple	Boston, Mass.

AFFILIATED

Bureau of Municipal Research, New York.

ASSOCIATE

Adams & Ruxton Construction Co., Springfield, Mass.; A. A. Adams. Representative.

Amies Road Co., Drake Bldg., Easton, Pa.; W. T. Newcomb, Representative.

Arabia Granite Co., Atlanta, Ga.; F. C. Mason, Representative.

Atlantic Refining Co., Philadelphia, Pa.; A. F. Armstrong, Representative.

Philip Bell, Magnolia Petroleum Co., Dallas, Tex.

Bessemer Limestone Co., Youngstown, O.

O. L. Culley, Magnolia Petroleum Co., Chicago, Ill.

S. J. Dalzelle, Representative Prudential Oil Corporation, Baltimore, Md.

Continental Public Works Co.; W. B. Spencer, Representative, 2 Rector St., New York.

B. Charles Hvass, New York.

John S. Lane & Son; A. S. Lane, Representative, Meriden, Conn.

J. B. Marcellus, Philadelphia, Pa.

C. C. Marshall, Representative Standard Oil Co. of N. Y., Cleveland, O.

Coleman Meriwether, Representative Lock Joint Pipe Co., New York.

Howard W. Morgan, New York.

North Carolina Granite Corporation, Mt. Airy, N. C.; Thos. Woodroffe, Representative.

R. W. Sanders, Representative Prudential Oil Corporation, New York City.

Westport Paving Brick Co., Baltimore, Md.

MUNICIPAL DELEGATES NOT REAPPOINTED

A. H. Biertuempfel	Newark, N. J.
G. W. Burke	Pittsburg, Pa.
Wm. Cardwell	E. Orange, N. J.
E. A. Christy	New Orleans, La.
L. V. Christy	Wilmington, Del.
Alex. Clark	Orange, N. J.
W. H. Connell	Philadelphia, Pa.
A. R. Denman	Newark, N. J.
Geo. Eager	Milburn, N. J.
C. A. Finley	Pittsburg, Pa.
M. A. Gantz	Troy, O.
A. W. Harrison	Livingston, N. J.
Jacob Haussling	Newark, N. J.
F. B. Knott	Newark, N. J.
C. F. Kraemer	Newark, N. J.
A. L. Lacombe	Irvington, N. J.
D. R. Lyman	Louisville, Ky.

R. F. Mattia..Newark, N. J.
Hans Mumm, Jr..Everett, Wash.
J. F. O'Toole..Pittsburg, Pa.
Wm. Pennington..Newark, N. J.
W. E. Rolfe..St. Louis, Mo.
L. M. Russell..Elkhart, Ind.
P. H. Ryan..Newark, N. J.
E. R. Ryman..Newark, N. J.
C. M. Shipman..Newark, N. J.
T. W. Smith..Newark, N. J.
H. C. Taylor..Wilmington, Del.
A. H. Terry..Bridgeport, Conn.
Wm. Tries, Jr..Newark, N. J.
J. H. Weatherford..Memphis, Tenn.
G. S. Webster..Philadelphia, Pa.
T. L. Willis..New Orleans, La.

DECEASED

Active

F. T. Elwood..Rochester, N. Y.
Foster Olroyd..New Orleans, La.

Affiliated

H. A. Wise..Kansas City, Mo.

DROPPED

Active

H. J. Bradshaw..Abilene, Tex.
H. L. Collier..Atlanta, Ga.
J. W. Crook..Paris, Tex.
F. P. Drane..Charlotte, N. C.
J. W. Flenniken..Knoxville, Tenn.
F. H. Frankland..Kansas City, Mo.
G. W. Hayler..Chicago, Ill.
H. W. Klausmann..Indianapolis, Ind.
R. J. Lewis..Ft. Madison, Iowa
J. B. McCalla..Knoxville, Tenn.
H. A. Naberhuis..Miami, Fla.
E. W. Quinn..Cambridge, Mass.
G. E. Shand..Columbia, S. C.
F. T. Shepard..Nutley, N. J.
W. S. Tomlinson..Columbia, S. C.

Associate

Boston Roman Road Co., Boston, Mass.
Buffalo Steam Roller Co., Buffalo, N. Y.
General Petroleum Co., San Francisco, Calif.
Hugh F. Gilligan, Newark, N. J.
Indian Refining Co.; J. H. Arnold, Representative, New York City.
McAvoy Vitrified Brick Co., Philadelphia, Pa.
Portland Cement Manufacturers Association; G. W. Myers, Representative, Columbus, O.
Wern Machinery & Engineering Co., New York City.
Wern Stone Paving Co., New York City.

MAIL RETURNED UNDELIVERED

Active

E. C. Aldrich..Auburn, N. Y.
Carl H. Bryson...Lima, O.
C. Winston Cooper..Wilson, N. C.
H. G. Lykken..St. Paul, Minn.
E. W. Meckley..Allentown, Pa.
S. D. Newton..Knoxville, Tenn.
G. A. Sherron..Los Angeles, Cal.
F. L. Smith..Rochester, N. Y.
W. H. Wilson...Park City, Tenn.

Affiliated

D. A. Hegarty...Houston, Tex.
L. R. MacKenzie..Clayton, Mo.
F. J. Soutar...Sioux City, Iowa

Associate

Creosoted Wood Paving Block Bureau, Chicago, Ill.
W. A. Curler, Representative Thomas-Hammond Machinery Co., Los Angeles, Cal.
E. J. Dewine, Representative U. S. Asphalt & Refining Co., Columbus, O.

REPRESENTATIVES OF ASSOCIATE MEMBERS NOT REAPPOINTED

M. J. Beistle...Cleveland, O.
Benj. Brooks...Kansas City, Mo.
Z. W. Carter...Boston, Mass.
C. V. Eades...Chicago, Ill.
W. L. Hempelmann..Chicago, Ill.
C. F. Hepburn..Chicago, Ill.
H. E. Lersch..New Orleans, La.
G. R. March...Philadelphia, Pa.
Geo. W. Myers..Columbus, O.
F. W. Patterson...Cleveland, O.
E. C. Sargent...Columbus, O.
O. G. Strother...Harrisburg, Pa.

Lightning Source UK Ltd.
Milton Keynes UK
UKHW010831211218
334381UK00013B/970/P